Philosophy and *The Hitchhiker's Guide to the Galaxy*

Philosophy and *The Hitchhiker's Guide to the Galaxy*

Edited by

Nicholas Joll
University of Hertfordshire, UK

First published 2012 by
PALGRAVE MACMILLAN

Palgrave Macmillan in the UK is an imprint of Macmillan Publishers
Limited, registered in England, company number 785998, of Houndmills,
Basingstoke, Hampshire RG21 6XS.

Palgrave Macmillan in the US is a division of St Martin's Press LLC,
175 Fifth Avenue, New York, NY 10010.

Palgrave Macmillan is the global academic imprint of the above companies
and has companies and representatives throughout the world.

Palgrave® and Macmillan® are registered trademarks in the United States,
the United Kingdom, Europe and other countries.

ISBN 978–0–230–29112–6

This book is printed on paper suitable for recycling and made from
fully managed and sustained forest sources. Logging, pulping and
manufacturing processes are expected to conform to the environmental
regulations of the country of origin.

A catalogue record for this book is available from the British Library.

Library of Congress Cataloging-in-Publication Data
Philosophy and The hitchhiker's guide to the galaxy / edited by
Nicholas Joll.
  p. cm.
Includes bibliographical references and indexes.
ISBN 978–0–230–29112–6 (pbk.)
1. Adams, Douglas, 1952–2001. Hitchhiker's guide to the
galaxy.   2. Philosophy in literature.   I. Joll, Nicholas.
PR6051.D3352Z84 2012
823'.914—dc23   2012008997

10 9 8 7 6 5 4 3 2 1
21 20 19 18 17 16 15 14 13 12

Printed and bound in Great Britain by
CPI Antony Rowe, Chippenham and Eastbourne

I dedicate this book to my mother, who loved *Hitchhiker's*. This book is also for my father. Through it, he might get a better sense of what my mother and I were always banging on about.

And it occurs to me that running a program like this is bound to create an enormous amount of popular publicity for the whole area of philosophy in general.

(Douglas Adams, *The Hitchhiker's Guide to the Galaxy*)

Contents

Preface

This book philosophises via the wonderful *Hitchhiker* books by Douglas Adams. But it does not mean to presuppose any knowledge of philosophy. So:

Don't Panic!

However, an *interest* in philosophical matters *is* required. Still, and as this book will show, *Hitchhiker's* is not above a little philosophy in the same way that the sea is not above the sky. Consequently, anyone who loves *Hitchhiker's* is liable to have *some* interest in philosophy.

For a fuller introduction to the book, please see the Introduction that follows. Now, since there *is* that Introduction, you might wonder why this preface exists. Well, I wanted to start with a short and friendly bit of text. For philosophy *can* be forbidding, even when, as in this book, pains are taken to make it accessible and intriguing. There's an additional reason for this preface, though. It's this. Traditionally one ends a preface with one's initials and location – and there was a location that I just *had* to get in.

N. J.
A café in Rickmansworth

Acknowledgements ('Thanks for All the Fish')

I have received a lot of fish from many quarters, as it were.

For encouragement and general support, I thank: my father Barrie; Liz Strang; my sisters Felicity and Louise; Nick Hale and family (Nick had the 'café' idea for the preface!); Charmaine Coyle and James Rodwell; Sarah Clark, Paula Grogan, Beck Pitt, Anne Raustøl, Jonathan Stibbs and Susi Taylor, and Brendan Larvor.

Quite a few people provided helpful comments on drafts of those parts of the book that I wrote (as against the parts I merely edited). Those good people are: Andrew Aberdein; Chris Belshaw, together with other participants of the 2011 Open University conference 'Thinking in the Open', at which I delivered an early version of chapter 2; Sarah Clark; Charmaine Coyle; Fabian Freyenhagen; Jerry Goodenough; James Rodwell; Ben Saunders; Ken Westphal; and Colin Westripp. (Acknowledgements for chapter 9, which I co-wrote with Alexander Pawlak, are to be found in that chapter.)

For information about things Hitchhikery and about Douglas Adams, my thanks to the following: Richard Beadle, Matthias Dörrzapf and George Watson (all of St John's College, Cambridge); Daniel Dennett; and various members of ZZ9 Plural Z Alpha, the official *Hitchhiker's* fan club, and especially therein David Haddock, Carrie 'Share and Enjoy' Mowatt, and my contributor and co-writer Alexander Pawlak.

Thanks also to my editor at Palgrave Macmillan, Priyanka Gibbons – and a big hand, of course, to all of my contributors, all of whom put a lot of effort into their respective chapters.

Despite all this help, any mistakes in my contributions to this volume – any signs that I do not really know where my philosophical or Hitchhikery towel is – are my responsibility alone.

Notes on the Contributors

> 'But who the devil are you?' [. . .] 'We [. .] are Philosophers.'
>
> (*Hitchhiker's Guide to the Galaxy*, chapter 25)

Andrew Aberdein is Associate Professor of Logic and Humanities at Florida Institute of Technology. Much of his research is concerned with the interplay of formal and informal accounts of human reason. He read the first *Hitchhiker* book as a ten-year-old schoolboy and has been a fan ever since. It was *Hitchhiker's* that first kindled his interest in philosophy, an interest that he has been delighted to be able to make his career – not least since he is so unsuited for employment in the customary alternatives: hospital porter, barn builder, chicken-shed cleaner, bodyguard, radio producer, or script editor of *Doctor Who*.

Timothy Chappell is Professor of Philosophy and Director of the Ethics Centre at the Open University; he is also a Visiting Research Fellow at the Department of Moral Philosophy in the University of St Andrews. He grew up reading *The Hitchhiker's Guide to the Galaxy*, and nearly always knows where his towel is.

Barry Dainton is Professor of Philosophy at the University of Liverpool. His research is focused mainly on consciousness, time and space, and the nature of the self. He often blames the primitive condition of his financial planning for the future on a curious but unshakeable suspicion that the Earth will shortly be demolished to make way for a hyperspace bypass.

Michèle Friend, a *Hitchhiker* fan from an early age, has since grown up to become a philosopher of logic and mathematics. She teaches lots of formal logic, and presents it as the ultimate form of escape from the brutish and nasty lives most humans are forced to lead.

Jerry Goodenough is Senior Lecturer in Philosophy at the University of East Anglia and an Associate Lecturer of the Open University. His research interests include 'thought experiments', philosophy of mind, and philosophy of – or via – film. He has been a keen science fiction fan since someone gave him a copy of Wells's *The War of the Worlds* when he was nine, and can still remember listening to the very first broadcasts of *The Hitchhiker's Guide to the Galaxy* on his car radio on the way home from work all those years ago.

Eloïse Harding is Ben Saunders's better half and the animal-rightsy part of the equation. She has been grappling with the question of 'animals who want to be eaten' for a while now. Her academic interests focus on political ideology, 'horizontal politics' and protest. She blogs at http://increasingveganicity. blogspot.com. And she likes ducks.

Nicholas Joll hails from near Rickmansworth and has taught philosophy at several universities, including the Open University and the University of Hertfordshire. He has various philosophical interests and, indeed, an interest in the nature of philosophy itself. He was as keen to produce this book as Ford is to go to parties.

Amy Kind teaches philosophy at Claremont McKenna College in the United States where, as she has found on more than one occasion, an infinite improbability drive would come in enormously handy. Although her inner science fiction geek only revealed itself relatively recently, she has since written articles appearing in *Battlestar*

Galactica and Philosophy and *Star Trek and Philosophy*. She is currently making plans to have attended the time travellers' convention that was held at the Massachusetts Institute of Technology in 2005 – and if the verb tenses of that sentence seem awkward, Amy refers you to Douglas Adams's remarks on the grammatical difficulties related to time travel.

Alexander Pawlak studied physics and philosophy in his quaint home town of Marburg in Germany. After gaining his degree in 1998 he began a career in science journalism and in 2002 he became editor of the membership journal of the German Physical Society. He has been a fan of *Hitchhiker's* since the 29th of April 1984, the day the first episode of the TV series was broadcast on German television, and in March 2000 he interviewed Douglas Adams for the weekly newspaper *Die Zeit*. In 2010 he published his book *Die Wissenschaft bei Douglas Adams* ('The Science of Douglas Adams'). He is not married and lives in Heidelberg. He is not a professional philosopher, either. Hence at several points in the writing of his contribution to this volume he found his head filled with a thousand wary philosophers shouting at him.

Ben Saunders is Lecturer in Philosophy at the University of Stirling. His academic interests focus mainly on democracy, which has been likened to two wolves and a lamb deciding what to have for lunch (*not* a procedure he recommends!), but he has also written pieces for *Soccer and Philosophy* and *Philip K. Dick and Philosophy*. He always takes a towel with him when travelling.

Introduction

Nicholas Joll

The Hitchhiker's Guide to the Galaxy is either:

- A hugely useful, informative and entertaining book, the standard reference work for all those struggling to make it from one part of the universe to another part of the universe on as little as 30 Altairian dollars a day. [. . .]
- A book/TV series/set of records/play/computer game/ towel which began life as a BBC radio series written by Douglas Adams.

(H2G2 entry for 'The Hitchhiker's Guide to the Galaxy')

The Hitchhiker's Guide to the Galaxy is a wholly remarkable book.

(*The Hitchhiker's Guide to the Galaxy*, chapter 8)

The Hitchhiker's Guide to the Galaxy – the guide within the *Guide*, I mean – *is* remarkable. It's remarkable because it was technologically prescient (i.e. ahead of its time). The Guide is a 'largish electronic calculator' that is connected to a 'Sub-Etha Net' and which can display 'any one of a million "pages" [..] at a moment's notice'. It can tell you 'everything you need to know about anything'.[1] Adams thought up the guide in the 1970s. Today, it is not so far from reality. For today we have portable devices that connect to the Internet; and the Internet is, for many people, an increasingly important source of information.[2] It *might* even be that, one day, our world will contain something like the 'Guide Mark II', that guide being a trans-dimensional, time-manipulating bird that declares itself to be all-knowing, all-powerful and extremely vain.

The Hitchhiker's Guide in the *other* sense – the collection of radio series, books, television programmes and more – is remarkable too, and not just because it contains the intergalactic Guide. Nor is it just that, in the *Hitchhiker* phenomenon, Adams created something remarkably funny and remarkably imaginative. *Hitchhiker's is* those things; and those are reasons why it has been, in at least many of its forms, such a remarkable commercial success. But, additionally: *Hitchhiker's* is remarkably *philosophical* and, indeed, a marvellous vehicle for popular philosophy.

The proof of this will be in the pudding. That is, the chapters that follow should amount to an extended justification for the view that *Hitchhiker's* is both philosophical and great for popular philosophy. Nonetheless, I explore those things here in this Introduction, as well. There are reasons why I do that – reasons why, so to speak, I anticipate the pudding. (There should be a saying along those lines. I fear there isn't, though. 'Counting your chickens' is as near as we get.) Here's a first reason. Exploring that stuff in advance – here in the Introduction – should serve to ease readers into the book. Secondly, that exploration will allow me to say a few things that don't get said in the chapters. I should note, too, something else that this Introduction does: it gives an overview of the rest of the book.

Here's what all this amounts to. The rest of this Introduction consists of these sections:

1. *Hitchhiker's* and philosophy
2. What *is* philosophy?
3. More on *Hitchhiker's* and philosophy
4. The project and point of this book
5. Overview of the rest of the book

Which of these sections are important? Which skippable? It depends.

If you find it *obvious* that *Hitchhiker's* is philosophical, then you might skip the first section. If you have a reasonable idea of what philosophy is, you could skip the second section. Section three goes further into how *Hitchhiker's* is philosophical. So if you think you know just *how Hitchhiker's* is philosophical, or if you are not really interested in the details of that, then by all means pass on by. If you are keen to launch straight into the book proper, then you could dispense with, well, the whole of the rest of this Introduction. That said, section 5 does contain some practical information about the book's glossary and suchlike. For my part, I find nearly all of the Introduction quite interesting. But then I would.

1 *Hitchhiker's* and philosophy

A biographer has said that Adams 'loved philosophical ideas, and had a natural grasp of them'.[3] So it would be unsurprising were *Hitchhiker's* to contain a philosophical idea or two. In fact, *Hitchhiker's* is stuffed full of philosophical ideas and of philosophical *questions* in particular. The most conspicuous of those questions is the 'Ultimate Question' of 'Life, the Universe and Everything'. But consider, also, the unfortunate whale that gets brought into existence by the Infinite Improbability Drive (in the first *Hitchhiker* book). The whale asks itself: 'Why am I here? What's my purpose in life? What do I mean by who am I?' (*Hitchhiker's Guide to the Galaxy*, chapter 18). Those too are philosophical questions. And *Hitchhiker's* contains more of that sort of thing. *Much* more. Let me give a sample of the philosophical questions that come up in *Hitchhiker's* – many of which will be at issue in this book:

- *Can machines think? Can they have emotions?* Consider, for instance, Colin the Happy Robot (in *Mostly Harmless*) and Marvin the very *unhappy* robot.
- *What is personal identity?* That is: under what circumstances are two persons actually one and the same person? Think of the encounter, in *Mostly Harmless*, between Tricia McMillan (who stays on Earth) and Trillian (the space-faring version of Tricia McMillan who changes her name to 'Trillian'). The last of the whale's questions ('What do I mean by who am I?') is relevant here too.
- *Is it alright to eat animals?* And, *How much does consent matter in ethics?* Consider here the animal that wants to be eaten (in *Restaurant at the End of the Universe*).
- *Is there a God? If there is (or were there) would He be above logic?* In the first *Hitchhiker* book, God 'vanishes in a puff of logic'.
- *Who or what should be given political authority?* Think here of the Galactic Presidency and, especially, of The Man Who Rules the Universe.
- *What sort of work – employment – is valuable?* Here one may cite the Golgafrinchams, the Vogon guard in first

book ('the hours are good [. . .] but now you come to mention it, most of the actual minutes are pretty lousy'), and Arthur as sandwich maker in *Mostly Harmless*. Note also the recurrent light abuse in *Hitchhiker's* of insurance, marketing and advertising.

- *What is the value, and nature, of art and beauty?* Think of the Vogons – of their poetry and of how they treat beautiful things.
- *What can we know, and on what grounds?* 'I've never met all these people you speak of. And neither, I suspect, have you. They only exist in words we hear. It is folly to say you know what is happening to other people. Only they know, if they exist. They have their own Universes of their own eyes and ears' (The Man Who Rules the Universe, in *Restaurant*, chapter 29).[4]
- *What is it to be at home?* Arthur stands out here. So does Douglas Adams himself, since he seems persistently to have felt somewhat out of place or out of joint.[5]

It is because these sorts of questions abound in *Hitchhiker's*, and because Adams presents them so engagingly, that, like the program run by Deep Thought, *Hitchhiker's* is so suited for popular philosophy.

Still: what is distinctive about these questions? What makes them philosophical? To use a formulation one might find in a Terry Pratchett book: what, when one really gets right down to it, *is* philosophy?

2   What *is* philosophy?

This is a difficult question, and one that philosophers, who disagree about just about everything, disagree about. But a short(ish), rough and fairly uncontroversial account goes as follows.

Philosophy consists in asking and trying to answer questions that have a particular and unusual character. That character consists in their combining two features. On the one hand, the questions at issue seem to admit of better or worse answers. In that way, they seem to be proper questions rather than pseudo-questions, nonsensical questions. So seemingly we can't just dismiss those questions.[6] On the *other* hand, these questions are ones we do not really know how to tackle. To specify that second characteristic a little: in trying to answer the questions, we have nothing obvious to go on save clear thinking, a desire to get to the bottom of things, and a history of past grapplings with the problem (except in the case of that rare thing, a *new* philosophical problem, in which case things are *really* difficult). We might sum up the whole idea with a line from the philosopher Ludwig Wittgenstein: 'a philosophical problem has the form: "I don't know my way about".'[7] Or, more simply, we might say: *philosophical issues are peculiarly baffling.* We might even refer here to Vroomfondel's 'areas of doubt and uncertainty'.[8]

One might wonder what *sort* of questions fall into this category, and, thus, into the domain of philosophy. Well, *ethical* questions do. For how are we to decide what is moral and what is not? Seemingly no survey or experiment or calculation will yield the answer. Indeed: just what does it *mean* to say that something is (morally) right, or wrong?[9] But there are other types of philosophical questions too. For there are questions that are not ethical (or at least not primarily so) but which are sufficiently baffling to count as philosophical. Examples are the remaining questions mentioned above in section 1 – the questions about whether machines can think, about God and logic, about what is to be at home, and so on. What makes *these* sorts of questions – these philosophical-but-not-ethical questions – so baffling? In the case of at least some of them, the answer, I think, is that they involve this rather boggling enterprise of trying to *tie things together into a comprehensive whole*. How are we to relate God (if there is one) to logic? How do – how *can* – merely mechanical or bodily things relate to thought and emotions and the self? And how do the various things we know, or think we know, fit together? (One question here is whether knowledge has foundations.) Such 'tying-together' questions yield another definition of philosophy. For we might say, with the philosopher Wilfred Sellars, this: philosophy is 'an attempt to see how things, in the broadest possible sense of the term, hang together, in the broadest possible sense of the term'.[10] (Or we might take that as a characterisation of at least the part of philosophy that is called *metaphysics* . . .[11])

Now, because philosophical questions baffle, quite a lot of philosophy is an attempt to *clarify exactly what is being asked about*. For example, when someone asks about the meaning of life, or about the 'value' of something they call 'art', or about God, what exactly do they mean to get at? Now, sometimes a philosopher, having pursued such clarification, concludes that some would-be philosophical question is not a proper philosophical question after all. The thought here can be that, upon close scrutiny, the question at issue reveals itself to be simply *bogus* – to be nonsensical. Or the thought can be that the question is not really a fundamentally *baffling* one, in that some discipline other than philosophy knows, at least in principle, how to handle it. Some philosophers apply this dismissive approach (in one or the other version) to a *whole bunch* of philosophical questions or to a whole area of philosophy. For instance, some philosophers hold that there is little left for philosophy to say in response to the question, 'What is knowledge?' once natural science has been given a good crack at the topic. More: every so often a philosophical movement arises according to which just about *every* philosophical question can be done away with.

A famous case of this tendency – a tendency one might call *anti-philosophical* – is the movement known as 'logical positivism'. According to logical positivism, philosophical statements were, literally, nonsense. But the philosophers – the *other* philosophers, ones who could not be called 'anti-philosophy philosophers' – tend to get their own back. For they point out the paradox. That is, they respond that the question of whether philosophy is nonsense, or any tool used to distinguish sense from nonsense, is *itself* philosophical.[12]

If you want to blither a bit upon reading that, please feel free.

3   More on *Hitchhiker's* and philosophy

There's more to say, even at a general kind of level, about how *Hitchhiker's* relates to philosophy. For one can ask the following question. Is *Hitchhiker's* philosophical *only* in that it alludes to philosophical ideas, brings up philosophical questions? I mean: does *Hitchhiker's* inhabit a kind of philosophical atmosphere, from which it might be possible to *condense* or *mould* philosophical ideas, but which *itself* has no philosophical substance? In short, does *Hitchhiker's* make any philosophical *claims*? In shorter: it is philosophically man or mouse?

The issue turns out to be involved. So if you want to say, 'Please, I think I am tired' (*Restaurant*, chapter 29), then feel free to skip to the next section. That next section stops messing around and imparts, with a reasonable but not excessive amount of detail, just what this book will be up to.

For those of you who are still here: there are some reasons to go for the 'mouse' verdict, i.e. to think that there can be little real philosophical substance in *Hitchhiker's*.

1. Adams once said: 'When you write something [. . .] you can place the tiniest piece of information you have so that

it sounds like the tip of the iceberg of a vast amount of knowledge. And very often it isn't.'[13]
2. Adams tried to deter someone from writing a thesis on the philosophical and scientific themes in *Hitchhiker's*, on the ground that it wasn't worth it.[14]
3. Adams seems not to have read much philosophy.[15]

None of this is conclusive, though. For, first, Adams was not always a reliable authority on his own life.[16] Second, it is possible that *Hitchhiker's* contains philosophical ideas Adams didn't really know he had, or which, for some reason, he didn't want to acknowledge. Third, one can have philosophical ideas without having read much philosophy. The moral might seem to be this one: the final authority for whether *Hitchhiker's* takes any philosophical line is *Hitchhiker's* itself, not anything biographical, not anything to do with Adams *the man*.[17] But a further complication pushes us back towards Adams himself. Let me explain. If it *is* the case that *Hitchhiker's* takes a philosophical stance, then probably that stance will be quite *implicit*. After all, *Hitchhiker's* is not a philosophical treatise; and Adams might have thought that 'plonking [philosophical ideas] unadorned into the text would induce instant tedium'.[18] Now, if philosophical claims *are* implicit in *Hitchhiker's*, then it makes sense to use Adams's views – views he expressed outside of his fiction – to help discern the philosophical content that lies within his fiction. So we *do* need to consider whether Adams himself was philosophically man or mouse.

I take as my point of departure one of Adams's many enthusiasms, namely, his enthusiasm for natural science.[19] Adams was interested, especially, in the life sciences. He even liked to note that his initials were DNA ('Douglas Noel Adams'). This love of science is reflected in the fiction. Witness all the jokes in *Hitchhiker's* about evolution. Witness too the Infinite Improbability Drive, eddies in the space-time continuum ('"Ah," nodded Arthur, "is he? Is he?"'), multiple dimensions, parallel worlds, and the WSOGMM (the 'Whole Sort of General Mish Mash' of worlds and dimensions and probabilities). Note also that quantum physics was an inspiration for the idea that it is impossible to know both the Ultimate Question and the Ultimate Answer.[20] Still, does this love of science have any particular philosophical significance (beyond the inspiration just mentioned)? After all, many contemporary philosophers are, in one way or another, scientific in their philosophising. One example: many of those working in the so-called 'philosophy of mind' make use of results from the brain sciences. There's 'the philosophy of science', too. The philosophy of science deals with philosophical problems thrown up by science as such (if 'science as such' exists – that's one of the problems) and by individual sciences. Also, many philosophers aspire to a quasi-mathematical rigour in their reasoning. There's something like an overlap, then, between science and philosophy. But there *is* something more to consider here, something more to consider in Adams's relation to science. That 'more' involves the 'anti-philosophy' outlook mentioned above (in section 2). Often, science inspires that outlook. When it does, the result is this idea: *many philosophical problems,* or at least many of the philosophical problems that actually make sense, *will turn out to be **solvable** by science.* This sort of view is sometimes called *scientism.*

There is some reason to attribute scientism to Adams. For one thing, he was *very* keen on science. His friend and biographer Nick Webb said that Adams's world view was 'based on science', in that Adams believed that science was where one should look for 'serious reflections and questionings about life'.[21] Further, *Hitchhiker's* can seem to suggest that philosophers are self-interested buffoons. Here the portrayal of Vroomfondel and his colleague Majikthise stands out. Further yet, Adams greatly admired Richard Dawkins; and

Dawkins once wrote, in a way reminiscent of the depiction of Vroomfondel and Majikthise, of people 'educationally over-endowed with the tools of philosophy'.[22] A final and less anecdotal consideration is part of a speech that Adams gave to the 'Digital Biota 2' conference. That part of the speech is worth quoting at length:

> So we may have accidentally stumbled upon the ultimate answer; it's the only thing, the only force, arguably the most powerful of which we are aware, which requires no other input, no other support from any other place, is self-evident, hence tautological, but nevertheless astonishingly powerful in its effects. [. . . I] put it at the beginning of one of my books. [. .] *'[A]nything that happens happens, anything that in happening causes something else to happen causes something else to happen and anything that in happening causes itself to happen again, happens again.'* In fact you don't even need the second two because they flow from the first one [. . . This is] a unique tautology in that it requires no information to go in but an infinite amount of information comes out of it. So I think that it is arguably therefore the prime cause of everything in the universe. Big claim, but I feel I'm talking to a sympathetic audience.

> (*Salmon of Doubt*, p. 129, my abridgement; the book reference is to *Mostly Harmless*)

I take the central idea to be as follows. *Howsoever counter-intuitive it might be, complex things can emerge, without outside help, from simple things; and this applies to evolution, to the original appearance of life itself, and, in fact, to everything.* This idea is scientistic if it means to claim that in principle science can explain absolutely everything such that no philosophical problems remain outstanding.[23]

The same speech contains something about *God*, too. In fact, the title of the speech is 'Is There an Artificial God?' Adams suggests that there is an artificial God, even though 'there isn't an *actual* god'. God is an entity 'we create [. .] to inform and shape our lives and enable us to work together' (*Salmon of Doubt*, p. 147). *God is a useful fiction.* Is this view simply atheism? It *is* atheism, but probably not simply atheism, or atheism of any simple sort. For fiction and falsehood are not quite identical. Fictions are false, yes; but they don't claim to be true. They are not *lies*. The point of a fiction is to do something other than tell the truth (other than tell the truth in any straightforward and literal fashion, anyway). The use that the fiction of God has for us, Adams is suggesting, is 'to inform and shape our lives and enable us to work together'.[24] However, there is some suggestion that we have *outgrown* this fiction, found *other* ways of doing those things. Matters are further complicated by this suggestion (*Salmon*, p. 140): money, too, is a fiction, albeit one that, like religion, has powerful effects because of our belief in it.

One can infer from all this stuff on God and science at least the following. It *does* seem fairly likely that *Hitchhiker's* contains some philosophical substance of one sort or another (even if some of substance might be scientistic and in that way anti-philosophical). Now, one may want to know, in more detail, what that philosophical substance is. Is the excavation of that detail – of more or less hidden philosophical substance – the project of this book? Is this that story, so to speak? *Partly* – as I shall now explain.

4 The project and point of this book

Broadly speaking, this book's project is to philosophise via the *Hitchhiker* books. The Preface said as much. But there is more than one way in which that project could proceed. First option: one engages with what one takes to be philosophical views expressed by the *Hitchhiker* books. Call that *philosophising* **with** *Hitchhiker's*. Second option: one uses *Hitchhiker* material as *occasions* for philosophy, i.e. use that material pretty much just as a *way into* philosophical topics, uses it as a stimulus or a springboard. One could call that *philosophising* **from** *Hitchhiker's*. Our book takes both approaches. Sometimes indeed both approaches operate within a single chapter. The chapters that most philosophise *with* – as against from – *Hitchhiker's* are, perhaps, chapters 2, 3 and 9.

But what is the *point* of any kind of philosophising via *Hitchhiker's*? Answer: doing so works rather well. But let me elaborate a bit. The point of this book is to do some philosophy, or at any rate to *introduce* some philosophy, in a way that (1) does justice to the philosophical aspects of *Hitchhiker's*, (2) is more accessible than most philosophical writing, (3) is not *so* accessible or popular that it ceases really to be philosophy. The last of these points means that, while this book is popular philosophy in the sense that it aims to be accessible, it is not quite what one might call, disparagingly, 'pop philosophy' (which is philosophy of the sort that, going by the book titles, Oolon Colluphid seems to write). Nonetheless, and as the Preface said, this book does not mean to presuppose any knowledge of academic philosophy.

5   Overview of the rest of the book

It is true, though, that most of the contributors to this book are professional philosophers. Those contributors are described in the 'Notes on the Contributors' section that immediately precedes this Introduction. After this

Introduction, the chapters begin. Those chapters are organised under four headings – thus:

Part I.   Ethics (two chapters)
Part II. The Meaning of Life (two chapters)
Part III. Metaphysics and Artificial Intelligence (two chapters)
Part IV. Logic, Method and Satire (three chapters)

The arrangement is not ideal: some of the chapters could fit under more than one of the headings; and some important topics get treated in more than one part. (God is one such topic. Artificial intelligence and the meaning of life are two others – even though those latter two topics figure in the titles of the parts.) But the classification does give a reasonable indication of what to expect where. In that same spirit, I shall, in a moment, give a summary of the chapters. First, though –

A word on the bibliography, glossary, indexes and the like

The chapters don't have separate bibliographies. Instead there's a unified bibliography at the end of the book. That bibliography is prefaced (p. 285) with stuff about just what's in the bibliography and what isn't, which I won't repeat here. The chapters do each have a section called 'For deeper thought'. Those sections list texts (books, chapters, articles) that should serve as routes further into the ideas of the chapter. All those texts are contained in the book's bibliography.

There's a book-wide *glossary*, too. It defines a bunch of philosophical terms. When a chapter uses a term – i.e. a word or phrase – which is in the glossary, that term is marked, in the chapter, with an asterisk. (Or rather the asterisk is stuck next to the *first*, and only the first, use of a term in a chapter. Normally, anyway.) So if you come across, say, 'normative*', that means that the word 'normative' is defined in the glossary. There are also four indexes: (1) an index of references to works by Adams; (2) an index of people, things and places from *Hitchhiker's* ('"The things," said Ford Prefect quietly, "are also people"' – *Restaurant*, chapter 16); (3) an index of (non-fictional!) philosophers, sages, luminaries and other thinking persons; (4) a general index, which contains everything else.

Lastly here, a few words on references. We refer to the *Hitchhiker* books by title or, after the first mention of a title, by a shortened version of the title (for instance, *Life* for *Life, the Universe and Everything*). When citing or quoting those books, we give chapter numbers, not page numbers. We avoid page numbers because the books have gone through many editions and the pagination differs between those editions. Anyway, the chapters in the *Hitchhiker's* books are short. So it is not very hard to find any bit of text. As our source for quotations, we have used the 'commemorative' editions issued by Pan in 2001.[25] Note that when we refer to something we call '*Hitchhiker's*' (or '*Hitchhiker*') the context should show whether the reference is to the first *Hitchhiker* book or whether, instead, the reference is to the whole *Hitchhiker* corpus/phenomenon. (You'll have become used to this already.) When referring to *other* things, i.e. *not* to *Hitchhiker* books, we gives references by author and title. I should perhaps add something that will be somewhat evident already, namely, that the present book does concentrate very much upon the *Hitchhiker's* books as against upon the radio series, television version, et cetera.

Now we've got all that out the way, here's the summary of the chapters.

Overview of the chapters of Part I, 'Ethics'

The very first chapter of the book is '"Eat Me": Vegetarianism and Consenting Animals', by Ben Saunders and Eloïse Harding. It explores the ethics of eating animals, with particular reference to the 'Dish of the Day' that confronts Arthur in *The Restaurant at the End of the Universe*. The authors first examine standard arguments for vegetarianism and then turn to the significance of consent. They argue that, while consent can make some acts allowable that would otherwise have been wrong, its force may be undermined when it is induced by the exercise of insidious power and, consequently, that Arthur may be best advised to stick to a salad.

The second ethics chapter is by me (Nicholas Joll). It is about an issue within the ethics of entertainment. Taking its cue from various passages in *Hitchhiker's*, but especially from one in *Mostly Harmless* about the character Random and the 'Lamuellans', I consider whether certain forms of violent entertainment are (i.e. should be) acceptable or whether they are harmful, or objectionable on some other score.

Overview of the chapters of Part II, 'The Meaning of Life'

The first chapter of this part of the book is by Amy Kind. Amy suggests that *Hitchhiker's* can be read as an extended meditation on the absurdity of human existence. She proceeds to consider a variety of philosophical responses to that apparent absurdity (*apparent* because one of the responses is to argue that actually life is not absurd). The best response, Amy argues, is one that owes much to Albert Camus, as well as to some more recent philosophers. The response in question – which Amy attributes to Adams himself, too – accepts that life is absurd but urges that the absurdity need not trouble us.

The second 'meaning of life' chapter is by Timothy Chappell. Starting from Douglas Adams's character Wowbagger the Infinitely Prolonged, the chapter develops a response to Bernard Williams's much-discussed argument that any eternal life that we might conceivably live would eventually become intolerably boring. Timothy, however, argues that an endless life need not be meaningless, and that the reasons why not have something to teach us about what gives meaning to a life of any length, finite or infinite.

Overview of the chapters of Part III, 'Metaphysics and Artificial Intelligence'

Jerry Goodenough's chapter (which is chapter 5) argues that Marvin 'the Paranoid Android' contradicts the science fiction norm and that we can learn from this. The traditional intelligent robots of science fiction fall into two categories. Either (1) they wholly lack emotions, or (2) they are cheerful in a mindless sort of way that makes one suspect they do not *really* have emotions. Now Marvin definitely has emotions, or the single emotion (if it is a single emotion) of being very depressed. This difference from the science fiction norm is informative. For it suggests a thought for which there are in fact good grounds. To wit: if there is to be any artificial intelligence that is *genuinely intelligent*, it would have to be capable of *real feelings* (a capacity that itself presupposes various other capabilities) – and thus capable of severe unhappiness.

Chapter 6 is by Barry Dainton. It's called 'From Deep Thought to Digital Metaphysics'. It starts from the idea that the Earth was 'commissioned, paid for, and run by mice' and that it and its inhabitants 'have formed the matrix of an organic computer running a ten-million-year research program' (*Hitchhiker's*, chapter 24). From this fantastical premise, Barry develops several mind-bending scenarios that, he argues, merit varying degrees of serious considera-tion. One possibility is that the Earth – *our* Earth – really is a computer. Another is that our whole universe is in fact a computer – that reality itself is fundamentally computa-tional in nature. Further: if indeed reality is fundamentally computational, then an accurate computer simulation of a world would *be* a world. The possibility of such simulations existing opens up the possibility of *universes within universes.* These universes (or sub-universes) might be run by aliens, or future generations of humanity itself. We might, in effect, be characters in a sophisticated computer game. Indeed: even if reality is *not* computational, there are reasons for thinking it is quite likely that we are living in machine-generated virtual realities – and hence that our world is not what we (ordinarily) take it to be.

Overview of the chapters of Part IV, 'Logic, Method and Satire'

The first chapter here is Michèle Friend's 'God . . Promptly Vanishes in a Puff of Logic'. Michèle examines the 'Babel Fish argument' against the existence of God. Strangely, this argu-ment does not figure on many philosophy syllabi (though I'm told that sometimes it is mentioned in philosophy teaching). However, that argument incorporates another argument – an argument *for* the existence of God – which *does* get studied a lot, namely, the so-called Argument from Design. Michèle examines both arguments (the Babel Fish one and the Design argument it incorporates) with, as she puts it, 'all the logical machinery [she] can summon'. In so doing, she provides a lesson in how to analyse arguments, together with some tuition in so-called formal logic. She adds some 'musings on Logic, God and the Universe', too.

Next up is Andrew Aberdein. His chapter takes its start from a problem that Adams encountered when composing the *Hitchhiker's Guide to the Galaxy* (in its original radio version). Adams has had the Vogon guard throw Ford and Arthur into space. It was incredibly unlikely that any ship would pass close by, and so potentially rescue them, before they died. So: end of story? No, because, via the Infinite Improbability Drive, the stupefying odds against rescue become the reason they *are* rescued. In this way, the problem is used to solve itself. Apparently Adams got this idea from watching a documentary on judo. In judo, I take it, one learns to turn the weight of your opponent against him (or her). Andrew explores other ways in which this 'judo principle' figures in *Hitchhiker's* and considers the way in which the principle has been used to treat philosophical problems – or, sometimes, problems that lie at the boundary between philosophy and science. The problems Andrew considers have to do with infinity, knowledge, artificial intelligence and multiple worlds. His chapter ends by relating the judo principle to the logic of *jokes*.

The final chapter, which is by Alexander Pawlak and Nicholas Joll, is about *Hitchhiker's* as satire. Actually – and rather to the point, given the business of this book – the argument is that *Hitchhiker's* is *philosophical* satire. In making that argument, Alex and I draw parallels between *Hitchhiker's*, on the one hand, and famous satires by Swift and Voltaire, on the other. Another topic we discuss is the relation between *Hitchhiker's* and other, or more traditional, science fiction. The chapter contains material on the meaning of life as well.

The most accessible chapters are, perhaps, chapters 1, 3 and 9.

Share and enjoy.

Notes

1. *The Hitchhiker's Guide to the Galaxy*, chs 3 and 5. Actually, 'the Sub-Etha Net' is not mentioned until the fifth chapter of *So Long, and Thanks for All the Fish* – though the 'Sub-Etha' itself, i.e. without the 'Net', gets mentioned earlier (in the aforementioned third chapter of *Hitchhiker's Guide*). One more thing here: text of the '[. .]' sort indicates an abridgment or ellipsis, i.e. that some words have been missed out from a quotation. This technique has an advantage over the more standard convention of writing '. .'. To wit: '. .' can obscure places where the quoted text itself contains '. .' – as in, for example, 'But the plans were on display . . .' (*Hitchhiker's*, ch. 1). I'm sorry this note is so dull. If you're looking for a more interesting one, I recommend, say, note 6 below. Or note 19 – that's a good one.

2. One thinks here of Wikipedia in particular, to which one may compare the following passage. 'In many of the more relaxed civilizations on the Outer Eastern Rim of the Galaxy, the *Hitchhiker's Guide* has already supplanted the great *Encyclopaedia Galactica* as the standard repository of all knowledge and wisdom [. .] though it has many omissions and contains much that is apocryphal, or at least wildly inaccurate' (*Hitchhiker's*, Preface). But there is also H2G2, from which I quoted above and which pre-dated Wikipedia. H2G2 is, in the words of its strapline, 'the guide to life, the universe and everything written by you'. H2G2 was produced by The Digital Village, a company co-founded by Adams. See further Doctorow, 'Wikipedia: a genuine H2G2 – minus the editors'.

3. Nick Webb, *Wish You Were Here*, p. 122.

4. I interpret 'Only they know, if they exist' as follows. Only those people know those things about what is happening to them, if indeed – i.e. on the presumption that – those people actually do exist. An *alternative* interpretation is: only those people know whether or not they themselves exist. Later in the same chapter the Man in the Shack says something even more cryptic: 'How can I tell [. .] that the past isn't a fiction designed to account for the discrepancy between my immediate physical sensations and my state of mind?' Now, there are various philosophical puzzles about the past. One of those puzzles – and perhaps the one the Man means to get at – is mentioned in a note to chapter 6 below. Note also that the shack-dweller may be intended as an answer to the problem that 'those people who most want to rule people are, ipso facto*, those least suited to do it' (*Restaurant*, ch. 28). Alternatively, he may be intended to show that the problem is insoluble, in that the only type of person who wouldn't abuse power, is someone so unworldly as to be useless.

5. I presume this is why Simpson called his biography of Adams 'Hitchhiker'. See also *The Salmon of Doubt*, pp. 148–50.

6. Actually, deciding which questions are proper ones is itself an eminently philosophical activity. To illustrate the difficulties in making such decisions, consider whether the following questions are proper questions, and, if not, why not.

   - What colour is a number – say, the number five?
   - Is the present King of France bald?
   - Does this tie (not just in someone's opinion, but really, objectively) go with this shirt?
   - Is cheese (objectively) nice?

7. Wittgenstein, *Philosophical Investigations*, section 123. Still, Wittgenstein (1889–1951) had his own rather particular account of just how that was the case. Exactly what that account was is a matter of some dispute. For a taster, though, see section 2c of my article 'Contemporary Metaphilosophy'.

8. *Hitchhiker's*, chapter 25. There's more on Vroomfondel later in this Introduction – and elsewhere in this book.

9. Some philosophers deny that ethical questions are proper questions. I consider a view of that sort of ilk towards the end of chapter 2 below. On the other hand, some philosophers *do* think that one can and should *calculate* to solve moral problems. The philosophers at issue are those, or some of those, who advocate 'consequentialism'. On consequentialism, see chapter 2, note 18. Still: since there is chronic and acute disagreement about all this, it seems reasonable to retain the original point that ethical questions are peculiarly baffling. On the very notions of ethics and morality, see the entries for 'ethics' and 'morality' in the glossary at the back of the book.

10. Sellars, *Science, Perception and Reality*, p. 1.

11. I mention metaphysics here mainly because I've used it in the title to one of the main parts of the book (as you'll find out if you keep reading this Introduction). For more on metaphysics, please see this book's glossary.

12. The philosopher most associated with the view I mention about science and knowledge is the North American Williard Van Orman Quine (1908–2000). As to logical positivism (which influenced Quine), it was a form of what I will discuss (in section 3 below) under the heading of 'scientism'. A famous passage by one of the inspirers of logical positivism, the Scottish philosopher David Hume (1711–76), gives a flavour of the positivist position:

   When we run over libraries, persuaded of these principles, what havoc must we make? If we take in our hand any volume; of divinity or school metaphysics, for instance; let us ask, *Does it contain any abstract reasoning concerning quantity or number?* No. *Does it contain any experimental reasoning concerning matter of fact and existence?* No. Commit it then to the flames: for it can contain nothing but sophistry and illusion.

(An Enquiry Concerning Human Understanding,
Section XII, p. 165)

13. Adams and Shircore, 'The First and Last Tapes', part 3.
14. Gaiman, *Don't Panic*, p. 158. See also section 7 of chapter 8, below. Now: so far as I know, that thesis (and I don't know what kind of thesis it was) was not written. However, a *different* thesis, on the same topic, *was*. That other thesis is a Master's thesis by one Kalle Häkkänen – a thesis submitted at the University of Jyväskylä, Finland.
15. Adams studied English at university – an undergraduate degree at St John's College, Cambridge. Later, he said that were he to have his time again, he'd do biology or zoology (Simpson, *Hitchhiker*, p. 30). Still, *Hitchhiker's* does contain a couple of allusions to actual philosophers or works of philosophy. See the mention of A. J. Ayer's *Language, Truth and Logic* in *So Long, and Thanks for All the Fish* (ch. 30) and the allusion to Voltaire, and thereby to Leibniz, in *Mostly Harmless* (ch. 6; on the Voltaire–Leibniz allusion, see further ch. 9 below). Additionally, some detective work by Alex Pawlak (*Die Wissenshaft bei Douglas Adams*, p. 291) has revealed a copy of Iris Murdoch's *Metaphysics as a Guide to Morals* on an Adams bookshelf. Moreover: 'Oddly enough, I [Adams] was offered a place in English and Philosophy at Warwick [. .] but that was before I was then offered a place at Cambridge. [. . .] I seem to remember having a great time doing the paper for Warwick. [. .] I was unexpectedly given this paper to do with no preparation expected or required and so it turned out to be fun to do' (Adams, 'Re: Get a professorship now, and beat the rush'). So Adams could have done English and philosophy but in the end just did English (at St John's, Cambridge). Mr George Watson of St John's College, who taught Adams, tells me that the syllabus Adams studied had little philosophical in it, and that, anyway, Adams was not especially likely to read anything on a reading list. In an affectionate obituary of Adams, Mr Watson says of him that, 'His mind was a lumber room, wholly disorganized and richly stocked' (Watson, 'The Cosmic Comic').
16. Here are some examples. (1) Adams's 'taxi/crowd' story – whereby the throng hindering his journey to a book-signing of *The Hitchhiker's Guide to the Galaxy* turned out to comprise his very own fans – is not in fact true. (2) Adams seems to have forgotten that he had read *The Plaine Man's Pathway to Heaven* (published in 1601), the author of

which was – and I kid you not – one Arthur Dent. (3) Adams doesn't seem to have come up with the idea of a Hitchhiker's Guide to the Galaxy whilst lying in a field in Austria. On all this, see Simpson, *Hitchhiker*, pp. 1–2, 93–4, 340, and Häkkänen, 'Physics and metaphysics in the Hitchhiker series', p. 5.

17. There's a little more on this point – this general point about the relation between author and the content of a work – in section 2.1 of chapter 2, below.

18. Webb, *Wish You Were Here*, p. 122. My addition.

19. A related Adams enthusiasm was technology, especially computers and especially, within that, Apple Macs. That technical enthusiasm was reciprocated. Apple recruited Adams – together with other luminaries – as an ambassador; and many more or less ordinary people who worked in technology were enthusiastic about Adams. Other Adamsian enthusiasms included: fast cars; restaurants; Bach, the Beatles, Pink Floyd and Dire Straits; California and Cambridge; Dickens and Wodehouse; Monty Python; parties; scuba-diving; and, or so it has been said, the 'whooshing' sound that deadlines make as they go by. (Note: this book itself was late. Slightly.) Adams was keen, too, on endangered species, and he did some thinking about them as well as acting on their behalf. Unfortunately, our book does not make much of this last interest. But, in addition to what chapter 1, below, says about animals, one can see Zimmerman, *Environmental Philosophy: From Animal Rights to Radical Ecology* and, in Adams's own output, *Last Chance to See* and 'Parrots, the Universe and Everything'.

20. For the connection with quantum physics, note the reference to 'Uncertainty' (capitalised) at the end of *Life*, and see Adams, 'Douglas Adams' Last Interview' and Häkkänen, 'Physics and Metaphysics in the Hitchhiker Series', section 6.3, p. 73. To get an idea of what quantum physics is about, see Rae, *Quantum Physics*. See also, on matters quantum, section 5 of the chapter below by Andrew Aberdein. General accounts of how *Hitchhiker's* makes use of science are Hanlon's *The Science of the Hitchhiker's Guide to the Galaxy* and Pawlak's *Die Wissenschaft bei Douglas Adams*.

21. The first quotation is from Nick Webb (Webb, 'Exclusive Interview with Nick Webb'). The second (quoted on p. 15 of Webb's *Wish You Were Here*) is from Adams himself, in a television documentary. That document is filed in the bibliography under 'Channel 4'.

22. Dawkins, *The Selfish Gene*, p. 278, note to p. 55. The people Dawkins means so to characterise are, he says (– says in the same note –), those philosophers who 'cannot resist poking in their scholarly apparatus where it isn't helpful'. He doesn't name names – with the exception of Mary Midgley, with whom he'd had a dispute, ill-tempered on both

sides, in a philosophy journal. Chapter 9 below has more on Adams's portrayal of Vroomfondel and Majikthise.

23. What of the use the passage makes of *tautology*? Roughly, a tautology is a statement that is true by definition. Now, 'Anything that happens, happens' is indeed true by definition; *but* the idea at issue here – the idea about complexity from simplicity – is not. Rather, that idea is true (if it *is* true) because of the way the world happens to be. One can compare evolution, which, as the speech points out (*Salmon*, p. 192), admits of this tautologous summary: that which survives, survives. This too unpacks into something non-tautologous, namely into a whole story about genes, bodily and behavioural traits, random mutation, and competition between organisms. However, there is something about both the theory of evolution and the complexity-from-simplicity idea that make them expressible – after a fashion – as tautologies. What that something is, Adams puts better elsewhere in *Salmon*, when he writes of 'the counter-intuitive observation that complex results arise from simple causes, iterated many times over' (*Salmon*, p. 124). Dennett's book *Darwin's Dangerous Idea* may have influenced Adams's thinking on this point (and see further section 2 of ch. 6, below). Adams met Dennett at a 1998 conference in Germany called *Der Digitale Planet*. Professor Dennett tells me that that was the only time he met Adams.

24. Seemingly Adams is proposing a version of what philosophers would call *anti-realism about religious language*. That view can be defined via contrast with a *realist* view of religious language. That realist view is this. Religious language means to be true in a straightforward or literal way. It aims at true assertions about a supernatural or ultimate reality. The anti-realist view of religious language denies that conception. Expressed more positively, the anti-realist idea is . . well, the view comes in various versions. The idea can be that religious language expresses a certain attitude towards the world, *or* that it expresses certain moral ideals, *or* that it is useful for achieving certain things – certain things not entirely to do with attitudes and ideals (and this seems closest to Adams), *or* that it does aim at literal truth, yet in so doing does not mean to be about anything supernatural and has its own standards of correctness. For more on such ideas, which are ideas with which some atheists rather fail to engage, see Moore and Scott, *Realism and Religion*, and Philips and Tessin, *Religion without Transcendence?*

25. For details of those books, please see the bibliography. There is at least one misprint in those editions. *The Restaurant at the End of the Universe* has 'Big Bank Burger Bar' instead of 'Big Bang Burger Bar' in ch. 17, p. 93. That error, which makes the bar rather less cosmic, has persisted into the more recent 2009 edition of the book.

Part I
Ethics

Part I
Ethics

1

'Eat Me': Vegetarianism and Consenting Animals

Ben Saunders and Eloïse Harding

Arthur, confronted with a bovine creature that apparently wants to be eaten in Milliways (*The Restaurant at the End of the Universe*, chapter 17), faces a moral dilemma. Should he eat it or shouldn't he? And what considerations might justify his refusal to do so? It seems, from the fact that he was willing to contemplate eating it, before it expressed its apparent consent, that he is an omnivore, who has either never seriously considered the ethical case for vegetarianism or who has done so but decided against it. It is strange, then, that he should show qualms about eating an animal that wants to be eaten and gives him not only permission but encouragement. As Zaphod observes, in one of his occasional moments of astuteness, this seems at first sight far less morally troubling than eating an animal that *doesn't* want to be eaten.

Perhaps Arthur's discomfort is because of unique features of his situation. One doesn't normally engage in pre-dinner chat with the animal that one is about to eat, and it might be that Arthur believes that this conversation shows that the animal before him is of higher moral status than he had hitherto assigned to animals. One question is whether there's something special about this particular animal that now speaks to Arthur, or whether the conversation he now has – aided by the Babel fish translator (*Hitchhiker's Guide to the Galaxy*, chapter 6) – shows that all cows[1] are more intelligent than Arthur had assumed. Depending on the answer to this question, it might be either that Arthur now has reasons to reconsider the ethics of eating meat generally, or simply that he has reasons to be uneasy about eating this particular animal.

One might think that, if Arthur has not already given serious thought to his dietary choices, this shows him guilty of serious moral negligence, but Arthur would hardly be alone in such failings. Most of us give very little thought to the fact that many of the decisions we face in our daily lives are, or at least involve, ethical questions. For the most part, our actions are habitual or dictated by social conventions. We rarely subject these conventions to ethical criticism. Widespread social practices may be quite unjustified though – as the example of slavery shows. It was only because a few individuals were willing to subject social norms to criticism that progress was possible. If we refuse to reflect seriously on the possibility that our treatment of animals is wrong, then we may be no better than those who refused to question the morality* of slavery.

In this chapter, we first reflect on the dangers of moral complacency and on the possibility that widespread social practices, such as eating meat, may be morally wrong. We then consider a number of distinct arguments for vegetarianism, which urge that we should never eat meat.[2] Then we turn to the specific and rather unusual case Arthur is presented with and examine the importance of consent. It is often the case that consent gives one permission to act in ways that would otherwise be wrong, but we note that there are serious problems where this consent has been manufactured, as in the case of the cow bred to want to be eaten. While the subject is complex, and the moral permissibility* of Arthur's eating the cow likely depends on further empirical* information that we do not have access to (like the quality of life that the cow enjoys or how its wants are manufactured), we conclude by noting that it is usually better to err on the side of not doing wrong. To eat the cow *may* be wrong, but *not* to eat it certainly isn't – despite its wish to be eaten, it has no right that Arthur eat it – so it is safer for Arthur not to eat it.

Singer's critique of moral complacency

Most of us, who aren't sociopaths or Zaphod Beeblebrox, don't even think about engaging in practices widely accepted as immoral, such as lying, cheating or stealing, to get what we want. On the other hand, few of us think seriously as to whether quite ordinary, socially accept-able modes of behaviour are in fact morally permissible. Is it morally wrong, for example, not to give more of our income to help people who are starving? Or to wear clothes produced by sweatshop labour? Or to take regular flights, though these contribute to global warming, which is likely to cause widespread suffering for many within the not too distant future? Eating meat is simply another instance of widespread behaviour that few pause to consider the morality of.

It's far from obvious that all of our habitual patterns of behaviour are morally justified simply because they're widely practised and eating meat may simply be another example of a widespread, but morally unjustifiable, prac-tice. If one wants to avoid complicity in such practices, then one must be prepared to assume responsibility for one's own choices and to speak out if need be. This is the position of contemporary animal rights activists, who have come to the conclusion that our treatment of non-human animals is deeply immoral and that a stand must be made against such barbaric practices. Since most animals cannot speak for themselves, we must speak for them. (The cow that can speak for itself, and wants to be eaten, is of course a problematic case!)

Not so long ago, racism, sexism and even slavery were considered acceptable by many societies. It was only because people were willing to stand back and criticise these social norms as immoral that progressive changes were possible. We shouldn't complacently assume that we have reached the end of our moral development. It may well be that our current social norms also permit instances of serious immorality, including perhaps the way that many of us treat animals.

The contemporary philosopher Peter Singer argues that, in many cases, our prevailing behaviours are indeed immoral. In one of his most famous articles (Singer 1972), he argues that we owe far more stringent duties to alleviate suffering and that it is unjustified to treat ourselves to luxuries such as designer clothes and bottled water while people in the Third World die of malnutrition or easily treated diseases, which could have been prevented if we instead donated the money to charities like Oxfam.

If we saw someone leave a child to drown in a shallow pond, for fear of ruining their expensive suit, we'd judge them to be immoral. But, Singer contends, most of us are guilty of taking a similar attitude towards those in the Third World. It's true that they're not literally dying in front of us, but we know that we can prevent suffering and death by donating our money to aid agencies. If you buy yourself a suit, instead of giving the money to Oxfam, then you're guilty of preferring your suit over a life that you might have been able to save.

Singer's moral views are pretty stringent. It seems that, on his view, most of us do wrong most of the time, if we're not actively working to alleviate global poverty. This view has been challenged, however. Critics have argued that, if morality were as demanding as Singer supposes, it would leave us little if any room to lead our own lives.[3] If we were morally required to do all that we could to combat global poverty, then it would be wrong for you to buy this book, when you could have sent the money to charity, or for us to be writing it, when we could have spent our time volunteering for worthy causes. While we should be wary of moral complacency, it's not clear that we should completely overturn our ordinary, common-sense beliefs.

Unfortunately, one belief deeply embedded in our ordinary moral outlooks is that it's wrong to cause gratuitous harm. We have our doubts about how much sacrifice should be required of us to aid distant strangers, but for the most part we agree that it would be wrong to inflict suffering on others for our amusement. It's one thing not to rescue hitchhikers – to leave them on their own – but quite another actively to subject someone to, say, a Vogon poetry reading.

In *Animal Liberation*, Singer argues that our widespread treatment of animals is wrong, even by these quite ordinary moral standards. We cannot justify the ways in which we use animals – in farms, zoos, research laboratories,[4] or even perhaps as pets – which often involve inflicting considerable suffering on them for the sake of trivial benefits on our part. We cannot, in this present discussion, address all of the difficult questions about the ethics of domesticating animals or using them for research. We shall confine ourselves to the matter of *eating* animals, including the associated practices of animal breeding and husbandry. We hope that this will shed light not only on Arthur's dilemma, whether to eat the willing creature before him, but also on wider questions about our treatment of animals.

Philosophers often seem to prefer questions to answers (*Hitchhiker's*, chapter 25). Most contemporary moral philosophers*, however, do seek clearer knowledge about our moral principles. One way of getting at this is through considering what we think about quite fantastic hypothetical examples, such as the one in which an innocent passer-by is wired into a famous violinist as a form of life support.[5] The case Arthur is presented with seems like a similarly useful test case. We may agree with Zaphod that, were eating animals ever permissible, it would most likely be so where the animal in question explicitly wants to be eaten. If we have doubts about eating animals even in this case, it might seem that it can never be justified. As we'll see though, matters aren't so straightforward. There might be quite different ethical objections to manufacturing animals that want to be eaten.

Arguments for vegetarianism

We have assumed that Arthur is ordinarily quite happy to eat animals in a variety of forms, provided that they don't put him off his meal by striking up a conversation with him first. Before we turn to why he might be particularly perturbed by the thought of an animal that wants to be eaten, it will be helpful to begin by asking why it might be wrong to eat meat in the first place. Ethical vegetarians (that is, those who are vegetarian for moral reasons) adduce a variety of reasons for objecting to our treatment of animals and not all agree on why they think meat eating is wrong.

Firstly, some object to the fact that eating animals necessarily involves killing them. We ordinarily think of murder as one of the most heinous crimes that we can commit, but why should this be restricted to humans and not also animals? This raises questions about the badness of death and killing. Many philosophers, such as Socrates and Epicurus, have questioned whether death is obviously a bad thing, likening it to a state of sleep or arguing that it is no worse than the non-existence that takes place before we were born.[6] We do not regret the fact that we weren't born earlier than we were, so why wish to die later than we will?

Responses typically focus on the fact that a shorter life means forgoing the goods that come with living.[7] This is equally true for both humans and animals. If we assume that most people live reasonably pleasant lives, then it's bad to die because it means being deprived of the benefits that would come from a longer existence. If animal lives include as many goods as human lives then this puts their deaths on a par with human deaths, since both involve the same loss. Killing an animal too deprives it of the rest of the pleasant existence it could have led.

It's sometimes suggested, though, that death involves more than the mere deprivation of future benefits. Killing a cow may deprive it of future pleasure, but if one were to substitute another cow in its place then the amount of good in the universe would not be affected. Nor would it make any difference to the cow if it was put in suspended animation and revived later, since the pleasures and pains felt by a cow do not depend on time. Humans, on the other hand, being the kind of creatures we are, inevitably make long-term plans. When we die, we are not only deprived of pleasures we could have had, but also risk the frustration of these plans. (Of course, this is not unique to humans – think how much worse the mice feel about the destruction of the whole Earth, after waiting almost ten million years to find the ultimate question of life, the universe and everything – but it is particular to higher animals.)

Since *most* animals don't have long-term projects, it can be argued that their deaths aren't as bad for them as human deaths. For these animals, a quick and painless death isn't such a bad thing, even if their suffering is bad.[8] Even if we accept this though, it doesn't mean that meat eating – the way it's currently practised by most people – is morally permissible. There might not be anything wrong *in itself* with killing an animal in order to eat it, but it might still be wrong to subject it to suffering in the process of slaughter or beforehand. The modern, commercial meat industry, unfortunately, is driven more by profits than animal welfare.[9] Factory-farmed animals are often kept in crowded, dark, dirty and generally inhumane conditions. It comes as no surprise that many caged animals seem as depressed as Marvin, given their miserable living conditions.

If animal suffering is bad, then treating animals in these ways is wrong, even if the simple act of killing them for food isn't itself wrong. This shows that even if eating meat *could* be morally acceptable, were the animals well treated, it isn't morally acceptable when that meat comes from factory farms in which animals are poorly treated. One needn't be a vegetarian to boycott products like foie gras or veal, which involve particular cruelty. Many people, if they saw the suffering inflicted on animals in order to provide us with cheap meat, would boycott all meat unless sourced from ethical, free-range producers. Thus, *even if you think there's nothing inherently wrong about **killing** animals for food, it doesn't show that our meat consumption is off the hook, morally, unless you're indifferent to animal pain and suffering too.*

It is generally accepted that pain and suffering are bad, so to cause unnecessary suffering to someone is wrong.

This seems to apply not only to human suffering, but also that of animals. The badness of suffering depends, it seems, on how it feels and not on anything distinctive to human beings. If animals feel pain in much the same way as humans, which seems to be the case at least for 'higher' animals, then that too is bad. To deny the moral relevance of animal pain simply because they are of a different species seems no more morally justified than denying the relevance of some people's suffering because they are of a different skin colour. In fact, some activists have coined the term 'speciesism' – popularised by Singer – to reflect the similarity of our attitudes to racism. We can't discount animal suffering simply because they're a different species, since species isn't relevant to the badness of suffering.

Thus, animal suffering is bad, but some have doubted whether animals really feel pain. If animals don't feel any pain then it's plausible that we can treat them as we wish, without wrong. René Descartes regarded animals as like automata, devoid of mental life (unlike those of the Sirius Cybernetics Corporation) and simply programmed to respond in certain ways to stimuli that we would regard as painful.[10] But, while there is of course significant variation between 'lower' animals like cockroaches and 'higher' ones such as primates, dolphins or mice,[11] it seems quite likely that those possessed of a central nervous system feel pain in much the same way that humans do.

We see that animals react to painful stimuli, just like we see other humans do. Now, it may be that we do not *know for certain* that animals feel pain. Perhaps we can never *know* what goes on in another being's head. Indeed, Zaphod doesn't always know what's going on in his own heads (*Hitchhiker's*, chapter 20). But this is hardly reason to deny that they feel pain. Firstly, this strategy would logically commit us to denying that other people feel pain too, since we can never know what they experience either, only judge from their reactions. Secondly, if we're not to be guilty of recklessness, we need to be pretty sure that animals *don't* feel pain, rather than simply uncertain that they do. This idea that one shouldn't take moral risks is one that we'll return to later.

Kant and using others as means

It seems that these considerations amount to a powerful case in favour of vegetarianism, even if we think that *killing* animals needn't be wrong, provided it is done painlessly. For, so long as animal suffering is bad – and it seems hard to deny this – then practices surrounding the meat industry, such as factory farming, are ethically dubious. Some animal rights activists go even further and object not only to killing animals or inflicting suffering on them but to *using* animals for our purposes, regarding it as a form of exploitation. On this account, it might be wrong even to keep animals as pets, as Trillian keeps caged mice on the *Heart of Gold* (*Hitchhiker's*, chapter 14), even if they are well looked after.

Many people, following the German philosopher Immanuel Kant, think that it's wrong to use people, or to treat them as 'mere means' to our own ends, even if it doesn't actually harm them.[12] We wrong people if we treat them in certain ways without their consent. This is supposed to explain the wrongness of lying or manipulation. Lying to someone to get them to do what you want is to use them for your ends without their consent. This is wrong, even if they end up better off as a result of the manipulation involved.

If we extend the same attitude to animals (which Kant would not have done himself) then, since they cannot ordinarily consent, there are many ways in which it is wrong to treat them. We might conclude from this that it is wrong to keep animals, even if they do not suffer at all. Such reasoning could take us beyond vegetarianism and into a case for veganism. Even if dairy cows, for instance, do not suffer from being milked, we exploit them by consuming what they produce.

According to this Kantian approach to moral thinking, physical harm isn't the most important thing from the moral point of view. We can wrong someone, even if we don't harm them – for instance, if we trespass on their property, without damaging anything or them ever finding out.[13] Moreover, we can harm someone without wronging them. In particular, if someone has consented to the way we treat them, then this may license actions that would otherwise be wrong. A patient's consent to surgery, for instance, permits a doctor to operate on them with a scalpel, even though this action – without consent – would constitute assault.

This returns us to Arthur's rather unusual dilemma. What should we say about eating animals if they could and did consent, as the animal in the Restaurant at the End of the Universe does? While this may seem an absurdly hypothetical example, of the sort philosophers love, what we say about this case may have implications for those like that of Armin Meiwes, the German computer technician who was tried in 2003 for cannibalism, after admitting to killing and eating volunteer Bernd-Jürgen Brandes.[14] If consent makes it permissible to eat someone, then we ought to acquit both Arthur and Meiwes. But if we *worry* about the cannibalism case, then perhaps that suggests that Arthur's doubts are well founded and we ought not to assume that it's OK to eat an animal that wants to be eaten.

The 'magic' of consent

As Zaphod observes, it seems better to eat an animal that wants to be eaten than one that doesn't. If morality forbids us from using other people in certain ways without their consent, then consent has the power to affect the morality of our actions. When Zaphod whisked Trillian away from that party in Islington, where she first met Arthur (*Hitchhiker's*, chapter 13), that would usually count as abduction. The fact that she consented, however, changes his action from deeply immoral to perfectly permissible. In other words, consent appears to have the power to alter the morality of our actions. Using others in ways that would otherwise be wrong becomes morally innocent when they give their permission.

A number of modern writers, such as Robert Nozick, who draw on the Kantian tradition, regard persons as having ownership rights over themselves.[15] Using my body in ways without my authorisation is therefore akin to borrowing – or stealing – my property without permission. Nonetheless, if I consent, then I allow you to use my body. Nozick goes so far as to say that people should be allowed to sell themselves into slavery if they wish – and so, presumably, would also allow people to volunteer to be eaten. (There's no accounting for what some people want.)

Consent can take a variety of forms. Sometimes it may be explicitly given, as by signing a contract, while sometimes it might be implicit in someone's actions or their lack of objection to what we do. Nonetheless, there are certain conditions that it must meet in order to be valid* – that is, to have moral force. Genuine consent must be informed and freely given, for example, so if we secure someone's consent only by drugging or misinforming them then that will not make our subsequent actions morally permissible.[16] Similarly if consent is secured only through threat of torture, such as a Vogon poetry reading, then it is invalid.

Before we return to the question of whether the cow that wants to be eaten meets the conditions for genuine consent, it's worth pausing to ask whether there are some things that one can never voluntarily consent to. John Locke held that individuals, as God's creations, had no right to take their own lives.[17] He thus concluded that they had no right to consent to an absolute monarch with power of life or death over them, since that could amount to forfeiting their lives, which they had no right to do. If there are acts that one cannot consent to, then any apparent act of consent will actually be null and void.

Without Locke's religious assumptions though, it's hard to see why certain things should be held so terrible that we cannot consent to them. What it's rational to consent to depends on one's context. You wouldn't usually consent to painful surgery, but may do so if it's necessary to save your life. Similarly, though one wouldn't usually wish to die, one might if suffering from a painful and terminal disease. Someone as depressed as Marvin might wish for euthanasia. One might also hope that one's death may do some good. If someone must volunteer for a dangerous mission, then it makes sense for someone who wants to die anyway to sacrifice themselves. One might even sacrifice oneself more directly – for example, one amongst a shipwrecked party might volunteer to be eaten to save the others. While we might find this somewhat repulsive, their consent makes the action morally different from the rest ganging up to eat them against their will.

There's no reason to think that one cannot possibly consent to being eaten. As the cow observes, it offers its own shoulder, because it has no right to offer anyone else's (*Restaurant*, 1980, chapter 17). If this is genuine consent, then it would seemingly make it permissible for Arthur to eat the cow. If he has his doubts, then presumably it's because he doubts whether this consent is genuine.

The consenting cow

The first thing that Arthur needs to do, when confronted by this apparently consenting cow, is to establish whether or not it is really capable of consent. It may be that, though the animal appears to be offering its consent, it is not really capable of doing so. It may be like a five-year-old child, who is capable of uttering the words, but lacks sufficient understanding of their significance for this to amount to valid consent. This is a matter of the animal's capacities and these are best gauged it seems by conversation.

If the issue is whether the animal is self-aware and rational, then that can be assessed by its ability to hold an intelligent conversation. This resembles the famous Turing test for artificial intelligence: a computer should be considered intelligent if one cannot distinguish it from a human in conversation, not that this shows much intelligence in many cases.

Some have even suggested that the capacity to enter dialogue with others is an important constituent of the scope of our moral concern, which would go some way to explaining why animals and even foreigners have often been afforded lesser moral concern in practice. It is only once we can enter dialogue with someone that the possibility of justifying ourselves to them arises. If we were able to communicate with dolphins, then we might have to explain why we keep them as we do. By expanding our scope for communication, then, the Babel fish appears to enlarge our domain of moral concern.

It seems that the animal in front of Arthur does indeed have the general capacity to consent. It's unclear whether this cow is more intelligent than others, or whether it's simply better able to articulate its preferences. Most cows can't speak for themselves, but this one's been bred to do so.

One might think that, being more intelligent, this cow would possess higher moral status than most of the species. That line of thought is dangerous, however, for it might suggest that Marvin – with his brain the size of a planet – would be of higher moral status than Arthur. Would this permit Marvin to kill Arthur for his pleasure? Surely not. Therefore, we shouldn't think that we can do what we like to animals, simply because they're less intelligent than us. At the very least, their suffering still matters, because the badness of pain doesn't depend on the intelligence of the sufferer.

If we accept that people can validly give consent to being eaten, however, then it seems that the same should be true for the cow. The next question for Arthur is whether consent *is* validly given in this particular case. If the cow consented only because it would otherwise be violently beaten, for example, then this would not be free and genuine consent. There's no reason, however, to assume that the cow is subject to such threats, misinformation or drugs. In other words, there's no temporary condition that explains – and invalidates – its consent to being eaten.

Three faces of power

Consent is not normally valid if extracted under duress, such as the threat of being ejected into space. This is a fairly obvious case of coercion, but it's also possible for power to be exerted in more insidious ways. In his book *Power*, the Marxist theorist Steven Lukes identifies what he calls three faces of power – that's one more than Zaphod's two faces and no more pleasant to look at.

Firstly, and most obviously, you can exert power over someone else by forcing them to do what you want and they do not. Threatening to blast someone with a Kill-O-Zap gun, for instance, might be one way of exercising power in this sense. Not all exercises of power are so overt though.

Power is exercised in a second way by what is sometimes called 'non-decision making', that is, shutting down the potential for an issue to be debated and encouraging the perception that it is a non-issue. If Zaphod gave Ford the options of coming with him to Magrathea or hanging around ZZ 9 Plural Z Alpha – former location of the Earth, before the Vogon construction fleet arrived – then he still exerts power by presenting Ford only with these choices and not, say, returning to Betelgeuse Five. Ford may pick the option he prefers, but his choice can be manipulated by Zaphod presenting him only with unpalatable options to choose between.

The third, and least obvious, form of power involves influencing what it is that others want. If we accept Karl Marx's view, that the workers in a capitalist society are under the sway of an ideology that prevents them from recognising their exploitation and leads them to passive submission,[18] then this would be an example of the third form of power. Thus, Lukes concludes, we only recognise this most insidious form of power if we shift our attention from whether people get what they want to whether they get what is good for them. The doors on the *Heart of Gold*, for instance, are happy to serve since that is all that they have been programmed to do (*Hitchhiker's*, chapter 11). That they cheerfully open and close for people does not, however, show that they are not oppressed, but perhaps how totally oppressed they are. Their very wants have been shaped by others and this is perhaps the most invidious exercise of power.

The cow that confronts Arthur in the Restaurant at the End of the Universe was intended to avoid complicated questions about the morality of eating meat, by wanting to be eaten.[19] The trouble is that, while consent might in theory legitimate eating someone, it might be wrong to breed an animal that wants to be eaten and Arthur might therefore have reasons not to eat it to avoid complicity in this practice.

Manufacturing consent

If the suppliers to the Restaurant at the End of the Universe thought that they could avoid moral controversy by breeding animals that wanted to be eaten then they were mistaken. While they may avoid one set of moral problems, they are merely embroiled in another about the ethics of breeding animals for a specific purpose and manipulating their wants.

It's often thought that creating children for a specific purpose, such as to act as donors for their elder siblings, is morally suspect because it treats them merely as means to that end and fails to respect them in themselves or their need for consent. We might still question the morality of this practice, even if the children in question were genetically engineered such that they wanted to donate their organs to their elder siblings. We ordinarily think it a fine, altruistic gesture for someone to give an organ to another, even a relative. But matters are more complex where that desire has been artificially implanted in the donor.

Similar worries might arise around the manufacture of animals with a desire to be eaten. Though we usually assume it's alright to raise animals for food, and that if they consent that makes eating them acceptable, engineering them so that they consent might be wrong in itself.

It's often remarked that such animals would not exist were they not produced for food. This may well be true, but it is only relevant if it is obviously better for them to exist than not to. To bring a child, or an animal, into existence only for a short, painful and meaningless existence – like that of the whale that plunges into the surface of Magrathea (*Hitchhiker's*, chapter 18) – is wrong. It might even be better for them never to exist. As we saw, one reason to object to eating meat is that many animals raised by the meat industry live in appalling conditions, so miserable that it is questionable whether they would be better off not to have existed at all.

The animals that have been bred to be willing food are, like 'saviour siblings', denied the right to an open future. They do not have the opportunity to direct their life as they wish, for it has already been mapped out for them (and they have been engineered to want this preordained course). Arguably, however, meaningful consent depends on the ability to say no. If one cannot refuse an offer, then one's acceptance of it loses its significance. So, that the cow is willing to be eaten doesn't establish the moral permissibility of Arthur's doing so, given that this consent was artificially manufactured to serve the interests of restaurateurs and their patrons. It's little different from raising people to be slaves, and then holding that the slavery in question is unobjectionable because they don't object.

Of course, Arthur himself isn't responsible for breeding the animal, so one might be tempted to argue that he wouldn't do anything wrong if he were simply to go along with its wish to be eaten. This overlooks the fact that it is wrong for us to be complicit in the wrongdoing of others. Arthur wouldn't himself be guilty of killing the animal, or of keeping it in inhumane conditions, but if others do this in order to satisfy his demand for cheap meat, then he is implicated in the wrongdoing. Similarly, if he is prepared to eat the consenting cow, then he is thereby complicit in the breeding of such animals.

There may be some truth to Zaphod's remark, that it seems better to eat an animal that wants to be eaten than one that doesn't, but this is true only when other things are equal. If Arthur were given the choice between eating a willing cow or an unwilling one, then he should probably prefer to eat the former. Nonetheless, other things aren't exactly equal here. Where an animal consents only because it is bred to do so, it's not obvious whether this consent outweighs the moral problems of breeding such an animal in the first place.

A final consideration: the precautionary principle

In summary, Arthur's choice – like many moral decisions – is a difficult one, requiring him to weigh the force of competing considerations. Firstly, there are all the usual reasons against eating meat, involving the wrongness of killing animals or subjecting them to suffering. These reasons seem at least partly offset by this particular animal's willingness to be eaten. Even if Arthur has doubts about the validity of its consent, the creature's cheerful disposition suggests that – unlike contemporary farm animals – it hasn't suffered in being raised for Arthur's plate. Indeed, the cow even points out that it has been exercising and force-feeding itself deliberately, to make its meat rich and tender.

On the other hand, this in itself can be seen as repugnant and strange, and thus invites moral inquiry. Arthur might be quite sensible to pause before eating a cow that's capable of talking to him. This is clearly no dumb brute. If the cow is capable of conversation, then it is presumably closer to human levels of intelligence and thus, *perhaps*, moral status. Granted, its consent to being eaten may carry some weight, but it is not obvious whether this is freely given, since the animal has been raised to want to be eaten. If this practice is *itself* morally dubious, then Arthur might wish to distance himself from it, rather than make himself complicit by enjoying its products.

As in most complex moral cases, there's no clear or simple answer to what Arthur ought to do. If there were, then acting morally – or, at least, knowing what morality required – would be easy. It's because real life presents us with a variety of complex and competing considerations, however, that powers of sensitivity and discernment are necessary. We need to think carefully – philosophically – through the issues at stake in a given decision in order to know what morality requires of us. Indeed, this critical thinking may itself be something that morality demands in complex situations!

In this case, Arthur is – quite understandably – unsure whether he should eat the cow, even though it wants to be eaten. Indeed, when the animal points out that many vegetables don't wish to be eaten, he becomes unsure even about a green salad and settles for a glass of water. In this, Arthur opts for a morally safe choice. Eating a living animal *might* be immoral, especially because we might be as mistaken about cows as we are about mice and dolphins, but eating vegetables or drinking a glass of water probably isn't – unless we're wrong about them too.

If Arthur were to eat the cow, then he might be doing something morally wrong. By not doing so, he's certain not to be doing wrong. If he wants to avoid wrongdoing, then it seems that he's better advised not to take this risk. It's true that he'll thereby upset the cow, which positively wants to be eaten, but, surely, the cow has no right that Arthur eats it (or that Arthur not upset it). While the cow's consent may waive Arthur's usual duty not to eat it, it doesn't place him under any *obligation* to do so. If he doesn't want to eat it, for whatever reason, then his refusal isn't itself wrong.

Where we are unsure whether a given course of action would be immoral or not, it is reckless to proceed anyway, if we have another alternative that avoids the risks. The 'precautionary principle' tells us to be cautious and avoid unnecessary risks. Where the potential harm is large, it might make sense to avoid even small risks. Even if the threat of catastrophic climate change is tiny, we'd be well advised to do what we can to reduce it further, since it would be terrible if it happened.

If we knew that Descartes was right that animals felt no pain, then we'd do no more direct wrong by torturing a cat than by kicking a stone. Since most of us would judge a cat torturer as immoral, it seems that most of us think animals do feel pain – or, at least, we're not sufficiently sure that they don't in order to justify wanton cruelty. On the other hand, that we're prepared to treat animals as we do suggests that we doubt that their suffering is as morally weighty as that of human beings. Given the choice between allowing the torture of a cat or that of a fellow human being, we'd let the cat suffer first, since that's not as certainly wrong.

The issue facing us – as well as Arthur – is what probability to attach to the hypothesis that animals suffer in morally relevant ways. The greater the probability we attach to this, the less risk we should be prepared to take. It seems that most of us think torturing animals is taking too big a risk for too little benefit. The question is whether the pleasure that we get from eating meat justifies the risk that we do wrong by raising and killing animals for our consumption. The answer is far from obvious.[20]

For deeper thought

For the classic defence of our moral duties to animals, see Peter Singer's *Animal Liberation*, which has been reprinted numerous times.

Various critics have attempted responses to Singer's arguments, defending favouritism towards our fellow humans (and maybe humanoid aliens). See, for example: Michael Leahy, *Against Liberation: Putting Animals in Perspective*; Roger Scruton, *Animal Rights and Wrongs*; and Bernard Williams, 'The Human Prejudice' in his *Philosophy as a Humanistic Discipline*.

There are many accessible introductions to the ethical issues around our treatment of animals, including Mark Rowlands, *Animals Like Us*, David DeGrazia, *Animal Ethics: a Very Short Introduction*, and Alison Hills, *Do Animals have Rights?*

Consent is rarely discussed in the context of animals, but for stimulating treatments of it in other cases see Neil Manson and Onora O'Neill, *Rethinking Informed Consent in Bioethics* and A. John Simmons, *Moral Principles and Political Obligation*, chapters 3–4.

Notes

1. The animal is described not, quite, as a cow, but as 'a large fat meaty quadruped of the bovine type' – 'with large watery eyes, small horns and what might almost have been an ingratiating smile on its lips' (*Restaurant*, ch. 17). For simplicity, though, we'll sometimes refer to it as a cow.
2. As to *fish*, we rather neglect them in this piece. But see note 20 below.
3. Miller, 'Beneficence, Duty and Distance'.
4. Of course, Singer – like Arthur, until corrected by Slartibartfast (*Hitchhiker's Guide*, ch. 24) – assumes that we're the ones experimenting on the mice. If the situation's actually the other way round, they might be wronging us.
5. This example occurs in Judith Thomson's 'A Defence of Abortion'. She hopes to avoid controversy over whether or not the foetus is a person, by arguing that you have no obligation to spend nine months serving as life support for the violinist, so nor must a mother let a foetus use her body for the same ends – she is quite permitted to choose an abortion, *even if* the foetus has all the same rights to life as a famous violinist.
6. Epicurus, 'Letter to Menoeceus'; Plato, 'Apology'.

7. Nagel, 'The Absurd'.
8. Tooley, ''Abortion and Infanticide'.
9. Singer and Mason, *Eating: What We Eat and Why it Matters*.
10. Descartes, *Discourse on the Method*.
11. The dolphins were, of course, aware of Earth's imminent destruction by the Vogons, even if humans failed to heed their warnings (*Hitchhiker's*, ch. 23). The fact that we wouldn't automatically have placed mice in the 'higher' group, without recognising that they are merely Earthly manifestations of hyper-intelligent pan-dimensional beings, suggests that we shouldn't be too hasty in our assumptions about what animals are capable of. Even crows have been shown to possess surprising abilities to use tools.
12. Nozick, *Anarchy, State, and Utopia*.
13. Ripstein, 'Beyond the Harm Principle'.
14. BBC, 'German Cannibal Tells of Fantasy'.
15. Nozick, *Anarchy, State, and Utopia*.
16. O'Neill, 'Between Consenting Adults'.
17. Locke, *Two Treatises of Government*.
18. Marx, 'The German Ideology'.
19. One might think that artificial meat would be a better solution, since it wouldn't involve any animal death or suffering. But the Nutri-Matic struggles to get a cup of tea right (*Hitchhiker's Guide*, ch. 17; *Restaurant*, ch. 2), so what chance steak?
20. Being mere humans, we might look to those more intelligent species for answers. Dolphins, of course, eat fish, so maybe pescetarianism is OK.

2
Mostly Harmless? *Hitchhiker's* and the Ethics of Entertainment

Nicholas Joll

> The villagers were absolutely hypnotized by all these won-
> derful magic images flashing over her [Random's] wrist.
> They had only ever seen one spaceship crash, and it had
> been so frightening, violent and shocking and had caused
> so much horrible devastation, fire and death that, stupidly,
> they had never realised it was entertainment.
>
> (*Mostly Harmless*, chapter 15)

Douglas Adams was interested in what entertains people. Witness several passages that I shall quote below and
also the wonderful *Mostly Harmless* passage that I have
reproduced above.[1] That interest in entertainment is
unsurprising. Adams was a comedy writer and, in person,
a raconteur. Now, what interests *me*, as a philosopher, and
indeed as a citizen, is this: *Hitchhiker's* prompts reflection
upon the *ethics* of entertainment (and, actually, that seems
to have been something that interested Adams himself as
well).[2]

This chapter unfolds as follows. I start by showing how
Hitchhiker's raises various questions within the ethics of

entertainment. (That's section 1.) Next I narrow the focus to *violent* (but fictional) entertainment and pose this question: *Is violent entertainment alright?* (That's section 2.) Then (section 3) I proceed to try to answer the question. There will be some jokes as well – or at least some quotation of wonderful stuff from *Hitchhiker's*. As for the endnotes (of which I have a few), they are mostly for the brave.

1   *Hitchhiker's* and the ethics of entertainment

Consider the following three passages.

> [. . .] 'I read [said Ford] of one planet off in the seventh dimension that got used as a ball in a game of intergalactic bar billiards. Got potted straight into a black hole. Killed ten billion people.'
>
> 'That's mad,' said Mella.
>
> 'Yes, only scored thirty points too.'
>
> Agda and Mella exchanged glances.
>
> (*The Restaurant at the End of the Universe*, chapter 34)

'So, ladies and gentlemen,' he [Max Quordlepleen, the host at Milliways, the Restaurant at the End of the Universe] breathed, 'the candles are lit, the band plays softly, and as the force-shielded dome above us fades into transparency, revealing a dark and sullen sky hung heavy with the ancient light of livid swollen stars, I can see we're all in for a fabulous evening's apocalypse!'

(*Restaurant*, chapter 17)

'The game you know as cricket,' he [Slartibartfast] said [...] 'is just one of those curious freaks of racial memory which can keep images alive in the mind aeons after their true significance has been lost in the mists of time. Of all the races on the Galaxy, only the English could possibly revive the memory of the most horrific wars ever to sunder the Universe and transform it into what I'm afraid is generally regarded as an incomprehensibly dull and pointless game.[']

'Rather fond of it myself,' he added, 'but in most people's eyes you have been inadvertently guilty of the most grotesque bad taste. Particularly the bit about the little red ball hitting the wicket, that's very nasty. [Refresher on galactic history: the 'Wikkit Gate' symbolised galactic concord; the Krikkiters, who used bats to propel little red grenades, destroyed both gate and concord.]

(*Life, the Universe and Everything*, chapter 12; 'refresher' added by me)

These passages can prompt one to ask this question: What is acceptable as entertainment? But they prompt two more specific questions too. *First*, the 'billiards' passage raises this question: Is it alright to *perpetrate violence* in order to entertain? *Second*, the Milliways and 'cricket' passages generate this question: Is it alright to *make use of* real violent events (which one has not brought into being) for entertainment?[3] Both of these specific questions are applicable to actual – 'real life', non-*Hitchhiker* – phenomena. *Apropos* the first question, think of gladiators, bullfighting, boxing and, insofar as they involve or aim to produce conflict, 'reality television' programmes. In the case of the second question, think of anything (films, books, TV programmes and also, in a way, satire) that makes entertainment from such things as actual earthquakes or actual terrorist attacks. But the question I want to pursue in this chapter is a slightly different – a *third* – one.

2 The question that will be at issue

The question I want to pursue is raised in an arresting way by the *Mostly Harmless* passage quoted above. It's this. Is it alright to present *purely fictional violence* as entertainment? There is a reason for focusing upon that particular question. To wit: it is the one people tend most to have in mind when they worry about, or defend, violent entertainment.

As it stands, though, the question is not precise enough. Actually, and though I want to avoid pedantry of superhuman or inhuman levels (see *Life, the Universe and Everything*, chapter 18, on Agrajag), the question needs honing on *three* fronts. Please bear with me, now, as I do that honing. To keep yourself going, you can look forward to reading section 3, which is a good bit and has Random in it. (Or, if you must, you could skip straight to subsection 2.4, which is called 'Conclusion to this section'.)

2.1 What is this thing called entertainment?

Part of the entry for 'entertainment' in the *Shorter Oxford English Dictionary* is: 'A thing which entertains or amuses someone, *esp.* a public performance designed to entertain people'.[4] This might suggest that almost anything that is in any way enjoyable is, just by dint of that, entertainment. However, the notion of *mere* entertainment, together with the dictionary's reference to amusement, indicate otherwise. They indicate that some things are too worthy or sophisticated to count as entertainment, or at least that those things are not entertainment in the same sense that many other things are. For entertainment, in some guises anyway, is solely about *amusement, relaxation or diversion*. And it is with that *type* of entertainment, or with entertainment so construed, that I am concerned. For what I wish to evaluate is fictional violence that *serves no serious purpose* – i.e. *mere* entertainment.[5] (Am I concerned, then, only with entertainment containing *gratuitous* violence? Not quite. For perhaps entertainment is gratuitously violent only if it aspires to be entertainment that is something more or other than violent; and not all violent entertainment does so aspire. For entertainment in which violence serves no serious purpose may not reflect a failed attempt to serve such a purpose but rather the lack even of an *attempt* so to do.)

Admittedly, just what counts as mere – or unserious – entertainment is moot. Take, for instance, Irvine Welsh's more disturbing stories (such as those in his collection *Filth*). Are *they* mere entertainment? What about the writings of the Marquis de Sade? Or the play *Shopping and Fucking* by Mark Ravenhill? There is a deeper problem too. On what sort of *ground* are we to decide the answers to these questions? Are we to go by intentions of the author? By audience reaction? *Likely* audience reaction? Or by some notion of 'the work itself', i.e. what there is to be found in the work irrespective of what people actually do find in it?[6] There's also the idea that something can be mere entertainment in *some* ways but not in others. I will leave these issues open. It will be enough that we have a rough idea of the kind of entertainment – the kind of mere entertainment – that will be at issue. That's the hope, anyway.

2.2 What violence is at issue?

Just what is *violent* entertainment? One might define violence as the 'exercise of physical force so as to cause injury or damage to a person, property, etc.' (That's the *Shorter OED* again.) Violent entertainment would then be entertainment that involved *that*. But there are many sorts of violence and various ways of representing violence. Now, again, this is not something I want to go too deeply into. But I can and will say, or stipulate, the following. I am concerned particularly with violence – fictional violence – that has the following characteristics.

- It has *people* among its (fictional) targets.
- It is what we might call moderate or severe in its *degree*.
- It contains quite a *lot* of such violence.
- Its presentation of violence is fairly explicit and/or frightening.[7]

These stipulations mean that the sort of entertainment at issue includes not only pieces that are extreme by almost anyone's reckoning, such as the films *The Texas Chainsaw Massacre* and *Saw*, but also milder (or at least slightly milder) pieces such as the book and film *The Girl with the Dragon Tattoo*, the film *Reservoir Dogs*, and the television series *Spartacus*. (In using these as examples, I am presuming that all these works are, more or less, mere entertainment. If you disagree with that classification of one or more of the cases, then you can supply your own examples.) I do *not* mean to be talking about, say, the novel *Moby Dick*, the television series *Battlestar Galactica*, or indeed (any version of) *Hitchhiker's* itself, even though all of those contain, in one way or another, more than a little violence. For – and irrespective of whether these works are mere entertainment, or the degree to which they are – they don't contain enough violence, or enough violence of the right kind, to fit my definition/interest.[8]

2.3 'Acceptability'?

I do not mean to ask about what people or some group of people think about the acceptability of fictional violence as entertainment. Rather the issue is one that philosophers call normative* and, more specifically, moral* or ethical*. That is, the question is whether or not people *should* find it alright – whether such entertainment is (to use the philosophical jargon) permissible*. Still: is our question about the ethics of *enjoying* – consuming – violent entertainment (of a certain fictional sort . .)? Or is it about *producing* such entertainment? (One could think here of the issues in the ethics of pornography.) Well, my main concern will be the *enjoyment* of such entertainment. But I will have something to say, too, about the morality of the production of entertainment violence.[9]

2.4   Conclusion to this section

The foregoing specifications have honed our question into the following one. *Is it permissible to consume moderate-to-severe explicit fictional violence as (mere) entertainment?* Now, that is a mouthful. So, normally, I shall write simply of 'violent entertainment' or of 'entertainment violence'. Still: is this *enough* specification? In one way, no. It won't suffice to make any conclusions that I reach easily applicable to specific pieces of entertainment. But that is alright. For our question about violent entertainment is a rather general one, and I am assuming that an attempt to answer that general question has a point.

End of pedantry.

3   Engaging the question via the *Mostly Harmless* passage

I pursue an answer to the question via the *Mostly Harmless* passage with which I began. Since I want to consider that passage in some detail, I start with a reminder of the background behind it. (Those who need no reminder can skip two paragraphs.)

By the time we reach the passage, Arthur has had yet another accident. This time, though, he has been lucky. Sort of. He is the sole survivor of the crash-landing of a spaceship onto the planet Lamuella. Lamuella has inhabitants who greatly resemble human beings. But 'the high watermark of Lamuellan technology' consists of 'a forge and a bakery, a few carts and a well' (*Mostly Harmless*, chapter 15). So Arthur is stranded. I say stranded. Actually, he's happy on Lamuella, and, anyway, he has a chance to leave, because Trillian arrives on Lamuella, and Arthur could have asked her for a lift. But he doesn't ask; and Trillian gives him her teenage daughter to look after.

Before she herself leaves Lamuella, Trillian tells Arthur that this child, her daughter, is also *his* daughter. Arthur paid for his travels in space by donating, among other things, sperm; and Trillian, who was the only remaining *Homo sapiens* besides Arthur, wanted a baby. Hence the child, whose name is 'Random Frequent Flyer Dent'. This name reflects both the journeyings of her father and all the toings and froings she herself has undertaken with her mother and which, it turns out, she resents. Now, Random is used to, and very keen on, hi-tech entertainment. Consequently she is very bored on Lamuella, which lacks the 'electric clubs' she repeatedly demands to visit. But she does retain one item of hi-tech entertainment: a television embedded in her wrist. On this she watches (can still pick up) exciting programmes about fictional spaceship battles. She shows the Lamuellans those programmes.

Let me now repeat the passage itself.

The villagers were absolutely hypnotized by all these wonderful magic images flashing over her wrist. They had only ever seen one spaceship crash [the one that brought Arthur to Lamuella], and it had been so frightening, violent and shocking and had caused so much horrible devastation, fire and death that, stupidly, they had never realised it was entertainment.

The central thing here is the imputation of stupidity. The passage calls the Lamuellans stupid for not realising that violence – fictional violence – can be entertainment. One might expand the point thus: much of the appeal of entertainment violence is that it affords the stimulating side-effects of stress or threat without the actual stress or threat; that is what the Lamuellans fail to realise. Crucially, though, the passage's criticism is somewhat *ironic*. The passage suggests there is something *right* about the Lamuellans' reaction to the entertainment. More specifically, the idea seems to be this: violence is *just not the kind of thing* that can – should – be entertainment.[10]

Can we make an *argument* out of this? One could venture the following. To think that violence can be entertainment is to make what philosophers call a 'category mistake' – it's to confuse a thing of one kind with a thing of a considerably different kind. However: here, that idea seems to boil down simply to an *assertion* that one should not make entertainment from violence – which is the very point that is in dispute. Thus, to try to indict violent entertainment on the basis of an alleged category mistake is to commit the fallacy called 'begging the question'*.[11]

Nevertheless, Adams, or his joke, does somewhat take the Lamuellans' side, or sympathise with them. There *does* seem to be a suggestion that somehow violence is not entertainment. The question now is whether more can be made of that idea. I begin upon that task by considering several more or less intuitive criticisms of violent entertainment.

4 Three objections to violent entertainment

4.1 The corruption objection

The first objection I consider is that violent entertainment *corrupts the character of those who consume it*. The objection comes in two varieties:

1. Violent entertainment desensitises: the more one is exposed to it, the less one is troubled by, and/or motivated to remedy or prevent, actual violence.
2. Violent entertainment is a significant cause of violent or aggressive behaviour.

Most of the relevant empirical* studies find that violent entertainment *is* desensitising. The same goes for the claim that such entertainment increases aggression. Indeed many claim that the evidence for that latter view has become incontrovertible. Nonetheless, and confusingly for those who, like myself, are not experts on such research, each claim (each of 1 and 2) has its critics.[12] But: if you believe that television or films or books never corrupt, then you have to believe they can never morally *improve* people either. But, if *that* is true, then much education – in the form of attempts to improve people through such things – is pointless. And/but presumably it isn't.[13]

4.2 The solidarity/decadence objection

The objection to which I give this name goes as follows. *Given that real people suffer from real violence, the enjoyment of violent entertainment is a breach of solidarity, or is decadent.* One can imagine someone putting the objection in this polemical form: you *enjoy* this stuff, as entertainment, when real versions of it occur everyday? Now, if we take the claim at face value, then we seem owed an account of *why* solidarity (or the avoidance of decadence) requires that we eschew violent entertainment. True, we might be inclined to accept the following: in a violent world, it would be *best*, because of solidarity, to refuse to enjoy violent entertainment. But it is not clear that people are *obliged* to make that refusal. There are other possible inter-pretations of the objection, though. One is that to enjoy violent entertainment is to manifest a character flaw. But that is the idea I will treat, now, as a *third* objection to vio-lent entertainment.[14]

4.3   The viciousness objection

The objection I have in mind here is expressed in the fol-lowing passage.

> A person who enjoys watching a girl graphically bludg-eoned to death by a blood-thirsty assassin is lacking a number of virtues, not least that of sensitivity. A whole-some reaction when faced with such images should be repugnance, not enjoyment. That the viewer is unlikely to commit such acts himself, or that the events are fic-titious, does not detract from the wrongness of the disposition.
>
> (Sokol, 'The Harms of Violent Imagery' p. 66)

But, still: why? Why believe that such enjoyment shows a lack of virtue – a lack of sensitivity, or, say, empathy or compassion? For, even though Sokol denies the relevance of this, it *is fiction* that is at issue. Well, here is one answer. Such enjoyment requires that one suspend one's compas-sionate attitudes. Yet why is *that* wrong, given that, again, the suspension applies only to fiction? Perhaps because the enjoyment of such fictional violence worsens one's reactions to actual violence.[15] But this would return us to – turn this objection into – the corruption objection.

5 Further analysis of the objections – and a further objection

The corruption objection seems the strongest of the three objections. That is for the excellent reason that what it alleges (in both of its variants) seems to be *true*, whereas the other two objections, so far as they do not collapse into the corruption objection, are problematic in one way or another. However, in certain respects the corruption objection is in fact *weak*. How that is so emerges from the *instrumental* character of the objection. An instrumental objection to something concerns the thing's ostensible *effects*. Contrast an *intrinsic* objection. An intrinsic objection targets the thing *as such*, irrespective of effects it may or may not have. This distinction will become clearer as I apply it, now, to the objections with which we have been dealing.

The corruption objection is that violent entertainment corrupts its consumers, either by desensitising them or by making them more aggressive. This is an instrumental objection because it concerns (alleged) effects of violent entertainment. The other objections have a different character. They are intrinsic objections. Consider the viciousness objection. That objection, which asserts that to enjoy certain forms of violent entertainment is to exhibit some vice(s), is silent about, and so does not mean to depend upon, effects. It says: 'To enjoy this sort of thing is vicious. Full stop.' Nor does the solidarity/decadence objection mention effects.[16]

We can now appreciate how the instrumental nature of the corruption objection makes it weak. It does so in two ways:

1. *It makes the objection hostage to empirical research.* Should it turn out that, actually, violent entertainment does not corrupt, or corrupts to a lesser degree than was thought, then the corruption objection collapses (or, in the second of the two scenarios just imagined, is weakened).
2. *The instrumentality of the corruption objection means it can't capture the idea we started from,* namely, the 'category mistake' idea that violence just is not entertainment. *That* objection to violent entertainment seems intrinsic. So, if that is the view one is trying to flesh out, then the corruption objection – and any instrumental criticism of entertainment – is useless.[17]

Still: our considerations have left it uncertain whether any stronger – any intrinsic – objection to violent entertainment is sustainable. Here's an explanation of *why* things have worked out that way. Instrumental objections are more likely than intrinsic ones to turn on *harm*; and it is *easy* to appreciate that something is bad because of harmful effects. (Actually, the particular instrumental objection that has been at issue, the corruption objection, alleges two types of harm: harm to the consumer and, through that, harm to others.) By contrast, the viciousness objection and the solidarity/decadence objection do not, at least in any simple way, involve harm. So perhaps we should conclude thus: if (– *if* –) violent entertainment is harmless or mostly so, then it is alright.[18]

But there is a further, and seemingly intrinsic, objection that one might make against violent entertainment. I call it *the cognitive failure objection.* It's this. *The enjoyment of some sorts of violent entertainment is a moral failing, because it is a certain kind of cognitive* (i.e. mental) *failing,* namely, *a failure to appreciate the nature of violence.* That is, if you enjoy fictional violence, you don't really know what violence *is.* But what does *that* mean? Presumably something like this: you don't fully appreciate the badness of actual violence, i.e. the humanity of (real) victims of violence, or the fact that violence *hurts* or causes damage.

If this objection could be made good, then, in a kind of judo move, it would turn a common defence of violent entertainment against itself.[19] Here is an instance of the sort of defence I have in mind. 'When we create our games we use a slapstick type of violence, we poke each other in the eyes and hit each other with frying pans like the old Warner Brothers cartoons.'[20] The counter-response – the judo move – is this: to fictionalise violence to the point of *trivialising* it is precisely to fail to appreciate what real violence is. Now, this turning of the defence against itself is applicable only to entertainment violence that *is* defended in that way, or that is intended as slapstick. Yet the cognitive failure objection itself (as against the 'judo move' that it suggests) seems set to target more entertainment violence than just the 'slapstick' variety. For the objection can be put like this. Even when entertainment violence does not present itself as slapstick, it *is* slapstick, because *to enjoy that entertainment is to act as if real violence were something like slapstick.* I will not pursue this objection any further. Nonetheless, I do think that the Lamuellans (and Adams himself?) were onto something; and this 'cognitive failure objection' might be a way to express what that thing was.

The next section of the chapter is the last. It's a kind of appendix, in that it contains two reflections of a kind that is somewhat different from, or broader than, what's been at issue above. Those reflections might prove slightly hard going. But I trust that they have more accessibility than a locked filing cabinet (stuck in a disused toilet, etc.).

6   Two wider reflections

6.1   Ethics, argument and censorship

One might think that arguing about the ethics of entertainment is pointless, on the basis that it makes no sense to argue about *any* ethical matter. A reason for thinking that latter thought, in turn, is this: one might think that ethics is subjective or relative. Let me explain.

The idea – which, *perhaps*, has some echo in *Hitchhiker's* treatment of the Krikkiters[21] – is this. One person, or one group, has one ethic; another person or group has another; *and it makes no sense to try to decide who is right.* That sort of thing is commonly said. The first difficulty with it, though, is knowing what it means. Is it just the idea that morals differ between persons and groups? If it is then ... so what? Mere disagreement about a matter does not show that there is no fact of the matter. (People have disagreed about whether the earth is round. Today, though, we have insurmountable evidence that it *is* round – and, even if we did not, that would not establish that there was no fact, which one day might be discovered, about the shape of the earth.) It makes more sense to construe the idea as follows. There is indeed no truth of the matter about morals, *no such thing as moral truth*; and disagreement about moral matters is one *reason* to believe that claim. The thinking goes like this. Were there moral truth, then surely we would have reached more agreement about it than we have.[22]

One challenge for this view – and it is a view that will return us, in a bit, to the topic of entertainment – is as follows. There might actually be quite a lot of agreement about morality. Or at least perhaps there would be such agreement were more people able to form their moral views under better conditions, i.e. without resentment, indoctrination, excessive peer pressure and the like. Note also the following. When people say that morality is relative to a group (say a society or a culture or a tribe), and, sometimes, when they say that morality is subjective, they mean to *preserve* the idea of moral truth, only a moral truth that is somehow only a truth 'for' the group or individual. This is a difficulty insofar as it is not the idea just mentioned (which was the idea that there was no moral truth), and so needs a separate defence. Worse, it is unclear that one can make sense of the idea of 'truth for'. There's also this: it is very hard to actually *believe*, or at any rate *act* on the belief, that one person's morals, or one group's morals, are as true (or false) as any other. So: anyone who wants to defend ethical relativism or ethical subjectivism (as the sort of approaches I have just considered are called) has their work cut out.[23]

Someone who rejects relativism and subjectivism is not thereby committed to any policy of forcibly changing people's behaviour. It *is* true, at least if relativism and subjectivism are false, that it makes no sense to say *both* 'I believe X is the moral thing to do' *and* 'I don't care whether or not other people do X'. But, on its own, that doesn't commit one to saying 'and the best thing to do is to *make* people do X'. One might hold, with John Stuart Mill, *both* that some opinions and ways of life are morally better than others, *and* that, if no one except the person him- or herself is harmed, then the state, and society, should not try to pressure people – by any means save argument – to change their opinions or ways of life.[24]

These thoughts bear directly on the ethics of entertainment via the issue of *censorship*. That issue is political. But, in order to decide what stance one should take upon it, one must have a view not just on the political matter of what intervention is justifiable, but also on the ethical one of whether there's anything wrong with violent entertainment in the first place. In that sense, the ethical matters considered in this chapter are prior to the political matter of censorship. Still: my next and final section considers whether, actually, there might be something inherently political about the 'ethics' of entertainment.

6.2 Politics, not ethics?

A different version of the idea that ethics as such is misguided goes something like this. Much or all ethics, quite possibly including the ethics of entertainment, is misguided *under current conditions*. The view can be elaborated as the following argument.

1. Many contemporary societies (and perhaps many or all past societies) very heavily shape the ethics of their members; and societies, in turn, are greatly shaped by their economies, and by the interests of the powerful and, perhaps, by technology. (Premise*)
2. People tend not to think very independently about ethics; and it is hard to change people's minds on ethical matters, howsoever strong one's arguments. (In these ways we resemble the electric monks in *Dirk Gently's Holistic Detective Agency*.) (Inference* from 1)
3. Insofar as ethics requires independent thought it is largely futile. For (i) *such thought is little to be found*, and (ii) *that approach treats the symptoms rather than the cause*. ((i) is an inference from 2. (ii) is an inference from 1, or perhaps from 1 and 2)

This argument is popular with the political Left.[25] There is a view of *entertainment* that tends to accompany or flow from the view. To wit: much entertainment, violent and otherwise, functions to *pacify* its consumers – in various ways and to various ends. One might think here of the screen-addicted 'boy-beast' in *The Long Dark Tea-Time of the Soul*.[26] And here again a defence of violent entertainment might be turned against itself. Perhaps it is a *bad* thing for entertainment to distract us from or give an outlet to our frustrations and resentments.

I won't really assess this position, but I do suggest there is something to its central idea. There is something silly in thinking about the ethics of entertainment without thinking about society. I add, too, a word about the production (the creation and/or distribution) of violent entertainment. If there *is* something wrong with some violent entertainment, whether because it pacifies or for some other reason, then its producers are culpable, or part of the problem, simply because they are the ones who produce it.

I conclude that the ethics (/politics) of entertainment is a big topic. Really big.

For deeper thought

1. There are various good *introductions to ethics*. One is the admittedly rather expensive *The Elements of Moral Philosophy* by James Rachels and Stuart Rachels.
2. *A way into the debate about the effects of media violence* is Murray's article 'Media Violence'.
3. *A classic text on censorship* – and, more widely, on what freedoms a society should allow its citizens – is Mill's *On Liberty*, which is passionate, rich and (fairly) readable.
4. For versions of the idea that much *entertainment is pacification*, one may see: Aldous Huxley, *Brave New World* (which is a novel); Huxley's *Brave New World Revisited*

(which is not); Neil Postman, *Amusing Ourselves to Death*; and Theodor Adorno, 'Free Time'.

Notes

1. Other relevant passages – ones that I do *not* quote below – include the account of the massed Golgafrinchams being entertained, at least initially, by Ford's rebukes to them (*Restaurant at the End of the Universe*, ch. 32). There's also the account, in 'Young Zaphod Plays it Safe', of how the islanders react to spacecraft. The latter story, which is great, is collected in *The Salmon of Doubt* and appears also, in a slightly different version, in Adams's *The Utterly Utterly Merry Comic Relief Christmas Book*.

2. This chapter's analyses of *Hitchhiker* material should support that point about Adams. But there's evidence of a more direct kind, too. In a non-fiction text reproduced in *The Salmon of Doubt* (pp. 122–3), Adams disparages contemporary entertainment as thoughtless and even as being resentful of those with knowledge. See also Adams and Shirley, 'A Talk with Douglas Adams', pp. 174–5, in which Adams tentatively expresses some views on violent entertainment.

3. Adams's *own* presentation of Milliways does this, after a fashion – in that Adams makes entertainment out of something (Milliways) that itself makes entertainment out of apocalypse. In so doing, Adams manages to get over two problems. (1) Apocalypses are not particularly funny. (Compare Byrne, 'Beware of the Leopard', p. 3.) (2) It seems impossible to observe an (*'an'?*) apocalypse. I owe point 2 to James Rodwell.

4. Shusterman's 'Entertainment: a Question for Aesthetics' gives the rather interesting history of the word 'entertainment'.

5. Amusement, relaxation and diversion are themselves serious insofar as they are *needs* or almost needs. So I should say: I am concerned with entertainment that serves nothing *more* serious than, or serves nothing serious *other* than, those things.

6. Sade serves as a good example since, though he may have written much of his work largely as personal fantasy, nevertheless, sometimes his work is thought to have important things to say. On the general issue of authorial intention – which is a topic within aesthetics* – one may see Gordon Graham's *Philosophy of the Arts*, pp. 207–13.

7. Differences in *medium* (film, book, play, computer game . .) and *genre* (horror, science fiction, comedy . .) matter too.

8. A complication: I have said that I mean to consider only 'purely fictional violence'; but any representation of violence will have at least *something* in common with violent reality. A 'disaster movie' that is

about an earthquake may not, at least at the particular date it happens to be shown, recall any particular earthquake. But it is still about earthquakes, which *do* happen. Similarly, a film that depicts torture may not mean to correspond to any particular actual instance of torture, and it might have no *exact* resemblance to any such instance, but it will have a lot in common with various of the actual, innumerable instances of torture that occur and have occurred. So actually the line between 'purely' fictional violence and real violence is blurry.

9. And what – a philosopher might ask – of *the mere existence* of such entertainment? (A philosopher *did* ask me this, namely, Chris Belshaw of the Open University.) Well: if it is bad to produce entertainment violence (of a certain sort), the *reason* for that might be that it is, indeed, bad for such stuff to exist. But, next: presuming that it is bad for such stuff to exist, is that *only* because its existence allows people to *enjoy* it (such enjoyment being itself, one might argue, bad)? I will leave that last, rather metaphysical* matter, here.

10. I am characterising the Lamuellans' *initial* reaction. Later, they come to enjoy the shows. Moreover, their storytelling leader ('Old Thrashbarg') becomes 'alarmed at the number of spaceship crashes he had to start incorporating into his holy stories if he was to hold the attention of the villagers'.

11. Or at least that is so until this employment of the idea of a category mistake is explained and justified. (The notion of a category mistake, or at least the phrase, owes to Ryle, *The Concept of Mind*, chapter 1. One of Ryle's examples is of someone who is shown around a university – shown its buildings and sports courts and grounds – and then asks, But where is *the university*?) As such explanation and justification, one might propose the following argument: (1) Entertainment is a good thing. (2) Violence is a bad thing. Hence (from 1 and 2) (3) It is confused to think that violent entertainment can *really* be entertainment. But this argument is unsound*. For, first: unless pacifism is true, then the second premise* (i.e. 2) is only *approximately* true (in that not all violence is bad, or at least not every instance of violence is worse than the available alternatives). Second: the inference to 3 is invalid*. For, in order for it to be valid, it requires a premise that is missing from the argument. To wit: (2b) *depictions* of violent things are themselves (and always) bad. Moreover, it is not at all clear that one should accept that extra premise. Doesn't that premise simply confuse fiction with fact? If so, we are back at the idea that it is the *Lamuellans* that make a mistake.

12. On 1, see, in *support* of the claim: Hurley, 'Imitation, Media Violence, and Freedom of Speech', p. 182; Scharrer, 'Media Exposure and Sensitivity to Violence in News Reports'; and 'Hostile and Hardened?' by Staude-Müllé, Bliesener and Luthman. For *opposition* to the claim,

see: Savage and Yancey, 'The Effects of Media Violence Exposure on Criminal Aggression; and Barker and Petley, *Ill Effects*. As to 2, see, in *support of it*: the Hurley piece (again); Murray, 'Media Violence'; and Cialdini, *Influence*, pp. 140–51. For *opposition* to 2, see (again) Barker and Petley's *Ill Effects*. Note also this. Apparently, in both the United States and the United Kingdom, the degree and amount of violence presented by (various forms of) mass media have increased, whilst various forms of actual violence have decreased. (See e.g. Bok, *Mayhem*, p. 4.) Lastly here: I do not deny that some fictional violence 'sensitises', i.e. makes one *more* alive to violence. But my notion of *mere* entertainment pretty much excludes such material by definition.

13. I adapt this argument from Kristol, 'Pornography, Obscenity, and the Case for Censorship'. Admittedly, this argument takes us away from the specifics of points 1 and 2.

14. Here's a further possible construal of the solidarity/decadence objection. When very bad things are prevalent, one should not wholeheartedly enjoy *anything*. Theodor Adorno (1903–69) seems to make that claim. See his *Minima Moralia*, part I, #5, 'How Nice of You, Doctor', p. 25. Roughly put, that passage claims this: even the enjoyment of a blossoming tree is, or should be, marred by the evils of the world. (Adorno would want to add the following. If the notion of solidarity has little force for most of us, then the problem is not with the idea but with us. The idea here is that ethics makes sense only given certain reactions to need or to injury. If we largely lack those feelings, then we cannot expect to make much sense of ideas, such as solidarity, that are rooted in them. My interpretation of Adorno on this latter point is influenced by, especially, J. M. Bernstein's work on Adorno.)

15. For a version of that answer, see section IV of Di Muzio, 'The Immorality of Horror Films'. Note also that there is a whole philosophical literature on how it is even *possible* for us to feel emotions for fictional characters. This problem is known sometimes as 'the paradox of fiction'.

16. The solidarity objection does have something *similar to instrumentality* about it – namely, its *conditionality*. The objection is conditional in that it says this: *given the state of things*, violent entertainment is a breach of solidarity, or decadent. Still, to be conditional is not to be instrumental. A further complication is that there are different ways in which an intrinsic objection can intend its 'full stop', as it were. That is because an objection that holds irrespective of effects may, or may not, be *definitive*. A definitive objection is an 'end of' objection. To say that I have a definitive objection to X is to say this (or at least that I, the objector, *think* that this is true): *whatever else can be said for X*, we shouldn't X/should not have X. Apply this to the viciousness

objection. Is the idea there that *nothing can outweigh* the wrongness (viciousness) involved in enjoying such entertainment? Well (1) probably that *would* be the intended idea, but (2) it *need* not be. The same two points hold for the solidarity/decadence objection. Note lastly that an *instrumental* objection cannot be definitive (at least not in any straightforward way).

17. This point is strengthened by the fact that the original thought intended itself to be a *definitive* objection (see note 16 above). If one takes that into account, there is a third way in which the corruption objection, as an instrumental claim, is weak. It is *open to counterattack* – in a way that a definitive objection isn't. If a *definitive* objection to violent entertainment can be made good, then that would trump any *defences* offered for such entertainment – such as the claim that it is cathartic, or salutary in some other way. For an account – and partial endorsement – of such defences, see Kreider, 'The Virtue of Horror Films'. On such defences compare also *Restaurant*, ch. 2: '"Well," he [Halfrunt] said, "I think this is perfectly normal behaviour for a Vogon, you know? The natural and healthy channelling of the aggressive instincts into acts of senseless violence".'

18. The moral philosophy* most likely to appeal to harm, whether entertainment or anything else be at issue, is 'consequentialism'. Consequentialism holds that the morality of something is entirely a matter of its consequences. See Pettit, 'Consequentialism' and Rachels and Rachels, *The Elements of Moral Philosophy*.

19. Andrew Aberdein's chapter discusses other 'judo' moves in philosophy.

20. Cliff Bleszinski, lead designer at 'Epic Games', in an interview with the BBC World Service, as reported here: http://www.bbc.co.uk/news/technology-11674368.

21. See, in addition to *Life, the Universe and Everything*, this: Adams and Shirley, 'A Talk with Douglas Adams', pp. 177–8.

22. J. L. Mackie's 'argument from relativity' (ch. 1, section 8 of his book *Ethics*) is a well-known version of that argument.

23. Perhaps 'truth for' some person or group X just means what person X believes. But then no claim about truth is being made. If a claim about truth *is* being made, then what is it? If it is the idea that two propositions that contradict each other can both be true, then how – without the 'illogic' circuits of an Electric Monk – are we to make sense of *that*?

24. As Mill was aware, there is a difficulty about how to define harm (or the *type* of harm that is/should be at issue).

25. Sometimes the Left – some might say: the far Left – extend the argument as follows. It only makes sense to say that someone ought to do something if that person *is able* to do the thing. So – if we accept

the reasoning above (i.e. points 1–3) – one can little *blame* people for their attitudes and actions (although it may be a practical necessity for individuals to apportion blame, and expedient for the authorities to do so, in that thereby they get a justification for punishing people and, perhaps, get to shift the blame away from themselves). Here we get into the issue of free will* and determinism*.

26. '"I have to tell you, kid," he said tersely, "your father's dead."¶ This might have worked if it hadn't been for a very popular and long-running commercial which started at that moment' (Adams, *The Long Dark Tea-Time of the Soul*, ch. 6).

Part II
The Meaning of Life

3
Life, the Universe, and Absurdity

Amy Kind

'But where are we?' said Ford, who was sitting on the spiral staircase, a nicely chilled Pan Galactic Gargle Blaster in his hand.

'Exactly where we were, I think . . .' said Trillian, as all about them the mirrors suddenly showed them an image of the blighted landscape of Magrathea which still scooted along beneath them.

Zaphod leaped out of his seat.

'Then what's happened to the missiles?' he said.

A new and astounding image appeared in the mirrors.

'They would appear,' said Ford doubtfully, 'to have turned into a bowl of petunias and a very surprised-looking whale . . .'

(*Hitchhiker's Guide to the Galaxy*, chapter 18)

One needn't encounter a sperm whale hurtling through the atmosphere to be struck by the absurdity of existence.

Although the grind of daily life might not often afford us the opportunity for quiet contemplation, many of us find that our minds are occasionally overtaken as we toss and turn some sleepless nights by questions such as: 'Why am I here?' or 'What's my purpose in life?' – exactly the kinds of questions the sperm whale itself pondered during its exceptionally brief existence. In the rare moments that we do have for reflection – and when we're not puzzling over the question of why we would spend so much of the time between birth and death wearing digital watches – it is hard not to be struck by a sense of our own deep insignificance in the vast universe as a whole.

Philosophers have long been preoccupied by the question of whether and (if so) why we are entitled to such sentiments. In his discussion of the absurdity of human existence, the French-Algerian philosopher Albert Camus famously noted that the question of life's meaning is the most urgent question that we face: 'There is but one truly serious philosophical problem, and that is suicide. Judging whether life is or is not worth living amounts to answering the fundamental question of philosophy.'[1] Ultimately, however, Camus condemns suicide as the coward's way out. On his view, the only real solution to the problem of our existence is to wholeheartedly embrace it; since we cannot evade or avoid the absurdity of our existence – for Camus *does* think that existence absurd – all we can do is to meet it with defiance.

If anyone is entitled to the sentiment that life is absurd, it's surely Arthur Dent. As he makes his way throughout the galaxy, most of the absurd things he can think of – and many that he cannot – end up happening to him. In *Hitchhiker's Guide* and its sequels, a trilogy (in five parts), Douglas Adams presents us with what can easily be seen as an extended philosophical meditation on absurdity.

A strong case is made, and remade, for the absurdity of the human condition. When it comes to the absurdity of our existence, we're really no different from the poor sperm whale plummeting towards a collision with the hard surface of the planet Magrathea (although we might have a little more time for reflection than the whale did).

But, as we will see, a strong case is also made that we can deal with absurdity without having to go so far as Camus-inspired defiance. In many ways, Adams's assessment of the absurdity of the human condition is similar to Ford Prefect's assessment of Earth and its occupants: it's mostly harmless. Adams's solution to the problem of absurdity strikes me as importantly correct, and this essay (which is itself a trilogy in five parts) thus works to defend it against several rivals.

Before we can look at these attempted solutions to the problem of absurdity, however, we must first get clearer on what the problem is. Thus, in the first three sections of this chapter, I attempt to flesh out the relevant notion of absurdity, and I explore several possible justifications for the claim that life is absurd. Having concluded that our sense of life's absurdity is in fact justified, the fourth section of this chapter surveys several attempts to deal with that absurdity. In the fifth and final section, I offer some additional considerations in favour of Adams's solution to the problem of absurdity. As it happens, that solution has much in common with the solution that Scottish philosopher David Hume proposed to a different problem, namely the problem of skepticism.

1 Infinity minus one

What exactly does it mean to say that life is absurd? Ordinary situations that strike us as absurd typically do so because of a fundamental mismatch between what we

aspire to and what actually happens. Consider the following examples loosely owing to philosopher Thomas
Nagel. A politician gives a passionate speech in support of
a motion she takes to be pending . . . but it turns out the
motion has already passed. Having finally worked up the
nerve to call the woman with whom he's infatuated, a timid
bachelor professes his love in a mad rush as the phone is
answered . . . but it turns out that he's only reached her
voicemail. After a long and drawn-out process, a leading
philanthropic organization announces their choice for their
new president . . . but it turns out that this individual has
been recently indicted for fraud. During a ceremony filled
with pomp and circumstance, the Queen solemnly knights
a noted public figure . . . but his trousers fall down during
the ceremony.[2] To Nagel's list of absurd situations, we might
add the following: A man accused of serially mass murdering a variety of life forms professes his innocence . . . but
it turns out that he does so with a rabbit bone entwined in
his beard.[3]

Abstracting from these examples, we might be tempted
to say that life is absurd because of a similar mismatch or
incongruity.[4] Like Arthur Dent, we often think there is a
deeper purpose to our existence; we routinely have that
strange and unaccountable feeling that something is going
on in the world, something big – and we just wish that we
could figure out what it was. But though we take our lives
to have some deep purpose or importance, it turns out that
there is none. It seems plausible to suppose that, just as the
aforementioned politician was mistaken in thinking that
her speech served some real purpose, so too are we mistaken – absurdly mistaken – in thinking that our lives serve
some real purpose.[5]

Philosopher Arthur Schopenhauer (1788–1860) has famously referred to this mistake as 'the vanity of existence',

a vanity that reveals itself, at least in part, 'in the infinite-
ness of time and space contrasted with the finiteness of
the individual in both'.[6] From the point of view of the
universe, we are but brief, inconsequential specks. Given
the vastness of the cosmos, there's no more significance
to our entire civilization than there is to a small walnut
in Johannesburg. After all, according to *The Hitchhiker's
Guide to the Galaxy*, 'Space is big. Really big. You just won't
believe how vastly hugely mind-bogglingly big it is' – and,
as Adams tells us, better minds than those responsible
for writing the *Guide* have faltered 'when confronted by
the sheer enormity of the distances between the stars'
(*Hitchhiker's Guide*, chapter 8).

In fact, someone forced to come to grips with this
actuality might literally be driven insane by the experience.
Recall the plight of those on Argabuthon who were unlucky
enough to be present in the courtroom when Prak testified.
A recalcitrant witness, Prak was eventually given a truth
drug to force him to testify truthfully. Unfortunately, too
much of the drug was administered, and when Prak was
ordered to tell the Truth, the Whole Truth, and Nothing
but the Truth, it turned out that hearing the truth in its
absolute and final form was a horrific ordeal. Eventually the
court was ordered sealed with Prak still in it, just to keep
everyone else safe from hearing what he had to say (*Life, the
Universe and Everything*, Epilogue).

In light of what we know about the events on Argabuthon,
it's no wonder that exposing people to the truth, and in
particular the truth about their place in the universe, makes
for an extremely effective torture device. Individuals who
enter the so-called Total Perspective Vortex 'are given just
one momentary glimpse of the entire unimaginable infinity of creation, and somewhere in it a tiny little marker,
a microscopic dot on a microscopic dot, which says "You

are here"' (*Restaurant*, chapter 10). The resulting shock completely destroys the victim's brain.

Except, of course, in the case of Zaphod Beeblebrox. But Zaphod, the only person we know of to have survived the Vortex fully intact, is not your typical victim, nor is his entry into the Vortex a typical one. His encounter with the Vortex takes place in a universe specially created for him by Zarniwoop, an executive at Megadodo Publications (the publishers of *The Hitchhiker's Guide to the Galaxy*). In that artificial universe, Zaphod is the most important person there is, and the perspective granted him by the Vortex thus simply confirms his own sense of himself as a terrific guy.

Unfortunately, most of us don't have access to Zarniwoop's services. But there might be another means of escaping the bafflement and discomfort caused by the recognition of our own insignificance with respect to the universe. Leo Tolstoy claimed, in the autobiographical 'My Confession', that it is only by way of religious faith that we can transcend our own finitude and thereby find meaning in life. According to Tolstoy, 'No matter what answers faith may give, its every answer gives to the finite existence of man the sense of the infinite, – a sense which is not destroyed by suffering, privation, and death.'[7]

A similar line of reasoning has led many others to turn to the comforts of religion. If God exists, and if God has a purpose for us, then the absurdity vanishes.[8] What better reason, then, to become a true believer? Theologian William Lane Craig has forcefully argued this point:

> If God does not exist, then life is futile. If the God of the Bible does exist, then life is meaningful. Only the second of these two alternatives enables us to live happily and consistently. Therefore, it seems to me that even if the evidence for these two options were absolutely equal,

a rational person ought to choose biblical Christianity. It seems to me positively irrational to prefer death, futility, and destruction to life, meaningfulness, and happiness. As Pascal said, we have nothing to lose and infinity to gain.[9]

Others have disagreed with theists like Tolstoy and Craig. For Camus, turning to religion to solve the problem of life's meaning is as much an evasion as suicide – in fact, he dismisses this option as *philosophical suicide*. In a sense, *Hitchhiker's Guide* offers a similar indictment of such a turn to religion – though, as we will see, it does so in a typically roundabout fashion.

2 Well that about wraps it up for God

There are two main ways that religion is thought to vanquish absurdity. The first is by offering us the prospect of immortal life, a suggestion I'll call the *Immortality Answer* to the question of life's meaning. Craig eloquently captures the basic point: without hope for immortality, 'man's life leads only to the grave. His life is but a spark in the infinite blackness, a spark that appears, flickers, and dies forever.'[10] In contrast, if God exists and bestows immortality upon us, then our flames need never go out.

But why, we might ask, does an immortal life solve the problem of meaning? The fact that life has a beginning does not seem to contribute to its absurdity, so why should there be anything absurd about the fact that it has an end? As tempting as it may be to think that there is something intrinsic to our mortality that makes life absurd, the proponents of the Immortality Answer fail to explain what that is. In the absence of any such explanation, it's not at all clear how we could escape absurdity even if we were immortal. In fact, immortality might even escalate life's absurdity; as

Nagel asks, 'would not a life that is absurd if it lasts seventy years be infinitely absurd if it lasted through eternity?'[11]

Adams offers a similar indictment of the Immortality Answer by way of his anecdotes about Wowbagger the Infinitely Prolonged. While Wowbagger initially finds immortality to be fun – he revels in the joy of taking risks and living dangerously – it eventually becomes rather wearying.[12] The only way that Wowbagger manages to cope with the tedium of his own immortal existence is by giving himself a purpose: he takes up the project of insulting the Universe by insulting each person in it, personally, one by one, in alphabetical order. Of course, as Wowbagger himself admits, this isn't a very good purpose, 'but it was at least a purpose and it did at least keep him on the move' (*Life*, chapter 1).

So much for the Immortality Answer to life's meaning – infinitely prolonging a meaningless life does not itself infuse that life with meaning. But there's a second main way that religion aims to offer us an escape from absurdity, which I'll call the *Higher Being Answer* to the question of life's meaning. According to this line of reasoning, the existence of a higher being allows us to participate in something greater than ourselves. By playing a part in God's plan for the universe, we secure meaning for our lives. Unsurprisingly, Adams thinks no better of the Higher Being Answer than he does of the Immortality Answer. As *Hitchhiker's Guide* elegantly demonstrates, the mere fact that we play a crucial role in the plan of some higher being – or higher beings – does not rid our lives of absurdity.

To see this, let's first suppose that the Sens-O-Tape material that Slartibartfast shows Arthur Dent is accurate; that is, suppose that we Earthlings *do* have a purpose. Our whole planet and our whole civilization was designed 10 million years ago when a race of hyperintelligent pandimensional beings needed a very powerful computer – 'a computer of such infinite and subtle complexity that organic life itself shall form part of its operational matrix' (*Hitchhiker's Guide*, chapter 28) – in order to calculate the Question to the Ultimate Answer, which, of course, is 42. Would our lives really be any less absurd if we, like Arthur, were to make this discovery? In fact, rather than vanquishing our sense of absurdity, this discovery would seem to underscore it. Moreover, the point here doesn't seem to rely on any particularities about what exactly the computer is calculating, nor on the fact that, in this case, the higher beings in question are the creatures we call *mice* (or at least, that's how they manifest themselves in our dimension)!

Philosopher Robert Nozick argues convincingly that the role we play in the plan of a higher being must be a central one in order for it to give our lives meaning. If we were to describe God's central purpose in analogy with the creation of a painting, says Nozick, then 'we do not want to play the role of the rag used to wipe off the brushes, or the tin in which the rags are kept. If we are not the central focus of the painting, at least we want to be like the canvas or the brush or the paint.'[13] This puts an important constraint on the Higher Being Answer. But the problem with the scenario of *Hitchhiker's Guide* is not that this constraint is unmet; we are a critical, in fact *the* critical, part of the mice's plan. Rather, the problem lies with the purpose itself.

Consider here an example of Nozick's that sounds like it could easily be drawn straight from the pages of an Adams novel. Suppose that the purpose of the human race, the purpose for which we were designed, is to provide essential nourishment to some hungry intergalactic travellers. No matter how good we taste to them, and no matter how much we are perfectly suited to fit their nutritional needs, learning about this scenario does not provide us with a satisfactory answer to the meaning of life.[14] Our lives would have a clearly defined purpose, but it can in no way furnish us with the sense of purpose that we seek. Playing a central role in the discovery of the Ultimate Question might be mostly harmless, but it otherwise isn't much better than serving as a food source. It's hard to imagine that any of us would find our lives infused with a sense of purpose that had been previously lacking, or that our lives would be in any way meaningfully enriched, simply by the discovery that we're serving as cogs in a giant calculating machine. Granted, our doing so ensures that our earthly lives have meaning *for the mice*. But it in no way ensures that our lives have meaning *for us*. Likewise, then, although it might be the case that our playing a part in God's plan for the universe has meaning *for God*, it's not clear how our lives would thereby have meaning *for us*.[15]

And things aren't any better even from the perspective of the mice themselves, creatures who share our interest in the meaning of life. In fact, the Ultimate Question that they are seeking, the quest that led to the creation of Earth, is itself a question about meaning. The mice have been searching for this question for over 10 million years, and the search has begun to weary them. As Frankie mouse confesses,

> Well, I mean, *yes* idealism, *yes* the dignity of pure research, *yes* the pursuit of truth in all its forms, but there comes a point I'm afraid where you begin to suspect that if there's any *real* truth, it's that the entire multi-dimensional infinity of the Universe is almost certainly being run by a bunch of maniacs.

> (*Hitchhiker's Guide*, chapter 31)

Thus, as Adams deftly suggests, the existence of a higher being isn't going to give us an escape from absurdity. There may be a higher being. We may be fulfilling some purpose that the higher being has set for us. But we have no way of being sure that the higher being itself is either benevolent or sane, and there's no way that any purpose that it has for us can give our lives meaning *for us*.[16] The Higher Being Answer thus fails. For Adams, like for Camus, seeking solace from absurdity in religion is really no solace at all.

3   Resistance is useless

But why should we be seeking any kind of solace, anyhow? Arthur's experiences during his travels throughout the galaxy may justify his own sense that life is absurd, but what about the rest of us? Those of us who have never been clued in to the facts contained in Slartibartfast's Sens-O-Tape records (and which, after all, are facts only within the fictional *Hitchhiker* universe) and who haven't suffered as Arthur has don't have access to a similar justification. So what reason do we have to believe that life is absurd?

One attempt at answering this question suggests that we can explain the absurdity in terms of the (alleged) pointlessness of our existence. Once we start to think about what our lives are like, day in and day out, our labors may seem to recall those of Sisyphus, the mythical man condemned to an eternal punishment of rolling a stone up a hill, only to have that stone roll back down so that he was forced to begin his task anew. Consider what philosopher Joel Feinberg has called *the supermarket regress*: Why do we wait in lines at supermarkets? So that we can buy food. But why do we buy food? So that we can stay alive and healthy. But why stay alive and healthy? So that we can work our jobs. But why work our jobs? So that we can earn money. But why earn money? So that we can buy food. And so on and so on, as Feinberg says, 'around the circle, over and over, with no "significant culmination" in sight . . . [T]he whole round of activity looks more like a meaningless ritual-dance than something coherent and self-justifying.'[17]

Sisyphus' labors are undoubtedly pointless, and thus to the extent that our efforts have the same basic contours as his, they may well be pointless too. (It is this pointlessness that the appeal to immortality, and the Higher Being Answer, seek to save us from.) But although there is definitely something absurd about a repetitive cycle of activity without real purpose, the notion of absurdity clearly extends beyond that of mere pointlessness.[18] Consider again the kinds of fairly ordinary situations that strike us as absurd. Professing one's love to an answering machine is indeed pointless, but the pointlessness of it doesn't completely capture why it's absurd. And we certainly can't explain the absurdity of appointing a notorious criminal to the directorship of a philanthropic organization in terms of the pointlessness of it. Rather, as we saw above, what makes these ordinary situations absurd is the fundamental incongruity inherent in each of them, an incongruity between our expectations for the situation and what the situation actually delivers. It might not be the height of fashion, but there's nothing intrinsically absurd about having a rabbit bone entwined in your beard, for example. Considered in light of your aspirations to present yourself as a man who's innocent of intentionally slaughtering animals, however, it's a different story. And when reflecting upon life as a whole, we might say something similar, might attribute a similar kind of absurdity.

This is precisely Camus' position. On his view, reality itself is not *intrinsically* absurd – rather, absurdity arises from the clash between the world's fundamental unintelligibility and 'the wild longing for clarity whose call echoes in the human heart'.[19] As Adams might put it, we want an answer to life, the universe, and everything, but the only answer available is 42. And even this deeply unsatisfying answer is produced only once the great computer Deep Thought works on the problem for seven and a half million years.

According to Deep Thought, the problem is not in the answer, but in the question. We're looking for clarity, but in this seemingly endless search, we don't even know how to properly formulate the question that we want answered. In the *Hitchhiker's* universe, at least, this isn't a limitation that we can do anything about. Recall Prak's remarks at the end of *Life, the Universe and Everything*: 'I'm afraid,' he tells Arthur, 'that the Question and the Answer are mutually exclusive. Knowledge of the one logically precludes knowledge of the other. It is impossible that both can ever be known about the same Universe.'

According to both *Hitchhiker's* and Camus, then, absurdity arises from the fact that the world is in principle unable to deliver on what we need from it; our desires for clarity and intelligibility can never be met. In contrast, Nagel offers a slightly different assessment of the absurdity of human existence. Although Nagel agrees with Camus that we should not locate the absurdity in the world itself, he disagrees with Camus that the absurdity arises from a collision between us and the world. Rather, on Nagel's view, absurdity arises from a collision within ourselves.

Unlike Zaphod Beeblebrox, humans (typically) have only a single head – but despite this feature of our anatomy, Nagel argues that we are nonetheless capable of taking two different perspectives on our existence. First there is what might naturally be called the *internal perspective*.[20] This is the perspective within which we ordinarily operate as we live our lives – the perspective within which we make decisions ranging over all sorts of things that we take to have considerable importance: what career to pursue, whom to marry, whether to have children, etc. From within the inner perspective, we approach our lives with a considerable degree of seriousness; these things matter to us. We typically look for justifications for the decisions that we're making, especially when the decisions seem to us to be particularly weighty ones. And the point is that many of these decisions do strike us as particularly weighty. These issues matter to us.

But, according to Nagel, we humans also have the special capacity to take up quite a different perspective on ourselves, what he calls the *external perspective*. From this perspective, when we take a step back and look at our lives from a perspective outside of ourselves, it is difficult to take our lives with the seriousness we adopt when we're operating within the internal perspective. Arthur seems to adopt this perspective after having instantaneously travelled two-thirds of the way across the Galactic disc on Slartibartfast's ship:

> 'It's a strange thing,' said Arthur quietly, 'that the further and faster one travels across the Universe, the more one's position in it seems to be largely immaterial, and one is filled with a profound, or rather emptied of a ...'

> (*Life*, chapter 6)

(Of course, it's easier to take the external perspective when Ford Prefect isn't around to interrupt.)

It's only when an individual is operating within the internal perspective that it seems a matter of critical importance whether she gets the next promotion at work or whether the fjords he's designed get the recognition they deserve. Things are different from the external perspective. Once I detach myself from myself and step outside of the context of my ordinary concerns, I see myself objectively as simply 'a small, contingent, and exceedingly temporary organic bubble in the universal soup'.[21] And from this perspective, it is hard to see how any of the things that I normally take to matter so deeply really even matter at all. The two perspectives thus inevitably collide, and according to Nagel it is this collision that accounts for absurdity:

> We cannot live human lives without energy and attention, nor without making choices which show that we take some things more seriously than others. Yet we always have available a point of view outside the particular form of our lives, from which the seriousness appears gratuitous. These two inescapable viewpoints collide in us, and that is what makes life absurd. It is absurd because we ignore the doubts that we know cannot be settled, continuing to live with nearly undiminished seriousness in spite of them.[22]

As Nagel himself notes, we cannot willingly abandon either of these perspectives. To abandon the internal perspective is simply to give up on life altogether, and Nagel thinks no better of this option than does Camus. Moreover, the seriousness with which we take our lives from within the internal perspective is equally unavoidable. As humans, we cannot simply move unreflectively from impulse to impulse. We have needs that must be satisfied, and we must make choices and plans in order to satisfy them. Even the least serious among us must take at least some things seriously. Lives do not simply happen; they must be *pursued*. And we can no more abandon the external perspective than we can the internal perspective – a capacity for self-transcendence is part of human nature.

This, says Nagel, is why the life of a human can be absurd, but the life of a mouse cannot.[23] Clearly Nagel has never met Benjy mouse and Frankie mouse, or else he's rejecting the assumption that mice are hyperintelligent pandimensional beings. But granting Nagel this assumption – assuming that mice are just that, mice – it does seem like we humans are stuck with absurdity. Resistance is useless, for absurdity is as much a part of the human condition as officiousness and callousness are a part of the Vogon condition.

4 Panic?

But what now? Suppose we accept the claim that life is not just absurd, but inescapably absurd. What, then, are we to do? Here Nagel and Camus give slightly different answers, and Adams seems to come down somewhere in between.

Camus is firm in his conviction that the absurdity of the human condition cannot be vanquished. We cannot stop wanting clarity and compassion from the world, as these desires – even needs – are built into our very nature. Nor can the world ever provide these things to us. But although we can't solve the problem of absurdity, we can deal with it by meeting it with the proper attitude. Camus makes this point by once again returning us to a discussion of Sisyphus, the absurd hero. Sisyphus has no choice but to undertake the labors assigned to him, but he does have a choice about the attitude he can take toward these labors. He might approach his stone with dread, grudgingly completing the arduous task of pushing it up the hill, his head hung in renewed defeat each time the stone rolls back down. But Sisyphus might also take a different attitude toward his fate. On Camus' view, 'there is no fate that cannot be surmounted by scorn'.[24] If Sisyphus adopts an attitude of scornful defiance as he takes up his task, he finds a way to take ownership of his fate. In doing so, his situation becomes no less absurd, and his stone-rolling becomes no less onerous, but the absurdity *itself* need no longer weigh him down. There's no escaping the fate to which he's been consigned, but by making it his own, he is able to achieve a certain heroic nobility.

The scorn Camus recommends may help dissipate the problem of absurdity temporarily, but I'm skeptical that it can be a satisfying solution for the long term. One problem is that it's hard to see how such an attitude can be appropriately sustained. Sisyphus might be able to muster up a scornful attitude through 50, or 100, or even 1000 trips up the mountain, but can he really maintain it indefinitely? And even if he can, how does it help? Insofar as the scornful attitude doesn't *erase* the absurdity – and Camus explicitly denies that it can – it doesn't seem to have the power needed to combat the kind of absurdity embedded in the human condition. Scornful acceptance may help us to feel better than self-pitying resignation, but that in itself is not saying much.

Nagel is also skeptical of Camus' assessment of how we should respond to absurdity, but for a different reason, namely, that it's an overreaction. According to Nagel, we don't need to adopt a defiant posture to solve the problem of absurdity; rather, we should instead simply reject the very assumption that there's a *problem* here that needs to be solved. The absurdity of our condition is essential to our lives as humans; indeed, says Nagel, it's 'one of the most human things about us: a manifestation of our most advanced and interesting characteristics'.[25] We cannot help but be engaged in our own lives, but we also cannot help but occasionally detach ourselves and look at those lives from an external perspective. Given these facts, Nagel concludes that we're better off being 'simultaneously engaged and detached, and therefore absurd, for this is the opposite of self-denial and the result of full awareness'.[26]

In a sense then, Nagel is encouraging us to embrace our absurdity. Because coming to recognize ourselves as absurd is a way of gaining insight into the truth about our own nature, it is not something to be regretted or resented. We shouldn't let it be cause for self-pity or despair, and dealing with it doesn't require us to be heroic or noble or scornful. There's not a problem but simply a deep irony in the fact that we cannot come to understand our own nature and place in the world without thereby developing a sense of absurdity.

Faced with this answer, we might wonder whether it's ultimately any more satisfying than the one offered by Camus. Scorn and defiance may not be the answer, but why is ironic embrace any better? In an essay that is sharply critical of Nagel's take on absurdity, philosophers Jonathan Westphal and Christopher Cherry worry that his proposed response to absurdity is rather limited. Not all of us have the temperament and sensibility to be satisfied by what Nagel has to say. Those of us already jaded about life might be willing to accept Nagel's assessment. But what about the rest of us? Suppose we were to learn that global warming is inevitably increasing at such a significant rate that Earth will be uninhabitable by humans within the decade. Were Nagel to tell us that we should stop viewing this as a problem because our inability to survive such temperatures is part of our very nature as humans, that seems unlikely to persuade everyone that the problem has been defused. In short, when something seems to be a problem, it doesn't much help to be told that the alleged problem, given that it derives from our very nature and is hence inevitable, is really only a pseudo-problem. Inevitable problems can still be problems!

On Westphal and Cherry's view, both Camus and Nagel are led astray by their whole approach to the problem, by their presupposition that our attitude to life 'calls for any defense at all'.[27] Their defenses, granted, are different. Camus attempts to solve the problem of absurdity, and Nagel attempts to defuse it. But what their differing approaches nonetheless have in common is the idea that absurdity needs to be taken seriously. In contrast, Westphal and Cherry offer up an intriguing alternative: we should simply *ignore* the problem altogether.

The Westphal–Cherry view is explicitly meant to be analogous to David Hume's famous response to a different philosophical problem, the problem of skepticism*. When we're confronted with the skeptic's arguments that we cannot really know anything about the external world around us, it can be an unpleasantly dizzying experience, much like experiencing one's first matter transference. Having had the rug pulled out from us like that – feeling, as Hume says, as if we're in the deepest darkness, completely deprived of all sense or reason – it's extremely hard to figure out how we can go on with daily life. If I don't know whether anything else, or anyone else, exists, how am I to live? One possible solution would be to behave like the Ruler of the Universe, a man who suspends all judgment on whether other beings exist and considers the whole of his Universe to be his eyes and ears. But talking to a table for a week to see how it would react doesn't seem like that appealing a way to live (*Restaurant*, chapter 29).

Hume's own response to the worries of skepticism may seem more palatable. Although there may be no way to reason our way to an answer to the skeptic, a different kind of response becomes available to us. Hume writes:

> Most fortunately it happens, that since reason is incapable of dispelling these clouds, nature herself suffices to that purpose, and cures me of this philosophical melancholy

and delirium, either by relaxing this bent of mind, or by some avocation, and lively impression of my senses, which obliterate all these chimeras. I dine, I play a game of back-gammon, I converse, and am merry with my friends; and when after three or four hours' amusement, I wou'd return to these speculations, they appear so cold, and strain'd, and ridiculous, that I cannot find in my heart to enter into them any farther.[28]

In Westphal and Cherry's view, we should take a similar attitude to worries about the meaning of life. It might be that we are unable to dismiss those worries intellectually, but that does not mean that we should allow them to torture us. Rather, we should leave it to life itself to restore the balance that has been disrupted by our questioning.

This Humean response is, I think, the one that best reflects the sentiments endorsed by Adams throughout the *Hitchhiker's Guide* series. Ultimately, as Ford Prefect remarks when he and Arthur Dent end up stranded on prehistoric Earth, contemplating the meaning of life is a frivolous exercise (*Restaurant*, chapter 34). We may not be able to help ourselves from doing it from time to time. We may not be able to avoid adopting a Nagelian external perspective, and we may not be able to stop ourselves from wanting clarity from Camus' cold and uncaring world. But fortunately, before we get too caught up in the murky depths of despair, the world finds some way to distract us (if not with some cute Golgafrinchams, then with something equally diverting).

5   Don't panic!

In fact, not only is the Humean response the one that best captures Adams's view, but it's also the one that offers us the most plausible assessment of how we can adequately cope with absurdity. While Sisyphus may guide Camus' thinking about absurdity, I think we'd do better to look to Slartibartfast. When Arthur starts to get excited at the prospect that there might be something outside of our Universe that would explain the happenings within it, Slartibartfast cuts him off. There may be such an explanation, he says, but who cares?

> 'Perhaps I'm old and tired,' he continued, 'but I always think that the chances of finding out what really is going on are so absurdly remote that the only thing to do is to say hang the sense of it and just keep yourself occupied.'

> (*Hitchhiker's Guide*, chapter 30)

In general, it's when we're bored with our lives that feelings of meaningless and absurdity take hold. One vivid example of this phenomenon can be found in Peter Singer's discussion of American housewives from the 1950s. Although such women had things easy compared to women of previous generations, or to women elsewhere in the world, it turned out that 'having it easy' wasn't a good thing; rather, the housewives found themselves increasingly dissatisfied with their lives. As Singer describes:

> The suburban housewife lives an isolated existence in her comfortable home, equipped with labour-saving devices that allow her to complete her daily chores in an hour or two. In another hour at the supermarket she can gather the week's food supply for the entire family. Her only role is to bring up a family, and her children soon spend all day at school, and much of the rest of their time watching television.[29]

Left with nothing – or not enough – to do, the housewives often found themselves suffering from malaise and ennui.

In Singer's view, the best way to escape this malaise is to get caught up in some worthwhile activity – to find what he calls a *transcendent cause,* i.e. one that extends beyond the boundaries of oneself.[30] Though, as Singer notes, there are many such causes, his own preferred route is by adopting the goal of living an ethical life, and in particular, of working to ease suffering. As a practical matter, if we're looking to ease our worries about the absurdity of the human condition, what seems to work best is simply getting out into the world and start doing something worthwhile.

I don't here want to defend Singer's own view about the kinds of projects that we should adopt. Rather, for our purposes, what's important is his claim – a claim that seems fundamentally correct – that people are least bothered by worries of meaningless and absurdity when they are caught up in activities that appeal to them. In doing so, they don't solve the problem of absurdity, or refuse to see it as a problem. Rather, they simply get so enrapt in what they're doing that they forget to be bothered by it – exactly as Slartibartfast recommends.

Ultimately, then, we don't need to be scornful, and we don't need to shake our fists at the world. Showing exquisitely judged outrage is a task best left to the President of the Galaxy; after all, that's his main job requirement (*Hitchhiker's Guide*, chapter 4). When we wake up each day, there's no need to engage in a ritualized early morning yell of horror. But we also don't need to be jaded or ironic. Rather, when we find the spectre of absurdity weighing us down, we'd be best served to find some way of ignoring it. One way is to grab another Pan Galactic Gargle Blaster and let it do its work. Having one may make us feel like we're having our brains smashed out with a lemon-wrapped brick, but at least it will stop us from thinking. Alternatively, we might decide to set ourselves a new project – such as learning to fly and communicate with birds, or mapping all of the stars, or trying to find out why all the dolphins disappeared from Earth. Some of these might prove more diverting than others (birdspeak, unfortunately, proves to be fantastically boring), but in finding something to do with our lives we manage to push worries of absurdity aside.

In short, then, the best attitude we can take towards absurdity is really one of benign neglect. When we're confronted with the philosophical melancholy that at times besets us all, what better to do than metaphorically stick your thumb out and hope to be carried along on an interesting journey. And, of course, don't forget your towel.

For deeper thought

Books and articles

Albert Camus, *The Myth of Sisyphus*. Perhaps the *locus classicus* for philosophical discussion of absurdity – it's as indispensable for anyone traversing this philosophical terrain as the encyclopaedic *Hitchhiker's Guide to the Galaxy* is to anyone traversing the galactic terrain.

William Lane Craig, 'The Absurdity of Life without God'. Craig defends the claim that there are two conditions necessary if our lives are to have meaning: God must exist, and we must be immortal. On this view, it is not possible for an atheist to live life both consistently and happily. Although he does not address it directly, Craig presumably rejects the argument for God's nonexistence presented by Oolon Colluphid's *Well That about Wraps it Up for God*.

Thaddeus Metz, 'Could God's Purpose Be the Source of Life's Meaning?' In Metz's view, the answer to this question is no. Many previous thinkers have argued this point by suggesting that God's having a purpose for us is incompatible with God's omnipotence (how could a God who needs us to fulfill a purpose for him be all-powerful?) or God's goodness (wouldn't God be disrespecting us by creating us with a specific purpose in mind?). Rejecting these arguments, Metz offers a different reason to show that God's having a purpose for us is incompatible with the God-centered view of life's meaning.

Thomas Nagel, 'The Absurd'. I don't know whether Nagel has paid his dues to the Amalgamated Union of Philosophers, Sages, Luminaries and Other Thinking Persons, but these works of his most definitely pursue the Quest for Ultimate Truth. In addition to grappling with the problem of absurdity, Nagel takes up other questions relating to life, death and living well.

Anthologies

Jonathan Westphal and Carl Levenson, *Life and Death*. An excellent (and inexpensive) collection containing many seminal contributions to the philosophical debate about the meaning of life. The readings are largely excerpted from longer works, including classic philosophical texts (such as Plato's *Phaedo* and St Augustine's *Confessions*) and classic works of literature (such as Shakespeare's *Cymbeline*). There are also several contemporary philosophical articles included in full. All foreign texts have been translated into English for those who do not have a Babel Fish.

E.D. Klemke and Steven M. Cahn, *The Meaning of Life: a Reader*. The works included in this collection, in contrast to the one by Westphal and Levenson, were primarily authored in the twentieth century. The book divides into three sections: the first comprises theistic responses to the question of life's meaning, the second comprises nontheistic responses, and the third comprises selections from authors who question the very question. Regrettably, none of the contributions are drawn from Oolon Colluphid's trilogy of philosophical blockbusters, *Where God Went Wrong, Some More of God's Greatest Mistakes* and *Who Is This God Person Anyway?*

Notes

1. Camus, 'The Myth of Sisyphus', p. 72.
2. See Nagel, 'The Absurd', p. 145.
3. Such was the unfortunate situation that Arthur found himself in when he was diverted to Agrajag's Cathedral of Hate – and, even worse, the bone in his beard does in fact belong to one of the life forms he's accused of murdering (*Life, the Universe and Everything*, ch. 18).
4. In a very interesting discussion of these kinds of examples, Joel Feinberg offers a useful and rich typology of absurdity. See his essay 'Absurd Self-Fulfillment'.
5. I will return to – and defend – this line of reasoning in section 3, below.
6. Schopenhauer, 'On the Vanity of Existence', p. 51. The gulf between infinitude and finitude is so great, in fact, that we cannot get from one to the other by simple addition or subtraction – hence, the humour when the computer on the Heart of Gold calculates an improbability sum of infinity minus one (*Hitchhiker's Guide*, ch. 13).
7. Tolstoy, *My Confession*, p. 14.
8. Michèle Friend takes up some related issues in 'God ... Promptly Vanishes in a Puff of Logic' (ch. 7 of the present volume).
9. Craig, 'The Absurdity of Life without God', p. 86.
10. Craig, 'The Absurdity of Life without God', p. 71.
11. Nagel, 'The Absurd', p. 144.
12. Wowbagger's plight is reminiscent of the famous arguments by philosopher Bernard Williams that immortality will always eventually become boring. See Williams, 'The Makropoulos Case: Reflections on the Tedium of Immortality'. Timothy Chappell argues, against Williams, that an eternal life *can* be meaningful (see ch. 4 in the present volume).
13. Nozick, 'Philosophy and the Meaning of Life', p. 226.
14. Nozick, 'Philosophy and the Meaning of Life', p. 227. Ben Saunders and Eloïse Harding take up some related issues in chapter 1 of the present volume.

15. A. J. Ayer makes precisely this point in his discussion of the meaning of life: 'For let us assume, for the sake of argument, that everything happens as it does because a superior being has intended that it should. As far as we are concerned, the course of events still remains entirely arbitrary. True, it can now be said to fulfil a purpose; but the purpose is not ours' (Ayer, 'The Claims of Philosophy', p. 200).
16. It turns out – in *Hitchhiker's* – that there is a Higher Being, but that he is only arguably sane. See the discussion of the Ruler of the Universe in section 4 below.
17. Feinberg, 'Absurd Self-Fulfillment', p. 163. Although Feinberg feels the allure of this kind of argument, he ultimately rejects it.
18. Feinberg, addressing this issue in 'Absurd Self-Fulfillment', argues that there are many different species of absurdity.
19. Camus, 'The Myth of Sisyphus', p. 76.
20. Nagel, 'The Absurd', p. 145.
21. Nagel, 'The Absurd', p. 210.
22. Nagel, 'The Absurd', p. 145.
23. Nagel, 'The Absurd', p. 150. Camus makes a similar point: 'If I were a tree among trees, a cat among animals, this life would have a meaning, or rather this problem would not arise, for I should belong to this world' ('The Myth of Sisyphus', p. 77).
24. Camus, 'The Myth of Sisyphus', p. 80.
25. Nagel, 'The Absurd', p. 152.
26. Nagel, *The View from Nowhere*, p. 223.
27. Westphal and Cherry, 'Is Life Absurd?', p. 103.
28. Hume, *A Treatise of Human Nature*, Book I, Part IV, Section VII, p. 269.
29. Singer, *How Are We To Live?*, p. 197.
30. Singer, *How Are We To Live?*, p. 218.

4

The Wowbagger Case: Immortality and What Makes Life Meaningful

Timothy Chappell

1 Wowbagger The Infinitely Prolonged

Wowbagger The Infinitely Prolonged was – indeed, is – one of the Universe's very small number of immortal beings.

Most of those who are born immortal instinctively know how to cope with it, but Wowbagger was not one of them. Indeed, he had come to hate them, the load of serene bastards. He had his immortality inadvertently thrust upon him by an unfortunate accident with an irrational particle accelerator, a liquid lunch, and a pair of rubber bands. The precise details are not important because no one has ever managed to duplicate the exact circumstances under which it happened, and many people have ended up looking very silly, or dead, or both, trying. . . . .

To begin with it was fun, he had a ball, living danger-ously, taking risks, cleaning up on high-yield long-term investments, and just generally outliving the hell out of everybody.

In the end, it was the Sunday afternoons he couldn't cope with, and that terrible listlessness that starts to set in at about 2:55 when you know you've taken all the baths you can usefully have that day, that however hard you stare at any given paragraph in the papers you will never actually read it, or use the revolutionary new pruning technique it describes, and that as you stare at the clock the hands will move relentlessly on to four o'clock, and you will enter the long dark teatime of the soul.

So things began to pall for him. The merry smiles he used to wear at other people's funerals began to fade. He began to despise the Universe in general and everybody in it in particular.

This was the point at which he conceived his purpose, the thing which would drive him on, and which, as far as he could see, would drive him on forever. It was this.

He would insult the Universe.

That is, he would insult everybody in it. Individually, personally, one by one, and (this was the thing he really decided to grit his teeth over) in alphabetical order.

When people protested to him, as they sometimes had done, that the plan was not merely misguided but actually impossible because of the number of people being born and dying all the time, he would merely fix them with a steely look and say, 'A man can dream, can't he?'

(*Life, the Universe and Everything*, chapter 1)

Wowbagger has a problem: how to make an infinitely long life meaningful.[1] His answer to this problem is studiedly perverse. Presumably, part of his reason for taking on the project he does is that everyone likes a challenge – and the project of insulting everyone in the universe, in alphabetical order, is really challenging even if you're immortal. Still, his response to the question 'How shall I make my life meaningful?' seems to be not so much an attempt to answer it as to stick two fingers up at it. Can anyone find anything less perverse to say about that question?

If the late and lamented Douglas Adams is to be believed, some beings can. The non-accidental immortals, the 'serene bastards' of Wowbagger's envy, have no trouble coping with everlasting life. Adams does not tell us *how* they manage to cope; which is a pity, because many contemporary philosophers, notably Bernard Williams and Adrian Moore, see a conceptual problem here.[2] They cannot conceive how anyone could cope with immortality, even in the rather minimal sense of 'cope' that Wowbagger manages. This chapter argues that their arguments fail. An eternal life, I argue, can be meaningful, and under the right circumstances, will be more meaningful than any finite life could be, because it would be free from a threat to meaningfulness that cannot be removed from any finite life. We therefore have reason to want eternal life lived under these circumstances. Moreover: in arguing for that point, I will present some ideas about what makes life – normal, mortal life – meaningful.

2 Human finitude and the threat of meaninglessness

We should not lose our sense of surprise at the claim that eternal life would be meaningless – even though, in our society, it is rather a clichéd paradox*, usually found alongside the 'tired fancy' that hell will be more fun than heaven.[3] We should stay surprised because, as a matter of common experience, it is not the prospect of immortality that most frequently and most familiarly threatens meaning. It is the opposite – the prospect of *mortality*, that does that:

> O dark dark dark. They all go into the dark,
> The vacant interstellar spaces, the vacant into
>   the vacant,
> The captains, merchant bankers, eminent men
>   of letters,
> The generous patrons of art, the statesmen
>   and the rulers,
> Distinguished civil servants, chairmen of many
>   committees,
> Industrial lords and petty contractors, all go
>   into the dark,
> And dark the Sun and Moon, and the
>   Almanach de Gotha
> And the Stock Exchange Gazette, the Directory
>   of Directors,
> And cold the sense and lost the motive of action.
> And we all go with them, into the silent funeral,
> Nobody's funeral, for there is no one to bury.
>
> (T. S. Eliot, *East Coker*)

Eliot's sense, like that of many others, is that a life lived 'in the valley of the shadow of death' – as all our lives ultimately are – is a life lived under the constant threat of meaningless-ness. As Shakespeare saw, the threat overshadows kings as well as the rest of us (*Richard II*, Act 3, Scene 2):

> ... for within the hollow crown
> That rounds the mortal temples of a king
> Keeps Death his court; and there the antic sits,
> Scoffing his state and grinning at his pomp,
> Allowing him a breath, a little scene,

To monarchize, be fear'd and kill with looks,
Infusing him with self and vain conceit,
As if this flesh which walls about our life,
Were brass impregnable; and humour'd thus
Comes at the last and with a little pin
Bores through his castle wall, and farewell king!

We might distinguish two sources of this meaninglessness. Let me take them in turn.

First, we are all constantly involved in projects and commitments,[4] in trying to get worthwhile things done or made,
in trying, if you like, to write some memorable poem on
the blackboard of the world. We think (and surely rightly)
that our lives will be less meaningful, the fewer worthwhile
projects we bring to completion or fruition: whether those
projects are philosophy essays, or friendships, or the great
concern of Shakespeare's first 19 sonnets, children. We are
all always under time pressure; I am writing these words
under time pressure. The ultimate source of that time pressure is not our line managers, nor the editors of the journals
where we want to publish, nor the Vice Chancellor, nor
even the chairman of UK academia's 'Research Excellence
Framework' (bless him). It is death: the pressure comes from
the fact that we have indefinitely many things we want to
do, and only a finite amount of time to do them in before
we die. How much better to be free of the time pressure that
our mortality imposes; to have, for these indefinitely many
projects, indefinitely much time.

The second way in which mortality threatens us with
meaninglessness is that it threatens to make a mock of
anything we *do* achieve. The thought here is more nebu-
lous, and more despairing. To sustain the last paragraph's
metaphor, it is that even if we do complete a good poem
or two on the blackboard of the world before we die, still it

will be wiped out not long after death wipes *us* out – leaving
nothing:

> All his happier dreams came true—
> A small old house, wife, daughter, son,
> Grounds where plum and cabbage grew,
> Poets and Wits about him drew;
> *'What then?' sang Plato's ghost. 'What then?'*
>
> 'The work is done,' grown old he thought,
> 'According to my boyish plan;
> Let the fools rage, I swerved in naught,
> Something to perfection brought';
> *But louder sang that ghost, 'What then?'*
>
> (W. B. Yeats, 'What then?')

'Man that is of woman born is of few days and full of
trouble'; 'Man's days are like the grass that flowers in the
field; the wind passes over it, and its place shall know it no
more' (Job 14: 1, Psalm 103: 15–16). We can get a sense of
the meaninglessness of life by looking at the vastness of the
universe and time and the shortness and littleness of us and
our projects.

> We cannot live human lives without energy and atten-
> tion, nor without making choices which show that we
> take some things more seriously than others. Yet we
> always have available a point of view outside the particu-
> lar form of our lives, from which the seriousness appears
> gratuitous. These two inescapable viewpoints collide in
> us, and that is what makes life absurd. It is absurd because
> we ignore the doubts that we know cannot be settled,
> continuing to live with nearly undiminished seriousness
> in spite of them.[5]

This bleak perspective might remind us in one way of the philosophy of Spinoza – and in another of the Total Perspective Vortex. On such a perspective, it can seem like there is *nothing* that we finite beings could do that could ward off the meaninglessness of our lives. And, of course, we can be tempted to take refuge from this sense of cosmic vertigo in the notion of immortality.

This second way to meaninglessness seems much vaguer and less compelling than the first. It seems to be *just* cosmic vertigo, as I called it, and no more; and vertigo is not a reason for thinking anything. If there is a thought behind the vertigo, it will be either a thought like Nagel's, about a clash between two viewpoints, or a thought about (roughly) our smallness and the universe's largeness. But Nagel's thought (to take this first) seems entirely uncompelling, and not because it can be answered, but because it *cannot* be answered. In fact, it is one of a very large set of equally possible thoughts none of which can be answered. It is possible to say with Nagel that, from the point of view of the universe, our lives are meaningless. It is equally possible to say that, from that viewpoint, our lives are rich with meaning; or that our lives are expressions of a mathematically elegant pattern; or that our lives are functioning parts of an overall mechanism that spells out the message 'Sorry for the inconvenience'; or that our lives, properly seen from the cosmic perspective, are just *funny*. All of these possibilities, and indefinitely many others, are just as real as Nagel's brow-clutching thought about ultimate meaninglessness. (In particular, Nagel's thought does not have science on its side. Science, as distinct from the dog-eared farrago of late-Victorian prejudices that we call scient*ism**, is professionally neutral between all these thoughts.) So these thoughts cancel out. The problem with Nagel's idea that 'the view from nowhere' is a challenge to our view of ourselves as significant is that there isn't just one 'view from nowhere'; there are indefinitely many, and bleak nihilism is by no means a guaranteed feature of them all. Or, to put the point slightly differently: the universe as such has no idea of significance. (Indeed, it has no ideas of any sort.) So, if we take, or try to take, the point of view of the universe, then we can say *nothing*, positive *or* negative, about significance (about the significance of one's own life, or of human life in general, or about any type of significance at all).

As for the thought about smallness, this is a non sequitur*. Just because we are small and the universe is big is, in itself, no reason to doubt that our lives can be meaningful or valuable; that is an illusion.[6] Quite simply, size is one thing, significance another. Which is one reason why, contrary to what some have perhaps thought, *being immortal* certainly could not ward off this kind of meaninglessness. Even if I were immortal, I would still be small in the grand scheme of things. Even if I were *big* in the grand scheme of things (as Zaphod is when he enters the Vortex), I could still, on any bad-enough day, work myself into a sense of the meaninglessness of my life; all it takes is a fit of *accidie*, one of those listless unhappy moods that we all fall into sometimes, where the reasons we have to act are the same as they ever were, yet we don't respond to them. This kind of threat to the meaning of a finite (or indeed an infinite) life is more a mood than an argument. Of this kind of threat to meaning Wittgenstein rightly said that 'The solution to the riddle of life is seen in the vanishing of the problem.'[7]

The first worry about the meaning of a finite life, to come back to that, is more substantial. To blend a Wittgensteinian image with the far older one of the Greek or Norse Fates, a good human life is a rope of overlapping threads, significant projects, some of which at any time are not yet fulfilled or otherwise still continuing.[8] Since the overlapping continues as long as the life continues good, we can't ever live long enough to fulfil all of these projects. This is a real problem about a finite life, and it is not just cosmic angst that makes us see it as a problem. Using our metaphor, the problem can be precisely stated. Wherever a good life is ended by death, there will always be broken strands, projects of meaning that are left unfulfilled. How much this fateful cutting of the threads will destroy the overall meaningfulness of the life depends on the importance of the threads that get cut. But wherever it occurs, it frustrates something important; for it is part of what it is to be living a good human life at any time, that at that time at least some important projects are under way in the life. The problem is *not*, then, that death as the ending of the finite life – the cutting of the rope – will destroy *all* the meaning of that life, or cast upon what was achieved a retrospective shadow of cosmic vertigo. But it is that, in Mick Jagger's words, 'you can't always get what you want', or in St Paul's, that 'creation was made subject to frustration' (Romans 8: 20). Mortality dooms us, if not to the frustration of every valued project we have, then at least to the frustration of some of our most valued projects. Insofar as we value those projects, and the possibility of taking on further equally valuable projects, we have reason to value the prospect of immortality as a way of continuing to pursue them indefinitely.

There are two points to notice here. First, I haven't just said that immortality is a way of always getting what you want. Maybe it is, maybe it isn't; what I have said leaves either prospect open, and therewith the questions that many will rightly want to raise about the very coherence of the notion of 'always getting what you want', especially if this is supposed to be possible, without significant modification or refinement of what we want, for everybody. I've said only that mortality is a bar (one bar among others) to achieving meaningfulness in our lives by way of our projects, and that therefore insofar as we have and want to have projects, we have reasons to want that bar removed. Secondly, I have implicitly denied a view that seems attractive to some, namely that the way to escape the threat to life's meaningfulness that arises from death's threat to our projects is, bluntly, to give up having projects. My contention that 'a good human life is a rope of overlapping threads, significant projects' rules out the possibility that a life of Buddhistic or ascetic renunciation, if this means a life where one gives up having projects, could be a *good* life. (In fact Buddhists and Hindus are rather elusive about whether they do mean this. Often what they seem to mean by their praise of *nibbana* or *moksa* is not that we should give up all of our projects, but that we should give them all up except for one very special project, the quest for enlightenment*.)

Another way of giving up on projects can also be dismissed. Some scientifically minded readers will no doubt have wanted all along to insist that immortality is unnatural for humans, because humans are by nature finite biological beings: it's part of the natural human life cycle for us to grow old, lose our grip on our projects, and fade away: 'it really is like going to bed at the end of a very, *very* long day'.[9] No doubt this conception of what it is to be human captures some parts of what we truly are. Elsewhere, I would contend that it does not capture *all*, and not the most important part, of what we truly are. But that opens up questions of theology: too big a subject for this small essay. And it is not our question here. As Williams agrees, our question is whether immortality could be desirable *even if* we were not just finite biological beings.[10]

My argument so far, to sum it up, has been this. A good human life is one in which a variety of projects and commitments are live at any given time, and a significant number of which are or have an excellent chance of being *successful* projects. While these projects may be each of limited temporal duration, they do not all finish at once – they overlap like the threads in a rope. There is, therefore, reason to want continued life at any moment of a good life, to enable the completion of those projects that are not yet complete. So as long as my life goes on being good, I have reason to want it to go on. So if my life is good, I have reason to value the prospect of immortal life, and to think that an immortal life lived by me not only could be a meaningful one, but would also be unthreatened by meaninglessness in a way that any finite life would necessarily be threatened.

Some people – perhaps the Heidegger of *Being and Time* is one – will respond that a life without death at the end of it would be meaningless because it would be *shapeless*. As we might almost put it, the prospect of dying concentrates the mind wonderfully; on the business of living. That sounds to me a bit like insisting that the only way to write a good philosophy essay is under exam pressure. Well, certainly exam pressure produces thoughts that wouldn't otherwise pop out so easily. However, it also leads us to loose thinking, to grabbing the first plausible idea that comes to mind, and to trying to work the question round so that we can answer the question that we wish the examiner had set. More pertinently perhaps, exam pressure also leads, at least in my own experience, to the thought 'This is all very interesting, but *I wish I had more time to think about it.*'

I see no reason why an endless life should be shapeless in any worrying way. Of course it is shapeless in one dimension, the forward dimension in time: though an endless life will *include* many completed narratives, it will never, itself, *be* a completed narrative. But this is not even to say that the life does not have a shape as the narrative it is so far. What gives it shape is, of course, the projects it contains. Those projects are already a very narrow selection from the huge range of logically possible* projects; they define the life down to particularity without needing any help from the limitation that death is. Another form of shape, if limits are thought to be a precondition of shape, is given by the temporal and spatial locatedness of any person at any time: my life and I are *here* and *now*, and cannot be anywhere else. Culture and nurture are kinds of shaping too … and so on. This seems enough shape to be going on with, without requiring that every life should be limited by mortality as well.

My point is not that an infinitely long life is better than a finitely long one simply because it contains more goods. For one thing, I do not believe, unlike John Broome for example, that the value of any life is simply a function of the goods in that life; lives, on my view, are not just receptacles for value – they have value in themselves.[11] For another, it isn't always true that 'More is better'. More of some goods can, familiarly, be less: wives, for instance. Rather, my argument is that from the viewpoint of the person living it, a good life means one where at any point some long-standing projects and commitments are continuing, others are coming to completion, others again are just beginning. When our lives are going well, we are carried forward into the future on the crest of a variety of different narrative waves. *Eudaimonia**, according to me, just is this busy variety, this engagement in a happy mix of interesting and absorbing commitments. We cease to be *eudaimones*, people who are living well, when our lives lose this structure. But the good life, because of its overlapping-thread structure, always continues to give us reasons to want its continuance: the good life is a narrative (or rather complex of narratives) that goes *on*. The logical pressure that I want to set up towards having reason to value immortality comes from this familiar feature of lived experience.

I do mean to claim that this experience – of wanting our lives to continue, and also of our lives *as going to continue* – is *familiar*. The condemned prisoner's thought, over his last lunch, 'This tastes good, I'd like this for lunch tomorrow too', and the jolt of realisation that for him there *is* no lunch tomorrow, has a peculiar horror to it; the horror comes from the way his future is closed in by his impending execution. (Compare a grisly Japanese joke: 'Why have you only bought a one-way pedestrian ticket for the suspension bridge?' 'Because when I get to the middle I shall throw myself off.') By contrast, normally happy people experience their futures as open, as of indefinite duration into the future. On my account, that's how a normally *eudaimôn* life is lived. If I simply present this account of *eudaimonia* rather than arguing for it, then that is simply because I think it is obviously true; I look forward to being told what's wrong with it.[12]

Nor, so far, have I made any assumptions about the kind of projects and commitments that a happy life is likely to contain. For all I've said, they could be any projects that will suffice to carry us forward into the future on a variety of different narrative waves. They could even be such modest projects as those noted by a rather depressive and not particularly *eudaimôn* character in Nick Hornby's *About a Boy*:

a few years ago, I was really, really down, and I did think about … you know [suicide] … it was always, you know, not today. Maybe tomorrow, but not today. And after a few weeks of that I knew I was never going to do it, and the reason I was never going to do it was because I didn't want to miss out. I don't mean that life was great and I didn't want not to participate. I just mean that there were always one or two things that seemed unfinished, things I wanted to follow through. Like you want to see the next episode of *NYPD Blue*. If I'd just finished stuff for a book, I'd want to see it come out. If I was seeing a guy, I wanted one more date. If [my son] had a parents' evening coming up, I wanted to talk to his form teacher. Little things like that, but there was always something. And in the end I realised that there would always be something, and that those somethings would be enough.[13]

The kind of projects and commitments that my argument needs need not be inexhaustible – need not be projects and commitments such that our participation in *any one* of them could go on continuing to be rewarding for ever. That possibility is, I think, real: more about it later. But its reality is vastly more than I need to show to establish my argument here. All I need is that it should be possible for us to have projects and commitments such that our participation in a *range* of them could go on continuing to be rewarding for ever. Now the world is a big place, and the range of worthwhile possible projects and commitments that it might afford us seems – as a matter of common experience – to be indefinitely and incalculably large. So if there is a reason why this is not possible, that needs arguing.

3   The Makropulos case: against the meaningfulness of eternal life

Bernard Williams seeks to argue it – to argue that it is impossible, in principle, for projects to make an immortal life meaningful – in his famous paper 'The Makropulos Case: Reflections on the Tedium of Immortality'. That paper considers a fictional character, Elina Makropulos. Elina is a bit like Wowbagger. She drinks an elixir of life and as a result remains at the biological age of 43 for three centuries. But, after those centuries, she finds that her life has become joyless and she decides to return to mortality by taking no more of the elixir.[14]

Williams makes his argument by a number of different tactics. His central argument, as I read it (other readings seem possible), consists of two conditions and a related dilemma. The conditions are these: for me to have reason to find any conception of eternal life attractive, (1) 'it should clearly be *me* who lives for ever'; and (2) 'the state in which I survive should be one which, to me looking forward, will be adequately related, in the life it presents, to those aims which I now have in wanting to survive at all'.[15] The related dilemma – more in a moment about how it is related to the two conditions – is this:[16]

> There are difficult questions, if one presses the issue, about this constancy of character. How is this accumulation of memories [i.e. the memories that the person at issue, one Elina Makropulos, has before she becomes eternal] related to this character which she eternally has, and to the character of her experience? Are they much the same kind of events repeated? Then … the repeated pattern of personal relations … must take on a character of being inescapable. Or is the pattern of her experiences not repetitious in this way, but varied? Then the problem shifts, to these various experiences and the fixed character: how can it remain fixed, through an endless series of very various experiences? The experiences must surely happen to her without really affecting her; she [any such person] must be, as EM [Elina Makropulos] is, detached and withdrawn.

As Adrian Moore puts it, in his recent re-presentation of Williams's argument: 'the conditions that must be satisfied for my life to continue to count as *mine* militate against the conditions that must be satisfied for it to continue to be a life worth living. Conditions of the former kind demand a constancy, and conditions of the latter kind a variety, that cannot be resolved.'[17] Briefly: if EM's life remains hers it goes round in circles; if it doesn't go round in circles it ceases to be hers.

Let us begin with the second horn of this dilemma. Why, if EM's infinitely long life *doesn't* ever repeat itself, must it cease to be hers? That is a question about the conditions under which we should be prepared to agree that we have the same life at two different times, i.e. the question of 'diachronic' personal identity* (of personal identity over time). Williams is assuming, apparently, that EM's life cannot be the same life (the life of the same person) at any two times unless there is a strong core of unchanged elements present at both times.[18] This can surely be challenged (and Williams does not try to argue it directly). Maybe a weaker condition about character or experience than this is enough for personal identity. Perhaps, for instance, we need only require an analogue of what Parfit calls *connectedness*, rather than an analogue of what he calls *continuity*.[19] On this account we do not require for sameness of person between times t_1 and t_2 that there should be at least one unbroken strand of experience or character that stretches all the way from t_1 to t_2. We require only that every strand of experience or character that is present at t_2 *overlaps* at least in part with at least one strand of experience or character that overlaps at least in part with at least one strand of experience or character that overlaps ... with some strand of experience or character that was present at t_1.

On this 'connectedness' conception of personal identity, there might be *no* strands of experience or character present in EM at t_2 that were present in her at t_1. *But* she would still count as the same person, because there is a certain continuity – the unbroken overlapping of threads. Thus the first condition mentioned above will be satisfied: by this account of personal identity, it will clearly be *her* who has lived from t_1 to t_2, and yet her life has both the variety and the constancy that Moore and Williams require. It is plausible that Williams's second condition for a meaningful life will be satisfied too. Whether 'the state in which she survives' at t_2 'is one which, to her looking forward, will be adequately related, in the life it presents, to those aims which she now has in wanting to survive at all' at t_1, will depend on what we mean by 'adequately'. Roughly, the relation will be adequate if when we describe EM at t_2 to EM at t_1 and ask her, 'Do you have reason to care that *that* should survive?', she can reasonably answer 'Yes'. But 'Yes' seems a reasonable answer where EM at t_1 and EM at t_2 are linked by continuity. EM at t_1 can defend her positive answer to the question 'Do you care?' by pointing out that EM at t_2 is, so to speak, her own future. If that is not enough for reasonable concern for a future, we need to hear why not.

So: the second horn of the dilemma crumples, unless we make some strong, and not particularly plausible, assumptions about the role of fixity of character in diachronic personal identity. Let us turn to the first horn. Why, if EM's infinitely long life *does* remain hers, must it go round in circles? The idea here is that only a finite number of things can happen to or be done by someone with a determinate character; so, if EM has a determinate character, then the things that happen to her or that she does would have to repeat themselves over an infinite time. I have said what I have to say about determinacy of character in considering the second horn; let us now worry about this notion of repetition. A simple response is just to deny on commonsensical grounds, as indeed I already have (in section 2 above), that there is only a finite number of things that can happen to or be done by any individual person. We could also go a little deeper, and point out that the notions of 'repetition' and of 'things that can happen' that are in use here are much too indeterminate.[20] If I climb the same mountain or hear the same opera twice, is that repetition? If I climb the same mountain twice by the same route (in the same weather?), or hear the same production of the same opera twice (with exactly the same cast?), is *that* repetition? Yes and No are equally good answers to both questions, because whether two time-ordered items count as instances of the same type, so that the latter item is a repetition of the former, depends on how we describe them.

It might be replied that the notion of sameness, and hence of repetition, that Williams's argument needs is simply whatever notion of repetition justifies *boredom* as a response to it. But this just opens up a different question, and a rather difficult one, as to what justifies boredom as a response to anything, repetitious or not. There plainly are sorts of repetition which in no way justify boredom as a response. 'Visions of Johanna' is only one among plenty of pieces of music that I am happy to hear again and again and again. That song does not bore me *just* because hearing it again is repetition.

We do not, I think, have a good philosophical theory of boredom.[21] Williams is rather going out on a limb when he famously remarks that it is a 'profound difficulty' to provide

> any model of an unending, supposedly satisfying, state or activity which would not rightly prove boring to anyone who remained conscious of himself and who had acquired a character, interests, tastes and impatience in the course of living, already, a finite life ... Just as being bored can be a sign of not noticing, understanding or appreciating enough, so equally not being bored can be a sign of not noticing, or not reflecting enough.[22]

I won't respond to this in the shoulder-shrugging way that a theist* might – by saying that heaven will simply be whatever it needs to be to overcome the problem of boredom that Williams identifies, and that it is no surprise if this is inconceivable to us, since after all the joys of heaven are *supposed* to be inconceivable.[23] Both these points seem correct to me; but I don't need to make them.[24] We have already seen that we can resolve the dilemma about *immortality* that Williams offers without bringing *heaven* into the discussion; and anyway, Williams has moved the goalposts. The challenge before was to describe a *life* which could be satisfying and meaningful for ever because of the *various* projects, commitments and activities that it contained; and I claim to have met that challenge. The challenge in the last quotation is different, and more demanding: it is to describe a *single* project or activity which on its own could give life meaning for ever. Since I believe that there are inexhaustible goods, and in particular God, I believe this second challenge can be met. But there is no need to meet it, if the first challenge can be met (as I've argued it can). To meet the first challenge is already to show that immortal life can be meaningful, and need not be unendurably boring, or indeed boring at all, without appealing to any such controversial claim as 'There is a heaven' or 'There are inexhaustible goods' or 'There is a God who is an inexhaustible good'. To meet the first challenge, one only needs the claim that the kinds of worthwhile projects and commitments that are available to us are *indefinitely various*, i.e. there can be no complete list of them. That claim does not sound controversial at all; it sounds like common sense.

But let me consider further the interesting concept of boredom. To begin with, boredom is apparently an implicitly relative notion: things are neither boring nor interesting in themselves, but only in relation to persons. I am justified in my boredom with X when X has nothing to offer *me*: when I am living out, as before, a variety of worthwhile projects, and the trouble with X is that it does not engage with these, and has no significant relation to anything that does engage with them. In this sense boredom is an essentially contrastive state: my being bored with X is a result of my being justifiably interested by something else. In another sense, of course, boredom might be more pervasive: there might be nothing that engages with my worthwhile projects because I *have* no worthwhile projects. In a third sense, I might be bored *of* my worthwhile projects: even though I have some, they fail to engage my interest.

Though boredom can happen in the second or third of these three ways, I doubt it can be rational, or justified, in either way. There is nothing rational about simply not having any worthwhile projects. (The right response to having projects that – like Wowbagger's – are not worthwhile is not just to get rid of them, but also to replace them with something that *is* worthwhile.) Having worthwhile projects, but not being moved by them, merely sounds like the kind of failure of *joie de vivre* (as it is well called) that I dismissed earlier as a mood rather than an argument. Some listless immortal might just give up having projects, or lose interest in the worthwhile projects that she has; but these would not be justified or rational forms of boredom.

So if there is to be *justified* boredom, as Williams's argument requires, it will have to be of the first, contrastive sort: A's boredom with X will be justified where A rightly judges that X has nothing to offer to A's worthwhile projects. From which it follows that only a person who *has* worthwhile projects can be justifiably bored by anything: if A is justifiably bored with X, then there is some Y with which A is, justifiably, *not* bored. Williams's vision of unending all-pervading boredom *which is justifiably felt* is an illusion.

4 Conclusion

I have presented a rather modest theory of what makes life meaningful, and used it to show the way out of Williams's dilemma about the meaningfulness (or, rather, meaninglessness) of eternal life. Contrary to Williams, a life *can* continue meaningfully for ever, without either repeating itself or becoming a different person's life, for the following reasons. Lives are meaningful when they contain a variety of different worthwhile projects; and there is nothing to stop the very same life from containing an indefinite variety of such projects, if our condition for 'the very same life' is a connectedness condition on character rather than (as Williams requires) a continuity condition. Moreover, Williams's key notion of 'repetition' is crucially indeterminate, and his account of boredom crucially underdeveloped; when we sketch an adequate account of boredom, it turns out that one of Williams's central theses, that boredom would be a rational response to any conceivable form of eternal life, cannot be defended.

And another thing: a further way of crumpling the second horn of Williams's dilemma

Section 3 argued that eternal life can be meaningful if personal identity is sustained by connectedness rather than continuity, and if, at each moment of eternity, we have an indefinite variety of worthwhile projects in our lives.[25] I did not require anything in particular about the nature of these projects, beyond their being worthwhile. In particular, I did not require that they should be inexhaustible projects – projects such that our participation in *any one* of them could continue to be rewarding for ever. I could have added this requirement. If I had, I would not have needed to deny Williams's account of personal identity as continuity of character, because if there are inexhaustible goods, then even a fixed character like EM's can go on getting more meaning out of them for ever. In short, we can meet Williams's argument either by combining an unfixed character with an indefinite variety of finitely satisfying goods, or by combining a fixed character with a finite variety of (at least potentially) infinitely satisfying goods.

So are there any inexhaustible goods, any goods that could be infinitely satisfying? That is the question I take up in this postscript.

The goods that are most central to human life – the enjoyment and practice of art, friendship and love, the contemplation of beauty, the practice of inquiry and discovery, philosophy itself understood as Aristotelian *theôria** (ironically enough for Williams and Moore): our experience of all these goods seems plainly inexhaustible. For each such good, enjoying it is something that I can *readily* imagine carrying on without any necessary temporal limit emerging from the structure of my experience and enjoyment of that good.

Notice that I can say this without even mentioning God among the inexhaustible goods. Yet God is, to put it mildly, a rather notable absentee from the Makropulos argument, given that according to most believers in the major historical religions, east and west, God is supereminently the central good that we enjoy in eternal life, through worship: worship being the contemplation of God's reality and the reception of his love.[26]

Here I will not argue a full case for believing in inexhaustible goods. My point is simply that the Makropulos argument, even if it takes a continuity view of personal identity, has no chance of success without a full case for *not* believing in inexhaustible goods. I see no sign of that. Without it, the possibility of meaningful immortality remains intact even if Williams is right to see personal identity as continuity of character rather than connectedness (or some even weaker condition about character). So too does the possibility, which is also worth pointing out, that something like a taste of eternity, an escape from time-boundedness, might actually be a part of the experience of plenty of goods that are well known not only to immortals more serene than Wowbagger, but even to us mortals: 'If by eternity is understood not endless temporal duration but timelessness, then he lives eternally who lives in the present.'[27]

For deeper thought

Thaddeus Metz, 'The Immortality Requirement for Life's Meaning'. This examines the thesis, proposed by Tolstoy in his text 'My Confession', that extinction – death without an afterlife – destroys any meaning one's life may have had.

Earl Conee and Theodore Sider, *Riddles of Existence: a Guided Tour of Metaphysics*, chapter 1, 'Personal Identity'. This chapter of this introductory book explores the question of (roughly put) what makes you you. This question was at issue in section 3 above.

One might also read Virginia Woolf, *Orlando: a Biography*. This wonderful and accessible novel is the 'biography' of a fictional character that lives – first as a man and then as a woman – through hundreds of years. There's a good film of the book, too.

Notes

1. This essay is a slightly revised version of Chappell, 'Infinity Goes up on Trial: Must Immortality Be Meaningless?' The changes are mostly in the service of making the piece more accessible.

2. See Williams, 'The Makropoulos Case: Reflections on the Tedium of Immortality' and Moore, 'Williams, Nietzsche, and the Meaninglessness of Immortality'.
3. 'Tired fancy' is Bernard Williams's phrase ('The Makropoulos Case', p. 94); I'd want to add 'analytic* untruth'.
4. 'Projects and commitments' is Williams's own phrase. Note that neither a project nor a commitment need be what Aristotle called a *poiêsis* rather than a *praxis*, a making rather than a doing, an activity with its outcome built into it as opposed to an activity with its continuation built into it. Both can be either. It is therefore implausible to suggest that all projects and commitments have a natural end built in to them. Some do, others don't. And anyway, my picture, as we'll see, is an overlapping-threads picture. (Note: not having a natural end inbuilt need not be the same thing as being inexhaustible.)
5. Nagel, *Mortal Questions*, p. 14.
6. 'Bertrand Russell [in *A Free Man's Worship*] went on about the transitoriness of human beings, the tininess of the earth, the vast and pitiless expanses of the universe and so on, in a style of self-pitying and at the same time self-glorifying rhetoric that made Frank Ramsey remark that he himself was much less impressed than some of his friends were by the size of the universe, perhaps because he weighed 240 pounds' (Williams, *Philosophy as a Humanistic Discipline*, p. 137).
7. Wittgenstein, *Tractatus Logico-Philosophicus*, section 6.521.
8. For Wittgenstein's image of the overlapping threads, see his *Philosophical Investigations*, section 67.
9. J. K. Rowling, *Harry Potter and the Philosopher's Stone*, p. 215. The impression created by this sentence is undermined by the next: 'After all, to the well-organised mind, death is but the next great adventure.' This presumably can't be true unless the mind is there to experience the adventure.
10. 'The Makropoulos Case', p. 89 ('these are contingencies').
11. For more on this see my piece 'On the Very Idea of Criteria for Personhood'.
12. My argument is not guilty, either, of a fallacy noted by Adrian Moore ('Williams, Nietzsche, and the Meaninglessness of Immortality', p. 313), the fallacy of confusing *always wanting that P* with *wanting that always P*. I have argued that if we are *eudaimones* then necessarily we always want that there should be a future for our lives. I have not argued that if we are *eudaimones* then necessarily we want that there should always be a future for our lives. We might not reflect that far. But if we do reflect that far, we are bound to see that *wanting, at any time T, that: P* leads by a natural piece of induction* to *wanting that: P at any T* – even if it is obviously not logically equivalent to it; just as

seeing a white swan every time you see a swan leads naturally to the supposition that all swans are white, even though it does not entail it.

13. *About a Boy*, chapter 30, p. 589 in *Nick Hornby: the Omnibus*.

14. 'The case of Elina Makropulos is adapted from Karel Čapek's 1922 play *Věc Makropulos* ("The Makropulos Case" or "The Makropulos Affair"), or perhaps more immediately from Leoš Janàček's 1926 opera which was based on that play' (Burley, 'Immortality and Meaning', p. 533 n. 12).

15. Williams, 'The Makropoulos Case', p. 91.

16. Williams, 'The Makropoulos Case', p. 90.

17. Moore, 'Williams, Nietzsche, and the Meaninglessness of Immortality', p. 314.

18. 'EM has a certain character, and indeed, except for her accumulating memories of earlier times … seems always to have been much the same sort of person' – Williams, 'The Makropoulos Case', p. 90.

19. Parfit, *Reasons and Persons*.

20. This same problem about indeterminacy undermines Moore's claim ('Williams, Nietzsche, and the Meaninglessness of Immortality', p. 327) that 'where allowing the subject to die would open up new possibilities of narrative, new opportunities for sense-making, and new ways of defying nihilism, preserving the subject would impose restrictions and constraints on subsequent interpretation that would impose an overall burden'. Going *any* determinate way rather than any other closes down some possibilities and opens up others. How are we to decide which possibilities it is more fruitful to leave open?

21. Nicholas Joll tells me that there is an admittedly rather exhausting analysis of boredom presented by Heidegger in the first part of his *The Fundamental Concepts of Metaphysics: World, Finitude, Solitude*.

22. Williams, 'The Makropoulos Case', pp. 94–5.

23. 'Eye hath not seen, nor ear heard, neither have entered into the heart of man, the things which God hath prepared for them that love him' (1 Corinthians 2: 9).

24. A related issue is raised by Nozick (*Anarchy, State, and Utopia*, p. 312 and foreword), who considers the difficulty of designing a political utopia that will satisfy its every member. Nozick regards this difficulty as an impossibility; he quotes Alexander Gray's remark that 'No utopia has ever been described in which any sane man would on any conditions consent to live, if he could possibly escape.' It is perhaps salutary to reflect that the question of the meaningfulness of immortality is usually debated as if it were a question solely for individuals. Presumably it is a social or political question too.

25. That is, *both* of these conditions – not just one or the other – must be met if eternal life is to be meaningful. Compare what section 2.3 in the chapter by Michèle Friend says about the fussiness of conjunctions.

26. If this is what worship is – as I contend: it would take another text to defend the contention – it should be obvious how odd it is to speak of an obligation to worship, or to look for grounds for this alleged obligation in, for example, God's maximal excellence, or the belief that he created us, or the claim that worship does us good. Is there an obligation to be in love? And if we do *not* love because the beloved is maximally excellent, or made us, or because it does us good to love – does that make love ungrounded? I don't think so; but for these claims – that is, for affirmative answers to those questions – see Bayne and Nagasawa, 'Grounds of Worship'.

27. Thanks to Tim Bayne, Mikel Burley, Sarah Broadie, Christopher Coope, Larry James, Adrian Moore, Adam Morton, Nicholas Joll and Yujin Nagasawa for comments.

Part III
Metaphysics and Artificial Intelligence

Part III

5

'I Think You Ought to Know I'm Feeling Very Depressed': Marvin and Artificial Intelligence

Jerry Goodenough

I still remember the first time I met Marvin. It was 15 March 1978 and the first broadcast of episode two of the *Hitchhiker's Guide to the Galaxy* radio series. From the moment I heard Stephen Moore's electronically modulated voice as Marvin, I was hooked, and he remains my favourite character in the show. Partly this has something to do with the surprise I felt, not just that a robot should have a personality of some sort but that it should be such a comically repellent one, marked by self-obsession, self-pity and hypochondria. Marvin plays no great role in the various narratives of the series (radio, book, film, etc.) but he is a great comic character in his own right.

Perhaps what makes Marvin so funny and interesting for me is that he confounds the expectations that science fiction has given us about robots and other 'artificially intelligent' beings. And he does so in a way that, when we think carefully about it, tells us a good deal about artificial intelligence and robotics in the real world. And trying to understand why Marvin is the way he is helps us to understand ourselves, the way in which human minds are put together and operate. These are the ideas that I shall pursue in the six sections that follow.

1   What are robots and what are they like?

A robot is an artificial being of some sort. Originally, robots were artificial in the sense that they were made entirely of mechanical, i.e. non-biological, materials. With the development in both science and science fiction, this picture rapidly becomes more complicated. As far back as Mary Shelley's 1818 novel *Frankenstein*, we see the artificial creation of a being made entirely out of biological material. (And a being who might be considerably unhappier than Marvin!) But the division between the biological and the mechanical has become increasingly blurred, in fact as well as fiction. So science fiction gives us, for instance, the film *Robocop*, starring a cyborg, a mechanical robot with an organic brain and nervous system transplanted from a dying human being. *Star Trek: The Next Generation* has Lieutenant Commander Data, an android with some organic components but with an artificial brain. In this way, science fiction manages to keep ahead of medical science which, over the last century, has managed to incorporate more and more mechanical devices into human bodies. But I want where possible to ignore this blurring and stick to the 'traditional' robot, which is a being like Marvin.

Robots in science fiction tend to come in one of two different sorts. The first of these, the archetypal robot, is sinister: such a robot lacks any personality, any emotional characteristics, and is often a threat to human beings. We can trace this view back to the work that gave us the word 'robot' – to Karel Čapek's 1921 play *R.U.R.* in which robots, which act as mechanical worker-slaves, rebel and ultimately exterminate humanity. Perhaps the most famous recent example is the Terminator – that is, the character played by Arnold Schwarzenegger in the film of that name. If there is one word that sums up the Terminator, it is 'implacable'. It is clearly capable of *reasoning* in some sense. Whenever it runs into an obstacle to its pre-programmed task, it is able to come up with a solution that removes or avoids it – *but* there is no point in trying to reason with it. It can't be persuaded out of its mission. (You might as well try to reason with a runaway bulldozer ...) And perhaps it is this that makes such things so scary. They have the outer appearance of humans (less so with ordinary robots, more so with those like the Terminator) while possessing entirely machine-like behaviour. They seem to lack any feelings, any kind of internal emotional life.

Other sorts of robot or computer have a friendly personality. Perhaps the earliest example of this in film was Robbie, the robot in *Forbidden Planet* (1956). Robbie was cheerful and helpful, as was another artificial entity, the computer HAL in *2001: A Space Odyssey* (1968). (Though HAL's warm personality and voice made him all the more sinister when, a little later on, he went mad and started killing all the crew!) But here, with the friendly robots, we may perhaps have a negative reaction, feel unsure or doubtful, because we have the intuition that this is not a *genuine* feeling being communicated but a mere automatic response. It has the external manifestation, the behavioural attributes, of a feeling, but there isn't, we tend to think, a real sensation causing it 'inside'. Let's take some examples from *Hitchhiker's*.

Consider first the insanely cheerful 'personality' of Eddie, *Heart of Gold*'s onboard ship's computer; far from reassuring the crew, Eddie annoys everybody. His excessively fulsome responses are often inappropriate to the situation. They are not the responses of a person, a sentient being aware of the gravity of the situation. (A real person probably wouldn't respond to the imminent destruction of the *Heart of Gold* and all on board by Magrathean missiles by starting to sing 'You'll Never Walk Alone'! – *Hitchhiker*, chapter 17. To be fair to Eddie, he is only a personality *prototype* and so perhaps the bugs haven't been ironed out yet and he – like some human beings – has difficulty in matching appropriate emotional responses to situations.) And the same can be said of the supposedly cheerful and helpful 'personalities' of *Heart of Gold's* other machines – tea dispensers, doors, etc. – which are all the wretched products of the Sirius Cybernetics Corporation with their 'Genuine People Personalities'. No wonder their complaints department 'now covers all the major land masses of the first three planets in the Sirius Tau Star system'! (*Hitchhiker*, chapter 17).

We find another friendly robot in Colin, the machine that assists Ford Prefect in *Mostly Harmless*. Colin's most notable feature – apart from his constant cheerfulness and desire to please – is his immense stupidity. If he has any kind of personality at all, it is that we associate with a Labrador puppy, one whose intelligence has not yet caught up with its enthusiasm and energy. (Though, to be fair again, much of Colin's 'personality' is the result of Ford's tinkering with his head with a piece of wire.) And there is an entirely unnecessary robot of a sort in the 'intelligent' and argumentative elevator in chapter 6 of *Restaurant*. Unnecessary, because a lift doesn't need a personality: it just needs to go up and down when you press the right button. And 'intelligent' only in the curious sense that it has been over-engineered, given both a 'personality' and an ability to see into the future which its personality can't handle .. In this, it resembles much existing consumer technology, which is made far more complicated than the average user needs. (Thankfully, the marketing division of the Sirius Cybernetics Corporation are a bunch of mindless jerks who'll be/who were the first against the wall when the revolution comes/came – depending on which century you are in when you read this, as *Hitchhiker* chapter 11 makes clear. Sort of.)

Then there is another sort of robotic character that has become popular in science fiction. I am thinking of the rather robotic (but actually flesh and blood, because Vulcan – or, more exactly, half-human, half-Vulcan) Mr Spock in the original series of *Star Trek*, and of Data in *Star Trek: The Next Generation*. Both of these characters argue at times that possessing emotions clouds one's ability to make judgements. They are supposed to be gifted with powers of reasoning to a high degree, but they lack empathy and any genuine sense of emotion. (Or perhaps, in Mr Spock's case, they lack the ability to *show* emotion: it is unclear whether Vulcans are trained to repress emotions or just to repress their expression.) We the audience are supposed to be entertained by this but without taking it seriously, for the story usually sides with Kirk or Picard in requiring that emotion be necessary for the making of correct decisions. Could these captains be right?

2   How do philosophers feel about feeling?

Historically philosophy has adopted a rather problematic attitude towards the relationship between rationality and emotions. Once we can get clear on how thinking and feeling are supposed to interrelate, we can better understand Marvin and what he tells us about ourselves.

Historically philosophers have argued that the emotions are a kind of bodily weakness that need to be overcome. We can trace this all the way back to the fourth century BC to Plato who has his character Socrates say, in the *Phaedo* dialogue, that the body must be transcended in order that the mind/soul may be capable of accessing pure reason, the idea being that our bodies actually *prevent* us from thinking or reasoning properly or gaining knowledge:

> [The body] fills us with wants, desires, fears, all sorts of illusions and much nonsense ... Worst of all, if we do get some respite from it and turn to some investigation, everywhere in our investigations the body is present and makes for confusion and fear, so that it prevents us from seeing the truth.[1]

This is a philosophical tradition that will last for millennia: we find it in the works of René Descartes in the seventeenth century.

According to Descartes, our conscious selves are entities that we know more intimately and more perfectly than we know our own bodies, and the reason for this is that we *are* our selves, non-physical entities, and are only loosely associated with our bodies:

> . . . I knew I was a substance whose whole essence or nature is solely to think, and which does not require any place, or depend on any material thing, in order to exist. Accordingly this 'I' – that is, the soul by which I am what I am – is entirely distinct from the body, and indeed is easier to know than the body, and would not fail to be whatever it is, even if the body did not exist.[2]

So: according to this mind–body dualism, that which is conscious and which reasons is something entirely separate from the physical biological body, fully separate in the sense that it could continue to be conscious and reasoning even if the body ceased to exist.

It was only towards the end of his life that Descartes got round to considering the emotions. In his last work, *The Passions of the Soul*, published in 1649, the year before his death, he categorises the emotions as generally the effect of bodies upon minds:

> . . . what is a passion in the soul is usually an action in the body. Hence there is no better way of coming to know about our passions than by examining the difference between the soul and the body.[3]

So the emotions are primarily bodily functions, caused by activities or events in our body. But then Descartes locates one possible candidate for an emotion *outside* of the body in a non-physical mind: that emotion or emotion-like thing, is volition or the will.

This move enables Descartes to avoid the traditional philosophical problem of free will* and determinism*. Since the will is located in the non-physical mind rather than in the physical body, it is not subject to the processes of physical causation and determinism; it is thus, Descartes infers, radically free. But just as importantly, a non-physical will enables Descartes to propound a philosophy whereby it is best if each of us (non-physical selves) can be in total control of our emotions:

> When the passion urges us to pursue ends whose attainment involves some delay, we must refrain from making any immediate judgement about them, and distract ourselves by other thoughts until time and repose have completely calmed the disturbance in our blood. Finally, when it impels us to actions which require an *immediate* decision, the will must devote itself mainly to considering and following reasons which are opposed to

those presented by the passion, even if they appear less
strong . . . the chief use of wisdom lies in its teaching us
to be masters of our passions and to control them with
such skill that the evils which they cause are quite bear-
able, and even become a source of joy.[4]

Note here Descartes' remarkable language, which seems to
characterise my emotions as something separate from me,
almost alien to me, capable of provoking actions against my
real interests. And so (that is, given that situation) I need to
develop my will in order to keep these emotions in check.
And this is an attitude towards the emotions that goes all the
way back to Plato and to the Stoic philosophers of the third
century BC. Under this view, the emotions are separate from
our thinking capacity: we can strengthen the latter with our
will in order to control these emotions. Spinoza – writing as
late as the 1670s – makes broadly the same kind of case. One
best achieves happiness when one is able to overcome one's
emotions and place one's reason firmly in control.

But other philosophers in the early modern period have
argued that, no matter how good our powers of reasoning,
they will always be subordinate to our emotions. David
Hume, for instance, in his *Treatise of Human Nature*, says:

We speak not strictly and philosophically when we talk of
the combat of passion and of reason. Reason is, and ought
only to be the slave of the passions, and can never pretend
to any other office than to serve and obey them.[5]

Hume's point here is that while reason can tell us what it is we
ought to do in order to bring about any particular outcome,
it can't make us do it. Reason lacks any psychic energy, so to
speak: it is inert. We need a passion, an emotion, a motivation,
a volition in order to move us into action. It is not enough

that I know that x is the best thing for me to do: I have to want to do x. Knowledge on its own won't propel me into action.

If Hume is right – and I think that here he is right – then the picture drawn by a long tradition of Western philosophy, from Plato and the ancient Greeks to Descartes, Spinoza and other more modern philosophers, is wrong. We need feelings as well as reason: in fact, reason itself won't work properly *without* feelings – as I will try now to show.

3   What can science tell us about emotions and reasoning?

In his 1994 book *Descartes' Error: Emotion, Reason and the Human Brain*, neurologist Antonio Damasio opposes the orthodox view of the relationship between emotions and reason. He presents that orthodoxy as follows:

> There has never been any doubt that, under certain circumstances, emotion disrupts reasoning. The evidence is abundant and constitutes the source for the sound advice with which we have been brought up. Keep a cool head, hold emotions at bay! Do not let your passions interfere with your judgement. As a result, we usually conceive of emotion as a supernumerary mental faculty, an unsolicited, nature-ordained accompaniment to our rational thinking. If emotion is pleasurable, we enjoy it as a luxury; if it is painful, we suffer it as an unwelcome intrusion. In either case, the sage will advise us, we should experience emotion and feeling in only judicious amounts. We should be reasonable.[6]

This sounds a lot like Plato or Descartes. Against this orthodox view, Damasio concludes from his neurological case studies that a reduction in the capacity to have emotions may be an important source of irrational behaviour.[7] He says:

> [E]motions and feelings may not be intruders in the bastion of reason at all: they may be enmeshed in its networks for worse *and* for better. The strategies of human reason probably did not develop, in either evolution or any single individual, without the guiding force of the mechanisms of biological regulation, of which emotion and feeling are notable expressions. Moreover, even after reasoning strategies become developed in the formative years, their effective deployment probably depends, to a considerable extent, on a continued ability to experience feelings.[8]

Damasio argues his case via studies of people who have experienced damage to the frontal lobes of their brain. The complicated role these parts of the brain play in relating our emotions and our reasoning first became clear to modern science with the case of Phineas Gage who, in 1848, accidentally inflicted an appalling wound to the front of his skull while working with blasting powder. A large metal rod was blown through his cheek and out of the top of his head, leaving a wound through the front part of his brain, the prefrontal lobes. What fascinated doctors about Gage was that he survived the accident, remained conscious throughout, and seemed at first to have suffered no ill-effects mentally. He could still talk, his memory was unimpaired, and so apparently were his powers of reasoning.

But as time went on, it became clear that the post-accident Phineas Gage was a very different person from his previous self. His emotional character was completely different and there were interesting – and distressing! – problems arising with his ability to reason. According to Gage's first doctor, John Harlow, he was now

> Fitful, irreverent, indulging at times in the grossest profanity which was not previously his custom, manifesting but little deference for his fellows, impatient of restraint or advice when it conflicts with his desires, at times pertinaciously obstinate, yet capricious and vacillating, devising many plans of future operation, which are no sooner arranged than they are abandoned . . .[9]

All of this was a considerable change from the pre-accident Gage who was famous for his 'temperate habits' and 'considerable energy of character'. He had had

> A well-balanced mind and was looked upon by those who knew him as a shrewd, smart businessman, very energetic and persistent in executing all his plans of action.[10]

But now his life went downhill. Gage was incapable of reading the moods of other people, of understanding them or behaving appropriately with them. Any understanding of his emotions and any control over them seem to have been destroyed along with his pre-frontal lobe. Though he formed many plans for new businesses and careers, they always came to nothing, for he was incapable of organising himself sufficiently to be able to bring these plans to fruit. It seemed as though he was incapable of any kind of sustained reasoning. It is no surprise that he wound up exhibiting his injuries in a circus freak show, dying of a major epileptic fit (presumably related to his accident) 13 years later at the age of only 38.

It is from the story of Gage, and from more recent clinical cases, that Damasio draws his conclusion that our powers of reasoning are intimately interwoven with our capacities for feeling and emotion. Within the complex structures of the human brain there aren't separate parts for feeling and for reasoning: often the two work together in the very same part, as Phineas Gage discovered to his cost.

This might lead us to wonder whether there is something wrong about the idea of beings like Mr Spock and similar entities that are supposed to be capable of pure reasoning without feeling. But Vulcans are biological creatures like ourselves: next we have to ask what role emotions might play for a *robot*.

4   Could robots have feelings?

Why might robots be thought to lack feelings? The traditional answer has been: because they lack organic bodies. The body is subject to all sorts of feelings that are uncontrollable – hence Socrates' desire to escape these feelings by abandoning his body. Thus an artificial creature that is essentially biological can still be expected to have feelings (and Frankenstein's creation is a strongly passionate creature).

But some science fictional artificial entities are biological (or part-biological like Robocop), some are supposed to be alien or part-alien creatures, and, in fact, the problematic relationship with emotion that one finds in *these* entities – the biological or alien ones – suggests that robots such as Marvin perhaps ought to have emotions. Perhaps the most famous exemplar of such problems is *Star Trek's* (fully biological) Mr Spock, half-Vulcan half-human, yet seeming to lack most of the emotions that human beings possess. Being unable to experience them means that he therefore lacks an understanding of how these emotions work and what influence they have upon human decision-making. Presumably a Vulcan's body has at least simple emotions – desires for food, sleep, etc. – and the fact that Vulcans exist (in the *Star Trek* universe, at least!) would seem to indicate that they are capable of reproducing, bringing up families, and so on, the sorts of activity that might generally be thought to involve some level of emotional attachment. Plus we see a clear emotional bond of some sort – friendship and respect – growing between Spock and Kirk.

Lieutenant Commander Data seems to fall halfway between Spock and Marvin since the *Star Trek* narratives aren't always consistent on the question of whether he is entirely mechanical or a partly organic cyborg. But Data has similar difficulties to Spock in understanding human emotions. How far is this true of Marvin?

Spock and Data in some ways resemble autistic humans, since these latter are often unable to understand emotions 'from the inside'. They suffer from what a leading autism researcher, Simon Baron-Cohen, has called 'mindblindness'. Such people are, as Baron-Cohen puts it, 'blind to things like thoughts, beliefs, knowledge, desires and intentions, which for most of us self-evidently underlie behaviour'.[11] Such autistic humans, while they may have high intellects and are some-times profoundly gifted in one way or another, suffer from severe reasoning problems, not least when they are trying to reason about other people. For many with this condition are unable to understand that another person has thoughts and feelings: they are, so to speak, unable to place themselves in another person's shoes and see the world through their eyes. (Mark Haddon's best-selling novel, *The Curious Incident of the Dog in the Night-Time*, gives an imaginative portrayal of what it must be like to be an autistic person.) This supplies us with a clue about Marvin, although – or rather just because – unlike Spock or Data, he never gives us any real reason to think that he may be autistic.

Marvin may not be good with people, but he does understand them. For Marvin *does* have emotions. True, whenever we see him, they are usually downbeat ones, but they are still emotions. The single exception to this may be Marvin's response to reading God's Final Message to his Creation: '"I think", he murmured at last, from deep within his corroding rattling thorax, "I feel good about it"' (*So Long, and Thanks for all the Fish*, chapter 40). These are Marvin's last words and are perhaps a recognition – via the Message – that idiocy and incompetence are built into the universe at its most fundamental level. Or perhaps not. Perhaps he's just looking forward to not suffering any more.

We ought not to assume that because robots have artificial bodies, they therefore cannot have emotions. They would plainly lack some emotions – sexual desire, hunger for food, etc. But it would seem probable that at the very least a robot would need a sense of *pain*. We may start by saying that it would be useful for a robot to be aware of any damage or malfunctioning in its 'body'. The great advantage of pain for human beings is that it has a strongly aversive quality that not only tells us that our body is damaged but forces us to do something about it. If I sprain my ankle, it takes an enormous effort to keep walking on it rather than sit down and rest it. (People born with the fortunately rare neurological condition of congenital analgesia have nervous systems that won't transmit pain signals. Far from being lucky not to have pain, they tend to lead short and difficult lives since they can damage their bodies and contract illnesses without noticing.) Something that was at least functionally equivalent to pain would be necessary to play the same role in the life of the robot, i.e. to advise it and protect it against bodily damage. So we ought not to be surprised, then, when Marvin complains '. . . and then of course I've got this terrible pain in all the diodes down my left hand side . . .' (*Hitchhiker*, chapter 13). Four books later, it is still there:

> [']I mentioned to you that I had this terrible pain in all the diodes down my left side? That I had asked for them to be replaced but they never were? ... See if you can guess,' said Marvin, when he judged that the pause had become embarrassing enough [good understanding of people there!], 'which parts of me were never replaced? Go on, see if you can guess.
>
> 'Ouch,' he added, 'ouch, ouch, ouch, ouch, ouch.'
>
> (*Fish*, chapter 40)

That no one takes Marvin's complaints seriously, that consequently his diodes are never replaced, is something to which we must return. In the interim, we must consider another point, that if Marvin is to have a real range of emotions, he needs to have something else: he needs to have a self, a personality.

5   Could robots have a self?

Let us assume that humans start to make robots in order to perform complicated jobs. We already have simple robots working for us, often in places where humans cannot safely go – in the radioactive parts of nuclear reactors, in deep-sea environments, and so on. Most of these robots are controlled directly by a human operator. One class of robots that isn't are the simple robot explorers that we have landed on Mars, where they potter around collecting data, taking pictures, and transmitting it all to us. The distance to Mars is so great that it wouldn't be possible to control these robots directly (by radio signals, for instance): the delay would be too great. So the exploring robots are capable of certain forms of behaviour such as avoiding dangers, finding ways around obstacles, and so on.

But is this really *behaviour*? For the computer brain built into these robotic explorers is *programmed* in certain ways such that it responds along certain preordained lines to certain stimuli – the presence of a large rock in its path, for example; and this is *not* really behaviour in that it lacks any kind of flexibility, any sense of intelligence or choice behind its movements. True, it *is* behaviour in the sense that what a wasp does when it repeatedly bounces against a window, trying to get out into the light, may be called behaviour. But it is certainly *not* behaviour in the same sense in which we use the term to describe the constantly responding ingenuity with which a cat seeks to track down its prey. The Mars explorers, then, are much more like wasps than cats. But some attempts at artificial intelligence construction are more ambitious. For instance, the 'Cog' project underway at the Massachusetts Institute of Technology is trying to map out the properties that an artificial entity would need to have in order to behave in the fuller, intelligence-requiring sense.[12]

For a robot to be capable of having genuinely complex interactions with its environment, it must have some conception of a self, if only in order to be able to locate itself within its environment. ('That thing is to *my* left'. 'From where *I* am, object A is further away than object B' and so on.) We see here that our perceptions of the world are relative in an important sense, in that they are all related to our bodies: we see things from where our eyes are located, hear things from where our ears are, and so on. And in order to be able to understand the world around us and react to it properly, we need to be able to relate these things to some sense of self. (Knowing that a large rock is about to fall on coordinates XYZ won't motivate me to action unless I also know that *I* am at XYZ!) Unifying all of the perceptions of a robot so that it has a subjective sense of a single perceiver is going to be important. (It is also going to be very difficult, since *this* problem – the so-called binding problem – is one that still baffles scientists trying to work out how *humans* unify all of their different perceptions into a single experience of the world.)

But a robot needs not only that sense of self but also a rather more sophisticated one. It must, for instance, be able to tell the difference between itself – its own body – and the world around it, something that even creatures as unintelligent as sea anemones can manage. (You don't want a robot that's looking for metal samples to start chipping pieces out of its own leg!)

But a robot's sense of self will have to be more sophisticated than this. One of the important features of *our* sense of self is our grasp of ourselves as *agents*. We are not just things to which things happen: from our earliest days in the cradle, we learn firstly that we can move our own bodies just by thinking about it, by wanting to do so, and then that we can use these movements to effect changes in the world. The next stage is that as small children we become aware of being automotive, self-moving, of possessing desires and other emotional states that cause us to embark upon actions. Of course, how we could create such a sense of agency in a robot is another question. Perhaps, like many other properties, it develops the more complex the other powers of the robot become.

Any robot that is going to be useful to us in anything like the sense of an independent being that can be left to operate on its own in a sophisticated and flexible manner must, at the very least, be able (i) to perceive (really to perceive, not merely to respond to sensory input in an automatic

146 *Philosophy and* The Hitchhiker's Guide to the Galaxy

fashion), (ii) to be aware of its perceptions, aware of them as its own, (iii) to be aware of itself as a thing located within the world that is the source of its perceptions, and (iv) to be aware of itself as a thing with aims, to be able to instigate actions rather than merely respond automatically to stimuli.

These four conditions are necessary but not sufficient* for a being that will have emotions, but there is another condition that we must consider, such that the five conditions may jointly be necessary *and* sufficient for having emotion. If we want a robot that is going to be able to *interact successfully with human beings* then it must have *some understanding of how human minds work.* In other words, the robot can't be the equivalent of an autistic person. It must have what philosophers call a 'theory of mind'. That is, it must have at least a minimal understanding of what it is to have a mind and a self, not just in its own case but in the case of others in the world around it. As far as we can tell with human beings, a full notion of others as selves usually comes along with our infant development of our own selves, and most of us achieve this by the time we are about four years old.[13]

6 So why is Marvin unhappy?

Why is Marvin unhappy? And why is it worthwhile asking that question? The answer to that second question is that working out how Marvin comes to be unhappy, what causes him to be unhappy in this way, again tells us something interesting about ourselves.

Let's summarise what we know must be true about Marvin. He is an artificial intelligent being of prodigious intellect, a fact of which he is aware. ('I have an exceptionally large mind' – *Hitchhiker*, chapter 11.) He is an agent with desires and self-awareness. (His strongest desire, as we shall see, is to be recognised as the special person that he is.) He is sensitive, and when not too self-absorbed, aware of the emotional states of other people. In fact, he is even aware of the effect on how his emotions affect the emotional states of other people, as this exchange with Ford Prefect makes clear:

> 'Don't pretend you want to talk to me. I know you hate me.'
>
> 'No I don't.'
>
> 'Yes you do, everybody does. It's part of the shape of the Universe. I only have to talk to somebody and they begin to hate me. Even robots hate me. If you just ignore me, I expect I shall just go away.'
>
> (*Hitchhiker*, chapter 34)

In order to see how a robot could become so unhappy, we need to look more closely at this notion of a self – at this logical or psychological construction that holds together, is the central binding point of, all of our mental properties.

If true possession of a self requires possession of the ability to know other people as selves, then this has important consequences. These were first explored by someone who wasn't interested in artificial intelligence and at a time when it wasn't a serious proposition: the eighteenth-century philosopher Jean-Jacques Rousseau. In his 1755 *Discourse on the Origin of Inequality* Rousseau describes how people come to live together in societies, and how this leads to all manner of social ills, including the social and economic inequality of the book's title.

What brings all this about, says Rousseau, is the development within us of *amour propre* rather than *amour de soi*.

Amour de soi translates literally as 'love of self', but by this Rousseau means that sense of self-awareness that even primitive or solitary animals have, the minimal sense of ourselves as something that feels and acts, as something that has crude desires to be satisfied. But when, according to Rousseau, we come to live in societies, to mix and inter-act with other people, *amour de soi* comes to be replaced or accompanied by the more sophisticated and problematic notion of *amour propre*. This term is harder to translate: it is often crudely translated into English as 'reputation' or 'vanity'. While it certainly includes these, it is a much richer and more complex notion than that. *Amour propre* concerns *how one is seen by others*. The idea here is that one becomes aware of oneself not only directly, through self-consciousness, but *indirectly*, through other people. We start to become able, as the poet Burns put it, 'To see oursel's as others see us.'

Amour propre in modest amounts leads an individual to self-confidence and reasonable ambition, but in larger amounts to the creation of the social vices. It is this latter, negative point that Rousseau stresses. Once in society, he says, we learn pretence. We learn to produce an inflated image of ourselves for others to consume – but which, ulti-mately, we ourselves consume. For we regard our honour or our reputation as an important source of our value. Thus we try to manipulate the image of ourselves that we present, in order to appear better, more powerful, more attractive and so on. Out of this, Rousseau contends, emerges all the evils of social life, power, social inequality, the class structure, consumer goods, the fashion industry and, as Douglas Adams pointed out in 1978, people who think they will look cool to others if they wear a digital watch . . .

If we make use of Rousseau's insight, we can now re-create the emotional life of Marvin. Marvin is enormously intelligent and capable of prodigious feats, mental and physical. His sense of self-awareness leads him to desire at least a certain level of admiration and respect for his qualities, but he doesn't receive it. In the course of the *Hitchhiker* narrative, he is mistreated in a number of different ways. His innate superiority, mental and physical, is never recognised by his companions. Worse, he is given only menial jobs to do:

> Here I am, brain the size of a planet and they ask me to take you down to the bridge. Call that job satisfaction? 'Cos I don't.

> (*Hitchhiker*, chapter 11)

His *amour propre* suffers, undermined by the apparently low image that the others have of him, an image that starts to reinforce the low image he has of himself. Despite his staggering mental powers, he is not respected. Worse, he is often ignored or forgotten, as when Marvin's human companions travel forward in time to the end of the universe for a meal, leaving Marvin behind for rather a long time:

> 'Five hundred and seventy-six thousand million, three thousand five hundred and seventy nine years . . . I counted them . . . The first ten million years were the worst . . . ,' said Marvin, 'and the second ten million years, they were the worst too. The third ten million I didn't enjoy at all. After that I went into a bit of a decline.'

> (*Restaurant*, chapter 18)

That he spends much of this time waiting outside Milliways Restaurant parking cars says a lot about how people treat Marvin. And him with a brain the size of a planet . . . Marvin's self-image seems to be the result of having always been treated like this:

> 'But I'm quite used to being humiliated,' droned Marvin. 'I can even go and stick my head in a bucket of water if you like. Would you like me to go and stick my head in a bucket of water? I've got one ready.'
>
> (*Restaurant*, chapter 17)

And this leads to a personality that depresses others who then avoid Marvin which then depresses him even more. So we see a kind of feedback loop here where things just get worse. In fact, Marvin is so miserable that he has become a universal hater, despising not only the humans who boss him around but also artificial life, and not just the Sirius Cybernetics Corporation's hideous doors and lifts with their 'Genuine People Personalities' but other robots too. There is almost a sense of satisfaction in the way that he lures the battle-machine robot into bringing about its own destruction. ('"What a depressingly stupid machine" said Marvin as he trudged away' – *Restaurant*, chapter 7.)

Marvin is so unhappy because he is so like us. In order to perform the tasks for which they are intended in science fiction, robots would have to possess many other human properties – many properties over and above those that they would *obviously* need to perform their tasks. That is, whilst various tasks evidently require at least some reason, machines that reasoned would require emotion, too. For without emotion reason goes wrong and finds it hard to cope with certain things, especially reasoning about other people's minds, motives, et cetera. But that means that, in giving robots emotion, one thing we would be giving them would be theory of mind, the sense of self necessary in order to relate to humans and to *their* respective senses of self. However, theory of mind inevitably brings along with it other qualities including *amour propre*, vanity, disappointment, disillusion, from which so far only humans suffer. And this ultimately is why Marvin is capable of feeling very depressed. In making him like ourselves, we inevitably have to make him so much like ourselves. And what ought to depress *us* is that these very same qualities are the ones that could have made Marvin happy – or at least, happier – if he had been treated as a person rather than a tool or a slave.

For deeper thought

Plato's dialogue the *Phaedo* is an important, but fairly accessible, presentation of the traditional view of the relation between the intellect and the emotions. See also Julia Annas, *Plato: a Very Short Introduction*, chapter 6. Descartes' version of the traditional view is given most fully in his text *The Passions of the Soul*. The best short guide to Descartes' writings on the mind is Bernard Williams's *Descartes*. Unfortunately, though, that book is rather difficult and no exception to the general rule that books on Descartes tend to say very little about his writings on the passions. A general introduction to Descartes is Tom Sorell's *Descartes: a Very Short Introduction*.

Works that *contest* the traditional view include Simon Baron-Cohen, *Mindblindness*, and Antonio Damasio, *Descartes' Error* and his subsequent *The Feeling of What Happens*. On *Hume's* contestation of the traditional view, see Barry Stroud, *Hume*, especially chapters 7 and 8.

Other sources for deeper thought include Mark Haddon, *The Curious Incident of the Dog in the Night-Time* and Rousseau, *Discourse on Inequality* (both mentioned above). Also, one might see Richard Hanley's *Is Data Human? The*

Metaphysics of Star Trek, and Daniel Dennett's *Brainstorms* and *Brainchildren*. Those two texts by Dennett are collections of essays, many of which consider the practical problems of artificial intelligence and the philosophical theories of mind that are necessary to deal with those problems.

Notes

1. 'Phaedo', 66c–66d. (Those characters – '66c–66d' – refer to headings given in the margins of editions – many editions, anyway – of Plato's works.)
2. Descartes, *Discourse on the Method*, p. 36.
3. Descartes, 'The Passions of the Soul', p. 218.
4. Descartes, 'The Passions of the Soul', pp. 403–4.
5. Hume, *A Treatise of Human Nature*, Book II, Part III, Section 3, p. 415.
6. Damasio, *Descartes' Error*, p. 52.
7. Damasio, *Descartes' Error*, p. 53.
8. Damasio, *Descartes' Error*, p. xii.
9. Quoted in Damasio, *Descartes' Error*, p. 8.
10. *Descartes' Error*, p. 8.
11. Baron-Cohen, *Mindblindness*, p. 1.
12. 'Cog' as a name is a play on the term 'cognition' and on the idea of machinery as involving cogs. There is a photo of Cog in Dennett, *Brainchildren*, p. 161.
13. Chapter 4 of Baron-Cohen's book discusses how psychologists explore and test for this development. As to why autistic children fail to achieve this development, that is still not well understood.

6
From Deep Thought to Digital Metaphysics

Barry Dainton

> I always think that the chances of finding out what really is going on are so absurdly remote that the only thing to do is say hang the sense of it and just keep yourself occupied. Look at me: I design coastlines. I got an award for Norway.
>
> (Slartibartfast, in *The Hitchhiker's Guide to the Galaxy*)

> And this computer, which was called the Earth, was so large that it was frequently mistaken for a planet – especially by the strange ape-like beings who roamed its surface, totally unaware that they were simply parts of a gigantic computer program.
>
> (*The Restaurant at the End of the Universe*)

The *Hitchhiker's Guide* series contains a wealth of brilliant and arresting inventions, many of which are philosophically intriguing. The argument from the Babel fish to the non-existence of God might be thought comparable with many in the theological literature.[1] Then there is the Hooloovoo, a 'super-intelligent shade of blue' (*Hitchhiker's Guide to the Galaxy,* chapter 4). Since intelligence is a remarkable and sophisticated phenomenon one might suppose that to possess intelligence a thing needs to possess inherent complexity – which a shade of blue manifestly lacks. But this reasoning is contestable. According to one venerable and still influential tradition, our own minds are housed in *immaterial souls*: things which lack internal complexity but not (presumably) intelligence.[2]

In what follows I will be focusing mainly on what (for many of us) is the most momentous and memorable of the discoveries made by Arthur Dent in the course of his galactic travels: the surprising news that the reason our planet was brought into being was to resolve a philosophical conundrum. The Vogons' destruction of the Earth to make way for a hyperspace bypass was not just a misfortune for the Earth's inhabitants, it was also a serious irritant to those hyperintelligent higher-dimensional beings who manifested themselves to humankind in the form of ordinary white mice. As Slartibartfast informs Dent:

> Earthman, the planet you lived on was commissioned, paid for, and run by mice. It was destroyed five minutes before the completion of the purpose for which it was built … Your planet and people have formed the matrix of an organic computer running a ten-million-year research program.

The Earth may have been paid for and run by mice, but it was not actually designed by the mice. The program itself was the creation of another computer (which the mice *had* built), Deep Thought. The latter was intelligent enough to work out that the answer to the Great Question 'of Life, the Universe and Everything!' was 42, but not intelligent enough to be able to provide the mice with an explanation as to what the Great Question really amounts to; hence their need for a still more powerful computer.

This is all big news – or would be if it were true. But could any of it be true? Is it really possible for a computer to take the form of an Earth-like planet? Could we all be parts of a gigantic computer program? Could a superintelligent computer be designed by a merely *intelligent* computer, or succession of such? Would a super-intelligent computer be able to answer *every* question? These are far from idle questions: over the past few decades they have been taken increasingly seriously by a growing number of philosophers, physicists and computer scientists. We do not yet have all the answers. But, as we shall see in this chapter, some progress has been made – and some highly intriguing possibilities have been uncovered.

1   Could the earth be a computer?

Most of us know roughly what lies inside the computers that most of us use every day: printed circuit boards, hard disk drives and – most crucially – the chips which contain the central processing units. It is the latter which do the actual computations, and they are remarkably complex devices: a recent (six-core) Intel i7 chip, for example, contains over a billion transistors, crammed into a thin block of metal and silicon which can easily fit in the palm of one's hand. Now, even if we overlook its massively greater size and mass, the Earth taken as a whole – with its oceans, atmosphere, mountain ranges, flowing rivers, its myriad life forms ranging from bacteria to whales, its human population with their villages and cities – obviously bears very little resemblance to the average desktop computer. Does this vast difference mean the Earth couldn't be engaged in the same kind of information processing as a desktop computer? Not in the least.

A desktop computer is an instance of what we can call a *universal classical computer* or 'UCC' for short. (Several other terms can be found in the literature, e.g. 'universal computing machine', 'universal Turing machine' – these all refer to the same sort of thing.) A UCC is a device which can store and manipulate patterns in accord with a stored set of instructions, otherwise known as the computer's program. The patterns usually take the form of sequences of presence and absence, or 1s and 0s, and the manipulations are themselves simple mechanical operations which require no intelligence or ingenuity to carry out; a typical manipulation might be 'make a copy of the sequence of symbols that are to be found at a location X, make a copy of these, and then store the copy at a location Y'. Alan Turing provided a precise characterisation of devices of this sort in an influential 1936 paper.[3] Turing went on to prove that a certain category of these devices, the *universal* classical computers, have the ability to run the program of any other classical computer. This property of universality means that anything one UCC can do, all the others can do too, given enough storage capacity and time. The basic operations of a UCC are quite primitive – no more than simple symbol shuffling – but their potential is vast: a UCC, or so it is generally thought, is capable of computing *anything* that can be computed at all.[4]

UCCs have another interesting feature, one that is very relevant to the ability of the Earth to be a UCC: it doesn't matter in the least what material they are made of. The UCCs we use in our everyday lives are silicon-based, but that is because contemporary silicon chips are small, reliable, robust and cheap to manufacture. Turing's own eponymous UCC was a mechanical device made of metal and paper – indeed, silicon chips had yet to be invented in 1936. A century earlier, Charles Babbage produced a design for an 'analytical engine' which it is now recognised had all the attributes of a genuine UCC. Babbage's projected engine would have been a fabulous steam-powered machine, the size of a house and composed principally of brass cog wheels. Alas, it proved too expensive to actually build, but we do have the design, and a campaign is currently underway to raise sufficient funds to construct a working model. In more recent times, Daniel Hillis and Brian Silverman built a functioning computer out of Tinkertoys in the late 1970s, and programmed it to play noughts and crosses. The main components in a set of Tinkertoys are wooden disks and spindles.

Clearly, if a UCC can be built out of just about *anything*, there is no reason why one couldn't be implemented in a whole planet. There are innumerable ways in which this could, in principle, be accomplished. The flow of traffic around our cities *could* also be a flow of data, with different distributions of traffic over the road network corresponding to different computational states – unbeknownst to us, the precise pattern of traffic is controlled (wholly, or only in part) by the planetary program. Alternatively, the computational action could be taking place on a smaller scale, for example in the chemical changes produced by bacterial activity in puddles and ponds, which jointly constitute a massively parallel computational system. Of course, it's not at all easy to see *how* the programmers are ensuring that what happens on (or in) the Earth conforms to the dictates of their program, but this does not mean that it isn't happening – and don't forget: it is safe to assume that the programmers (Deep Thought in the case of *Hitchhiker's*) are *vastly* more intelligent than ourselves.[5]

2   Universes = computers?

UCCs are an important kind of computer, but they are by no means the only kind. An interesting and potentially relevant alternative are the machines known as *cellular automata* (or 'CA'). These come in a wide variety of forms, but all the essentials are on view in the simple cases. A basic two-dimensional CA consists of a grid whose component cells can be in either of just two states, 'on' (or 'live') or 'off' (or 'dead'). All changes in the grid are discrete: with each new cycle – with each tick of the system's clock – the contents of each cell either remain the same, or change, depending on the state of the immediately surrounding cells. A CA's *program* consists of nothing more than the rules which determine how the contents of a cell change (or don't change) in response to its surroundings.

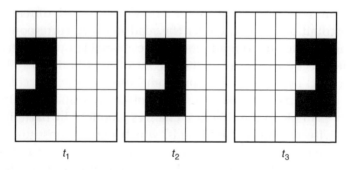

A simple example of a 2D cellular automaton showing the condition of a grid world at three successive times; the shaded cells of the grid world are 'live'. Note how the depicted structure is both stable and mobile: it is occupying distinct spatial locations at t_1, t_2 and t_3.

In the case of the most famous two-dimensional CA, namely John Conway's 'game of life', the rules are as follows: (i) live cells with two or three neighbours survive, but those with fewer than two neighbours die (as if by loneliness), and those with four or more neighbours also die (as if by over-population): (ii) if a dead cell acquires three live neighbours it changes to a live cell. These rules are not very complex, but they are enough to give rise to a wondrous range of complex configurations, some stable and persistent, some transient and dynamic, some stable and dynamic. That the game is called 'the game of life' is entirely appropriate: the changing configurations in some of Conway's life worlds often look distinctly – and eerily – organic in nature.[6] Impressively, it has been proven that a fully functional universal computer can be generated and sustained *within* many types of CA, including Conway's. However, CAs more complex than Conway's are possible: in more complex CAs the grids can have three or more dimensions, and their cells are not confined to just two conditions.

The ability of CAs to generate impressive complexity from great simplicity has led some of those studying these systems – those most familiar with their miraculous-seeming capabilities – seriously to speculate that our entire physical *universe* might be a single vast cellular automaton, of three or more dimensions. It is not difficult to appreciate why: the universe manifestly houses a great deal of variety and complexity; and science has revealed that there are remarkably simple natural laws underlying this variety. And this is precisely what one would expect *if* the universe, at bottom – at the smallest of scales – just *is* a CA. The German computer pioneer Konrad Zuse was an early advocate of this doctrine: he suggested that the entire cosmos might be a CA in his *Rechnender Raum* (translated as *Calculating Space*). Edward Fredkin, who went on to lead the Information Mechanics

Group at MIT, also started to find this idea appealing in the 1960s, and by the 1980s had become a firm advocate of it. More recent proponents of the universe = computer hypothesis include Stephen Wolfram and Seth Lloyd.[7]

Inspired by his new metaphysical* vision, Fredkin launched a new discipline that he named 'digital physics'.[8] Since one of the main aims of this discipline is to clarify and assess the intelligibility of the claim that the whole universe might be a computer, a more apt label might have been 'digital metaphysics' – and indeed, Fredkin later came to prefer to talk in terms of 'digital philosophy'. There are very different ways of construing the claim that 'the universe is a computer', ways which are not always clearly distinguished, but which need to be. At its weakest and most metaphorical, the claim is simply that for some purposes it can be fruitful to view the universe *as if* it were a computer following a program. Construed in this way, the doctrine is not particularly contentious, or interesting. A stronger and more interesting claim is that the universe actually *is* a computer. The easiest, but not the only, way of making sense of this is to suppose that at the very smallest scale the universe is a CA. The ever-changing patterns of elementary particles in space and time are, if this view is correct, patterns of activity in the grid of a vast cellular automaton. (This is how I will usually construe the doctrine in what follows.) A still stronger claim is that the physical world is informational *all the way down*, and hence that the universe is nothing but a flow of information. Fredkin inclined to this super-strong version of the view – he regarded information as 'more concrete' than anything else, and some eminent physicists are of the same opinion, including the very influential John Wheeler:

> It is not unreasonable to imagine that information sits at the core of physics, just as it sits at the core of a computer.

It from bit. Otherwise put, every 'it' – every particle, every field of force, even the space-time continuum itself – derives its function, its meaning, its very existence entirely – even if in some contexts indirectly – from the apparatus-elicited answers to yes–no questions, binary choices, bits. 'It from bit' symbolizes the idea that every item of the physical world has at bottom – a very deep bottom, in most instances – an immaterial source and explanation … in short, that all physical things are information-theoretic in origin.[9]

The notion that information is itself the most basic ingredient of the physical world, more basic than matter or energy, is certainly an intriguing one, but much remains unclear. Could fundamental reality consist of nothing but patterns of difference – Wheeler's basic 'bits' – without there being any underlying substrate or stuff that these differences exist within? It is not clear, to say the least. So unless and until these doubts have been resolved, the viability of the Fredkin–Wheeler proposal will remain in question.

Another of the aims of digital physics is more purely scientific: establishing that there is no incompatibility between the scientific laws that we need to explain the macro-scale observable world, and the hypothesis that the universe is a computer running through its program. This is by no means a trivial task. Many of the laws of orthodox physics assume that reality is *continuous*, i.e. that space and time are infinitely divisible, that physical magnitudes such as energy or momentum are to be measured using the real numbers (and so infinite decimals). But if the universe is digital it must also be *discrete*: both UCCs and CAs are finite state machines that are incapable of accommodating the infinite complexity of real numbers, or continuous space and time. Digital physicists hold that this limitation is by no means an insuperable problem. If the cells of the universal CA are sufficiently small in size – perhaps of the order of the Planck length of 1.6×10^{-35} metres (or about 10^{-20} times the size of a proton) – then the universe could easily *appear* to be continuous at the macro-scale even if in reality it is discrete. Whatever the truth of this matter, it may be some time before we are in a position to ascertain what it is. For we will be able to decide with confidence whether or not reality is discrete only when physicists reconcile quantum theory (our best theory of the very small) with general relativity (our best theory of the very large). That said, string theory and loop quantum gravity are two of the most promising candidates for a 'theory of everything' that achieves this reconciliation, and both theories reject at least some of the continuities of orthodox physics in favour of discreteness.

Digital physics may have serious advocates, but it should also be registered that some physicists, including some of the very best, are far from being persuaded of its merits. Nobel prize-winning particle physicist Steven Weinberg points out that since the hypothesis has not (so far) given rise to any new predictions, there is no reason to prefer it to more orthodox alternatives. Weinberg also offers this pointed diagnosis of why some find the doctrine so appealing: 'I can't see any motivation for these speculations, except that this is the sort of system that Wolfram and others have become used to in their work on computers. So might a carpenter, looking at the moon, suppose that it is made of wood.'[10]

3   Foundations and hierarchies

The universe = computer doctrine remains controversial, at least if construed literally rather than metaphorically, but it is by no means the absurdity it may initially seem.

What is for certain is that if Fredkin, Wolfram and the other proponents of digital physics-cum-metaphysics *are* correct, then there are some interesting philosophical consequences. By no means the least of these is the possibility of *nested worlds*.

I noted earlier that all universal computers (or UCCs) are able to run the same programs, which means that any such machine can replicate or emulate any other. This is why an Apple computer running a version of OS X can devote a part of its resources to emulating a computer running a version of Windows; within this virtual Windows environment an emulation of an early-generation games machine might be running, allowing its owner to spend a few minutes playing *Space Invaders* or *Pac-man* (or even the original *Hitchhiker's* textual adventure game).[11] What goes for operating systems goes for physical universes – or at least it does if a physical universe just is a computer following a program.

Our universe is a good deal more complex than any computer game – or at least, any of our contemporary computer games (more on this shortly) – but it is possible to estimate how much computational power would be needed to generate it. Seth Lloyd has calculated that to create the entirety of our universe from the Big Bang until now a computer would need to perform some 10^{120} operations. That's a very big number, but it's still a finite number. Hence a computer capable of performing more than this number of operations – ten times as many, say – would be powerful enough to generate a much bigger universe of its own. It will be handy to have a name for this hypothetical bigger universe: let's call it U$^+$. If U$^+$ were actually to exist, then it could contain a computer which generates and constitutes a somewhat smaller universe, U. The latter could easily be *our* universe – let's suppose this is the case. Since U is a self-contained cosmos in its own right, then, unless they were informed otherwise its inhabitants would naturally suppose that U is the sum total of creation. But as it happens, in this instance they are very much mistaken.

The scenario of universes nested within other universes may seem odd, but it is perfectly possible if the computational universe hypothesis is true: the computer which constitutes U^+ (and also U) is simply behaving in the same way as a contemporary laptop which is running a game while simultaneously carrying out various other tasks (such as running a word-processing program, a web browser and downloading a movie or two). And it needn't stop here. A still larger computer U^{++} could contain the whole of U^+, along with all the sub-universes it contains, U included. There is no obvious reason why, in principle, this hierarchy of nested universes – or, if you prefer, 'levels of reality' – can't continue upward indefinitely.[12]

Now, the term 'universe' is used in different ways. It can be used to refer to the totality of what exists, but it can also be used to refer to the entirety of our spatio-temporal system and its contents. To mark this distinction we can use 'UNIVERSE' when talking about the former, and 'universe' when talking about the latter. If the totality of what exists comprises a multitude of distinct spatio-temporal systems – or 'parallel universes' as they are sometimes called – then the UNIVERSE contains many universes. Some cosmological models – eternal inflation, for example – entail a multiverse of this kind. The universe-as-computer hypothesis does not guarantee the existence of a multiverse, but it does open up the possibility of one.

Mostly Harmless (chapter 3) tells us that the *Guide* has 'had a great deal to say on the subject of parallel universes. Very little of this is, however, at all comprehensible to anyone below the level of Advanced God.' The *Guide* goes on to say that the first thing to realise about parallel universes 'is that they are not parallel'. This claim is not true of all parallel universes: the so-called 'brane-worlds' of string theory, for example, can be parallel, albeit in a higher spatial dimension. But what the *Guide* says looks to be true of *nested* computational universes. If these are spatially related to one another at all – and this is by no means obvious – they certainly do not lie parallel to one another; rather the relationship is that of inclusion or containment.

If a computational multiverse does exist, we have to face an uncomfortable fact. Since all of the nested universes are perfectly real physical universes, all as real as *this* universe, there is no reason to suppose that our universe exists at the ground level. It is far more likely that we exist somewhere in the undistinguished middle of the hierarchy of universes, i.e. nowhere special at all.[13] Alternatively, perhaps the hierarchy lacks *any* ground level: it may go on upwards to infinity, with each universe being computationally generated by a computational process which is itself computationally generated, without end. (This is the digital-metaphysical version of the famous 'it's turtles all the way down' scenario.) And of course there is this further option: some higher agency, an individual person or perhaps a whole civilisation, may have created the hardware and software which constitute our universe for some as yet inscrutable purpose of their own. In an interview with Robin Wright, Fredkin revealed that he is drawn to just this hypothesis:

'What I'm saying is that there is no way to know what the future is any faster than running this [the universe] to get to that [the future]. Therefore, what I'm assuming is that there is a question and there is an answer, okay? I don't make any assumptions about who has the question, who wants the answer, anything.' Does he mean that there's something out there that wanted to get the answer to a question? 'Yeah' Something that set up the universe to see what would happen? 'In some way, yes.'[14]

Fredkin's digital metaphysics and Adams's fictional world as described in *The Hitchhiker's Guide to the Galaxy* here coincide, almost exactly. The only difference, as far as I can see, is that Fredkin's *über*-programmer doesn't take the specific form of a race of hyperintelligent pan-dimensional creatures who manifest themselves to us as white mice.

4   Programmed worlds: should we be worried?

Should we be troubled by the thought that our entire universe might be a gigantic computer? Commenting on this possibility, Kevin Kelly observes that 'no one wants to see themselves as someone else's program running on someone else's computer. Put that way, life seems a bit secondhand.'[15] This seems right – I suspect many of us do find this an undesirable scenario. But precisely why?

The underlying worry, surely, is *not* that our universe might have been causally generated by events in some other universe, rather than its being uncaused or self-caused. Few of us would be greatly concerned if we discovered that the Big Bang was caused by, and constituted of, matter that had fallen into a black hole in some other spatial dimension. No, the unease derives from the idea that our universe was created not by some perfectly natural physical process but rather by some *intentional agent* (i.e. something that has intentions and other mental states). Or more accurately, a *non-divine* intentional agent. Many people are not only untroubled by the thought that we are the creations of an all-powerful, all-knowing and benevolent God; they positively welcome it – and are profoundly disappointed if or when they come to believe that this isn't in fact the case.

The perturbing possibility is that we are acting in accord with the dictates of a program created not by a God, but by beings very much like ourselves who happen to have highly advanced computer technology at their disposal, and who are engaged in some world creation as a hobby – perhaps the adolescents in their technologically more advanced civilisation enjoy computer games as much as their counterparts in ours.

Quite how much autonomy we would have in a deliberately designed computer-sustained universe depends on the character of the program. If it grants us full freedom of choice, i.e. if it allows our psychological systems and personalities to develop in a natural unforced manner, and our decisions are generated by our own psychological systems, then we have as much autonomy as we believe we have. Alternatively, if the program dictates our every thought and move, then we have no autonomy whatsoever. In these latter circumstances it *seems* to us that we are acting freely – the program ensures this – and hence we believe that we are free agents. But in reality we are not. What is disquieting is that if we are leading programmed lives then *we have absolutely no way of knowing which of these possibilities obtains*.

There are also worries of a more practical kind. Although it's true that (other things being equal) we would prefer to have lives that are not pre-programmed, it's also true that a pre-programmed life is, in many cases, preferable to non-existence. *But* if our universe is nothing more than an adolescent's plaything, we are all entirely at the mercy of their whims; the appearance on the scene of a new game or fashion – or the onset of simple boredom – could easily spell the end for us. Our longevity is hardly assured even if we are playing some grander role in the scheme of things. Would the mice have continued to pay for the maintenance of the Earth if it had managed to complete its 10-million-year program, and come up with the answer they were seeking? It seems unlikely. Life in a computer-generated universe is precarious and unpredictable.

The notion that, to a greater or lesser extent, we are leading 'second-hand lives' may be worrying in some respects, but you may not find yourself gravely troubled by it. For the scenarios presented so far all rest on the hypothesis that the entire physical world is a computer. This may not be the absurdity it initially seems – it may even be logically possible*. But since this hypothesis is also highly controversial it is quite possible, perhaps very probable, that our universe is *not* merely a computer running a program. However, this does not mean that we are out of the woods. For even if the universe itself is not a computer, it still *contains* computers; and as we'll now see, the universe doesn't have to *be* a computer for advanced computer technology to threaten our ordinary ways of thinking about the foundations of our existence.

5   Virtual lives

In chapter 5 of *The Restaurant at the End of the Universe*, Zaphod overhears an irate hitchhiker, railing against the *Guide*, say: 'I've even heard that they've created a whole electronically synthesized Universe in one of their offices so they can go and research stories during the day and still go to parties in the evening.' This would certainly be a useful way of eliminating the inconveniences of space travel, though there would surely be problems in keeping the synthesised universe in sync with the real universe – which is perhaps, in part, why the *Guide* is as fallible as it is. In Chapter 12 of *Restaurant* we discover that Zarniwoop has been hiding (protecting his secret about The Man Who Rules the Universe) in an 'electronically synthesised universe' of his own, handily concealed in his briefcase. When asked by Zaphod how it differs from the original, Zarniwoop tells him there is no virtually no difference: 'they are identical. Oh – except that I think the Frogstar Fighters are grey in the real Universe.'[16]

It seems safe to assume that the 'electronically synthe-sised' universes Adams is talking about in these passages are being generated by computers – indeed, they are instances of the nested universes we encountered earlier. If Zarniwoop is right in his claim that the artificially generated universes are (almost) *identical* to the real universe, then they will have the same intrinsic nature as the real universe, and so be themselves physical worlds in their own right.[17] But there is another possibility: perhaps the synthesised universes are entirely lacking in physical reality – perhaps they just *appear* to be physical universes to those who inhabit them. In other words, perhaps these universes are 'virtual worlds', i.e. computer-generated environments that don't really exist, but seem to. In the scenarios that we have looked at in sections 3 and 4, computers have been generating human levels of mentality and consciousness by a clear and direct method: they have been generating entire *physical* universes, and these universes contain ordinary human beings, and hence ordinary mind-sustaining human brains. However, this is by no means the only way in which computers may be able to significantly influence, or perhaps even produce, conscious minds and human-type experiences. Some of the proposed methods of creating these *virtual* worlds are more radical than others. We will start by looking at the less radical versions.

Until quite recently so-called virtual reality technology was expensive and confined largely to research laboratories. The user would don a sizeable helmet, put on some hefty gloves, and these would be connected to a computer which would generate high-resolution images on the helmet's internal screen. When shown (say) a vase on a tabletop, then, if the user moved their hand towards the vase, they would see an on-screen simulated 'virtual' hand moving towards the vase; if they grasped the vase, feedback sensors in the glove would generate the sensations of pressure similar to those which would be felt if a real object were being held. Subjects almost unanimously reported that having (what seemed to be) a physical presence in their virtual environments greatly increased their sense of really being *in* these virtual spaces. Thanks to advances in processing power and miniaturisation, there is no longer any need for bulky equipment to experience something approaching this depth of immersion. Mobile phones equipped with video cameras, and enabled for 'augmented reality', can produce similar effects (albeit minus the tactile feedback), as can video games – e.g. Microsoft's *Kinect*. But the relevant technologies are in rapid development, and it will not be too long before computers interact with our brains in a more direct fashion: not through our sensory organs, but via *neural interfaces*. Game controllers which detect and respond to one's brain waves via sensors in a comparatively unobtrusive headset are already being sold to consumers.[18] It will probably not be too long before more sophisticated surgically implanted neural interfaces will allow a computer to act directly on the brain's sensory cortices, allowing them to generate fully lifelike auditory, visual and bodily experience, corresponding to whatever their program dictates. It might even be that future neural interfaces have the ability to control the cognitive, linguistic and emotional centres in the brain. Computers would then not just be able to provide you with high-resolution, fully lifelike sensory experiences of any kind they choose, they will also have complete control over what you think and feel – even down to the language you speak (or seem to speak).

If this technology becomes available, scenarios along the lines of that exploited in the *Matrix* movies will become possible. In those films, the vast majority of the human race are forced to live out their lives in a shared or communal virtual world that is created by a computer that is plugged directly into their nervous systems. The physical objects in this simulated world (which seems just like *this* world) have no reality except for their appearances in the plugged-in subjects' experience, and the code in the computer program which is controlling the simulation. The tables, chairs, roads, pavements and buildings these subjects encounter – along with their own bodies, at least as these feature in their virtual environment – have no existence as properly *material* things; they are thus quite unlike their counterparts in the computational worlds we were considering earlier, which *do* contain properly material things.[19] *Matrix*-style communal virtual worlds may be possible, i.e. worlds in which whole populations of subjects inhabit, and interact with each other within, a shared virtual environment – as they already do, to a limited degree, in massive multiplayer online role-playing games (or 'MMORPGs') such as *Second Life*. A computer might also generate a *private* virtual world for just one individual, or a small group; in such a world the vast majority of people appearing within the simulated environment are wholly machine-generated. And of course, people might opt to 'visit' these virtual worlds voluntarily, for shorter or longer periods, as they see fit.

6   More radical (and more disturbing) scenarios

This is all rich food for thought, but we are not yet done: a far more radical kind of virtual reality might be possible. The *computational theory of mind* (CTM) has it (as does 'functionalism'* in some guises) that our minds are themselves software entities, running on the hardware of our brains. What goes for our minds goes for *all* minds: to make any kind of mind all you need is a program of the right kind. If the CTM is correct – and a good many (though by no means all) philosophers of mind believe that it is – then a program for a human mind could be run on a silicon-based computer, or a computer composed of brass cog wheels and powered by steam.

If the CTM is true we have to confront some quite remarkable possibilities. The typical human brain is a highly complex object, containing as it does some 100 billion neurons, many of which connect up to hundreds or thousands of other neurons. Nonetheless, it is possible to estimate the computational power of a typical human brain: it is of the order of 10^{14}–10^{17} operations per second. Our faster supercomputers are currently capable of 10^{15} operations per second, and even an average laptop can manage 10^9. We cannot be sure that the recent rapid rates of increase in computation power – a doubling (roughly) every two years – will continue indefinitely into the future. Even so, no one seriously doubts that computers which have vastly more computational power than a human brain will be available, probably quite cheaply, before very long. If hardware isn't a problem, the software undeniably is: since we are a long way from understanding how our brains function, even if we had the right sort of hardware, at present we are not in a position to be able to furnish it with the software which would enable it to run a human-type mind. But this limitation may not be insuperable: we are learning more about the brain all the time. Relying on thousands of detailed scans of rat brains and a powerful supercomputer, the Blue Brain project has managed to produce what seems to be an accurate simulation of a 10,000 neuron cross-section – including 10,000,000 interneuronal interconnections – of the rat cortex. This is still a long way short of simulating an entire *human* brain, but Blue Brain's project leader estimates that this will be possible by 2020.

If the software problem *can* be solved, then predicted future hardware developments will make possible all manner of large-scale simulations of human minds. If we converted the mass of an Earth-sized planet into a single computer, it would be capable of between 10^{32} and 10^{45} operations per second. This would be enough to simulate all the mental activity – reproduce all the *experiences* – of the 100 billion humans who have ever lived in a little under two minutes. A computer with the mass of a larger planet could do the job in a fraction of a second, using only a small proportion of its computational resources.[20]

Evidently, if future generations of humankind have access to computers with anything approaching this sort of power, then provided the software problem has been solved, they could easily run very large numbers of simulations, each of which includes vast numbers of simulated lives. Indeed, it could very easily be that the total number of simulated human lives is vastly greater than the number of non-simulated human lives. For this to be the case, all we need suppose is that our descendants have the *will*, as well as the *means*, to create simulations in the required quantities. If we suppose they do, then we are faced with an awkward conclusion: if simulated lives greatly outnumber non-simulated lives, isn't it far more likely than not that *our own lives* are simulated too?

Let's go through this more carefully. As Nick Bostrom represents our predicament, we have no option but to accept that at least one of the following propositions is true:[21]

1. The human species is very likely to go extinct before reaching a technologically advanced stage, i.e. a stage at which it can simulate large numbers of human-type lives.

2. Any technologically advanced civilisation is extremely
   unlikely to run a significant number of simulations of
   their own history (or variations thereof).
3. We are almost certainly living in a computer simulation.

Since the possibility that humankind will go extinct in
the not too distant future certainly cannot be ruled out,
(1) is a definite possibility. But let's suppose our species
does avoid extinction, and goes on to develop technology
which makes it possible to simulate very large numbers of
human lives. If you think that our descendants won't use
this technology – i.e. if you accept (2) above – then there's
nothing to worry about. But if you think (2) is unlikely to be
true, there's a lot to worry about: if simulated lives greatly
outnumber real lives, it is far more likely than not that our
own lives are simulated. Alas, if our descendants are anything remotely like us, it is very unlikely that they will be
able to resist running large numbers of relevant simulations.
Just think of how historians, political theorists, economists,
government agencies and military planners would be able
to benefit from running variants of our history to see how
adopting certain policies would have played out. And that's
before we get to religious cults, utopian (or dystopian)
political movements, and the future equivalents of our contemporary Russian oligarchs – why settle for a sports team
when you can have a whole world to play with?

So we have to face up to the facts: if we think it likely that
humankind will have a long and successful future, then we
should also believe it quite probable that we ourselves are
living in a simulation. But there is more. For with this possibility all the perturbing considerations surveyed in sections 3 and 4 immediately enter the frame, albeit in a new
key. Since simulations within simulated worlds are possible,
so too is a hierarchy of *nested*, but *virtual*, universes. These

virtual universes would not be fully physical universes in the manner of the computer universes postulated by Zuse and Fredkin, but they would *seem* real to their (simulated) inhabitants – and of course the *experiences* of these inhabitants would themselves be fully real. We should accept that there is no particular reason to suppose that we exist at the foundational level of reality. We must also confront the disquieting aspects of leading 'second-hand lives', and the potential loss of autonomy this brings with it – not to mention the menace of imminent shutdown. The lot of a simulated being is, in many respects, far from an enviable one.

At this point you might be thinking as follows. 'Ah, but there's hope. The alleged threat of simulation depends on future computers being able to simulate entire human lives in vast numbers. But this all rests on the CTM, the thesis that mentality is a wholly computational phenomenon. But suppose it isn't: suppose human consciousness requires human *brains*, and can't be reproduced in a computer, however it is programmed.' It is true that the CTM is a much-disputed doctrine.[22] But even if it should prove false, there remain the other, less radical forms of virtual reality we encountered in section 5: the forms which involve computers acting *on* brains, via neural interfaces and the like. If this technology becomes very advanced, it may well be possible for suitably programmed computers to control every aspect of one's consciousness. This is all that is needed to give rise to simulation-related worries.

To illustrate: let's suppose that our species flourishes over the next few centuries, and develops – and uses – very advanced neural implant-based simulation technology. As a part of their normal education, future generations of schoolchildren will all spend a few hours hooked up to powerful virtual reality generators finding out *exactly* what it's like to be an ordinary inhabitant of the early twenty-first century. When they are enjoying these educational 'trips', they will be quite unaware of what is really going on: they will believe themselves to *be* ordinary twenty-first-century people, leading ordinary non-simulated lives. (Recall the 'exactly'!)[23] So for hundreds of years, *billion upon billion* of children enjoy streams of consciousness which are (for a few hours) very much like that of a real twenty-first-century person. If the number of simulated twenty-first-century-like streams of consciousness outnumber the real twenty-first-century stream – and this is by no means out of the question, for the numbers soon add up – do you have any grounds for being confident that your current experience is real rather than simulated?[24]

The problems posed by the simulation scenarios we have been considering in this section are novel, philosophically speaking. Descartes wondered how one knows one's experience accurately reflects reality. Can you rule out the possibility that your current experience is a hallucination induced by some demonic power? But while it is impossible to rule this sort of bare possibility out, there is also no reason to take it particularly seriously. As we saw at the end of section 4, in the eyes of many (though not all) the Fredkin–Zuse thesis that the universe is a computer has a similar status: yes, it's a possibility, but we haven't (yet) been given enough reasons to take it seriously. In contrast, the hypothesis that you are living in a computer-generated virtual world is grounded in *reasonable empirical* predictions* concerning future technological possibilities. Let's suppose the universe is pretty much as you ordinarily believe it to be, i.e. that there really is a planet Earth, inhabited by human beings, and the course of human history is broadly as you suppose it to be. These beliefs are not beyond question – we can't rule out Descartes' evil demon, or innumerable other bare possibilities – but nor are they unfounded: they are confirmed by your current experience, and what you remember experiencing. Let us suppose that you also believe, after giving careful thought to recent technological trends and human psychological traits, that powerful simulation technologies are likely to be both developed and used in the not too distant future. It follows at once that you should also believe that it is quite likely that your own experiences are simulated rather than not. Why? Simply because if your beliefs about your world are true, simulated human lives will very probably outnumber non-simulated human lives, perhaps by a considerable margin. Of course, it would be different if your life were distinguished in some way which renders it less likely to be simulated than most. But is it?

This empirically grounded threat to our ordinary certainties has only recently begun to be appreciated by contemporary philosophers, and no doubt interesting responses to it will be forthcoming. In 'The Matrix as Metaphysics', David Chalmers has argued that it is a mistake to view the hypothesis that you are living in a large-scale communal simulation as a *sceptical** threat to the truth of your current beliefs. If the hypothesis is true, then the vast bulk of your ordinary beliefs (e.g. that you are living in a three-dimensional material world, that London is the capital of the UK, that Yuri Gagarin was the first human in space, and so forth) will still be true. This is because your *world* – the one you seem to be living in, the one you can perceive and act on – is a perfectly real and objective world: properly construed, the thesis that your world is virtual is a *metaphysical* claim about its *underlying* nature, not about the truth of particular things within it. Is Chalmers right about this? Certainly, it is hard to see why anyone who believes that reality itself is informational all the way down – in the manner of Fredkin and Wheeler – could have a reason for *not* agreeing with Chalmers. However, those who believe that a non-computational substrate lies at the base level of reality may find this diagnosis less than compelling: aren't tables and chairs that are made of this primordial matter *more properly physical* than their digital counterparts in virtual worlds?

In any event, given Adams's long-standing interest in both computers and computer games, I have no doubt that he would have been amused by this turn of events: to find serious-minded contemporary philosophers taking seriously the notion that we might all be characters *in* a computer game.

For deeper thought

Bostrom, N., 'Are You Living in a Computer Simulation?' For more on the argument discussed in section 6.

Chalmers, D., 'The Matrix as Metaphysics'. A detailed defence of the claim that virtual worlds should be thought of as real.

Gleik, J., *The Information: a History, a Theory, a Flood*. A highly readable introduction to the information age.

Wolfram, S., *A New Kind of Science*. For more (much more) on cellular automata.

Notes

1. Though of course, for the argument to work Babel fish would have to actually exist. For more on the 'Babel Fish Argument' see the chapter by Michèle Friend.
2. Hooloovoo mentality – assuming it is logically possible* – raises other philosophical issues. Is there one Hooloovoo mind, or many? It depends on how we conceive of colours. If we view particular instances of colour as individual entities in their own right (or as philosophers sometimes call them 'tropes'*) then each instance of the relevant

shade of blue would be a distinct mind. If, in contrast, we view colours as *universals**, then all instances of the relevant blue are numerically identical*, such that there is just one Hooloovoo mind – but that mind will be located, at any one time, at multiple locations. Those familiar with ancient philosophy will note the interesting similarities between the latter conception of mind and the Aristotelian notion of active intellect.

3. It is here that the eponymous *Turing machines* make their first appearance. These theoretical devices are curious beasts. Since they require an unlimited storage capacity, actually building one is beyond our capabilities. Yet in other respects they are primitive: Turing envisaged them as having a long paper tape for a memory and a mechanical read–write head. In any event, as Turing demonstrated, these abstract automata are very well suited for exploring the most general properties of computers.

4. This is the *Church–Turing thesis*, which is often misconstrued; for further detail see the relevant *Stanford Encyclopedia of Philosophy* entry: http://plato.stanford.edu/entries/church-turing/. Note also that since the central processors in ordinary desktop computers and laptops are UCCs, in principle they too can compute anything that can be computed – although in practice they will be constrained by their storage capacities.

5. In a perfectly deterministic* universe there would be no need for post-construction interference from the programmers: it would be sufficient to select (and precisely engineer) a suitable initial configuration and then let nature take its course.

6. By way of an illustration, the simplest mobile structure in Conway's game is called 'the glider', another is known as 'the eater'. Here is someone describing how they can interact:

> An eater can eat a glider in four generations. Whatever is being consumed, the basic process is the same. A bridge forms between the eater and its prey. In the next generation, the bridge region dies from overpopulation, taking a bite out of both eater and prey. The eater then repairs itself. The prey usually cannot. If the remainder of the prey dies out as with the glider, the prey is consumed.

> (Poundstone, *The Recursive Universe*, p. 38)

Anyone interested in seeing some of this for themselves should note that there are examples of Conway's game of life which can easily be found on 'YouTube'.

7. Wolfram, *A New Kind of Science*; Lloyd, *Programming the Universe*.

8. A collection of Fredkin's work is available at http://www.digitalphilosophy.org/.
9. Wheeler, 'Information, Physics, Quantum: the Search for Links', p. 5.
10. Weinberg, 'Is the Universe a Computer?'
11. Amongst other computer-related projects, Adams contributed to an interactive fiction game based on the *Hitchhiker's* universe released in 1984, and the *Starship Titanic* game released in 1998.
12. The hierarchy can also extend in the other direction: *downward*. Our own universe is easily large enough to contain a computer which is sufficiently powerful to generate another physical universe, U^-, somewhat smaller and simpler than our own, but still with impressive breadth and complexity. U^- could in turn generate the smaller U^{--}, which in turn generates the smaller U^{---}, and so on.
13. Hayes (in his 'Computational Creationism') aptly calls this the 'Computational Copernican Principle'. Just as it is a mistake, not least of hubris, to suppose that we exist at a privileged *spatial* location (e.g. right at the very centre of the universe – though, actually, some Ancient Greeks believed the centre to be a lowly place) it is equally a mistake to suppose we exist at a special location in the hierarchy of nested worlds (e.g. right at the bottom, at the foundational level).
14. Wright, *Three Scientists and their Gods*, p. 69. Interpolations in the original.
15. Kelly, 'God is the Machine'.
16. But as some readers will recall, it turns out that there is another important difference – one which has to do with Zaphod himself.
17. On this reading, Adams is – in effect – subscribing to the strong (but not super-strong) form of the universe = computer doctrine, at least in regard to the synthesised universes in question.
18. For example, Emotiv's *EPOC*, which is a 'high-resolution, neuro-signal acquisition and processing wireless neuroheadset. It uses a set of sensors to tune into electric signals produced by the brain to detect players' thoughts, feelings and expressions and connects wirelessly to most PCs.' See http://www.emotiv.com/store/hardware/epoc-bci/epoc-neuroheadset/.
19. Or at least this is the natural way to construe this state of affairs – we shall see later that it is not the only way.
20. When Marvin complains of having a 'brain the size of a planet' does he means that his brain *is as powerful* as a planet-sized computer? If so, then his remarkable brain would be capable of running simulations of human history, of the kind envisaged here.
21. Bostrom, 'Are You Living in a Computer Simulation?'
22. John Searle's 'Chinese room' thought experiment is one of the most-discussed arguments against the CTM. For more on the Chinese room, see http://plato.stanford.edu/entries/chinese-room/.

23. And as Bertrand Russell was fond of pointing out, if you only sprang into existence five minutes ago, but with a full complement of memories similar to your actual memories (and no knowledge whatsoever of your all-too recent creation), you would assume you were a normal person with a normal past life. (The Sperm Whale of *Hitchhiker's* which improbably comes into existence above the surface of an alien planet lacks any memories of a past life – which is one of the main reasons why it finds its life as puzzling as it does.)

24. See Dainton, 'On Singularities and Simulations', for more on this theme – and virtual worlds generally.

Part IV
Logic, Method and Satire

7

'God . . . Promptly Vanishes in a Puff of Logic'

Michèle Friend

Introduction

There are some things that suddenly vanish: balloons, single socks and, perhaps, chesterfields. But, at least in the *Hitchhiker's* universe, nothing truly disappears. Things just get moved through some sort of time singularity and pop up again somewhere else. Well, almost nothing. God vanishes, at least according to *The Hitchhiker's Guide to the Galaxy*.[1] But then God is not really a 'thing', is He? He's quite a special entity, having, allegedly, created all of the 'things'. He's also supposed to be all-powerful. So, how is it that God could 'vanish in a puff of logic'? In this chapter I propose to examine the relevant passage, and the argument leading up to it, with some care and all the logical machinery I can summon. (But don't panic! It won't be too painful.)

In section 1, I'll set out the argument for the conclusion that God does not exist. Then I'll examine it carefully in section 2. During the course of the examination, I shall introduce a number of fancy words, distinctions and technical concepts. We can think of these as conceptual tools – or, if we are feeling more combative, 'philosophical weapons' – which refine our analysis and reasoning. In the final section (section 3), I'll draw some general conclusions about the place of God and logic* in Adams' s *Hitchhiker* universe.

1   The argument for the vanishing of God

I shall begin by reproducing the relevant part of the text. Then, in order to analyse the argument, I shall set it out in 'standard form'. To put an argument into 'standard form' is just to organise the argument so as to draw out its 'form'. The form of an argument is revealed by identifying 'premises'*, 'inferences'* and a 'conclusion'.

1.1   The argument as we find it in the text[2]

'The Babel fish,' said *The Hitchhiker's Guide to the Galaxy* quietly, 'is small, yellow and leech-like, and probably the oddest thing in the universe. It feeds on brainwave energy not from its own carrier but from those around it. It absorbs all unconscious mental frequencies from this brainwave energy to nourish itself with. It then excretes into the mind of its carrier a telepathic matrix formed by combining the conscious thought frequencies with nerve signals picked up from the speech centres of the brain which has supplied them. The practical upshot of this is that if you stick the Babel fish in your ear you can instantly understand anything said to you in any form of language. The speech patterns you actually hear decode the brainwave matrix which has been fed into your mind by your Babel fish.'

'Now it is such a bizarrely improbable coincidence that anything so mindbogglingly useful could have evolved purely by chance that some thinkers have chosen to see it as the final and clinching proof of the *non*-existence of God.'

'The argument goes something like this: "I refuse to prove that I exist," says God, "for proof denies faith, and without faith I am nothing."'

'"But," says Man, "The Babel fish is a dead giveaway, isn't it? It could not have evolved by chance. It proves you exist, and so therefore, by your own arguments, you don't. *QED*."'

'"Oh dear," says God, "I hadn't thought of that," and promptly vanishes in a puff of logic.'

(*Hitchhiker's Guide to the Galaxy*, chapter 6)

1.2 The argument in 'standard form'

When putting an argument in standard form, we turn the argument into a series of steps. When we do that, we try to respect the order of the argument as it is given in the text as much as possible. We set out the premises we are given. We list the inference moves that are explicit in the text. Moreover, we add any *implicit* premises. Implicit premises are *assumptions* made by the proponent of the argument – ideas that the argument seems to presuppose in the background. The translation into standard form ends with the announcement of the conclusion of the argument, using the favourite word of the logician: 'therefore'.

With most arguments given in a text, it is not obvious how to put the argument into standard form, and this text is no exception. Putting an argument into standard form is an acquired skill and one that involves judgement. For example, we have to guess what implicit assumptions are being made. Moreover, here – as in many cases – it is not clear that there is only one correct standard form. Indeed, in section 2.7 we shall consider an alternative way of formulating part of the argument. Here, though, I present what I think is a plausible attempt:

1. The Babel fish – which is small, yellow, leech-like, and fits into the ear – is probably the oddest thing in the universe and is mindbogglingly useful. For it feeds on the brainwave energy of its host and translates any language that the host hears into something the host can understand.

(Premise)

2. Anything that is pre-eminently odd and mindbogglingly useful cannot have come into existence through the random processes of evolution.

(Premise)

3. We have a proof that God exists.

(Inference – from 1 and 2)

4. God says: 'Proof denies faith, and without faith I am nothing.'

(Premise)

5. God tells the truth and abides by his own pronouncements.

(Implicit premise)

6. God is – *nothing* – according to the principles He endorses! He vanishes in a puff of logic.

(Inference – from 3, 4 and 5)

Therefore:

7. God does not exist.

(Inference – from 6)

Now that we have put the argument into standard form, we can analyse it logically – that is, analyse it step by step.

2 Analysis

2.1 Step 1: The nature and character of the Babel fish

The argument begins with a description of the remarkable Babel fish. But, within this description, we should distinguish the descriptive claims from evaluative judgements.

The descriptive claims include the fact that it is yellow, leech-like, etc., feeds on brainwaves and translates when placed in an ear. Descriptive claims are straightforwardly true or false (in this case, true or false according to the fiction).

In contrast, 'evaluative judgements', as I am using the term here, are more subtle. One evaluative judgement within premise 1 is that the Babel fish is 'probably the oddest thing in the universe'. This is not just a straight descriptive fact. Its truth depends on an evaluation. The evaluation depends on our making a comparison with other things in the universe. The trick for spotting that it is an evaluation lies in the words 'probably the oddest'. The 'probably', here, marks what statisticians call a 'subjective probability'. That is, the probability is based on knowledge and is a sort of epistemic* estimate. For, whether we deem the judgement of oddness to be true depends on what we know. The way we arrive at such a judgement is to make a rough scan of all the odd things in the universe *we* happen to know about, and, if we find one that is pretty odd, and indeed more odd than the rest, then, *as far as our knowledge of the things in the universe goes*, that thing is the oddest. So, two people knowing about a different array of things in the universe might come up with different candidates for 'oddest thing'. Apart from different people having different knowledge and experiences to draw on, there is another aspect to the subjectivity of the judgement. In making the judgement, we are invoking a particular *measure* of oddness, and that particular measure can also differ between people. For example, oddness in terms of evolutionary processes might be more important than oddness in terms of shape, or colour. So: even if two people knew of all the same things in the universe, one might judge *this thing* more odd than *that*, and the other person might judge *that thing* more odd than *this* because they are using *different measures*. Similar considerations apply to the idea – also to be found in step 1 – of 'mindboggling usefulness'. This is the second evaluative judgement. Not all things are equally useful to all people. A logic handbook is very useful for me, but it is not so for everyone, except in 'logic handbook throwing competitions' as practised in the more remote parts of the galaxy.[3]

Now: because evaluative judgements include a *subjective* element, determining their truth is a subtle matter, and consensus might never be reached. For this reason, the evaluative judgement is a weakness in the argument, since we can make up alternative measures. Exercise: next time someone in casual conversation makes a claim that something is 'best', or 'most useful' or 'most ugly', or 'strange' or what have you; challenge them by using another measure (of what is best, or most useful, or whatever). This exercise in argumentation can lead to hours of distraction and heated debates. Warning: heated debates can turn violent. For reasons of personal safety, concede *before* suffering injury.

2.2   Step 2: 'Anything that is pre-eminently odd and mindbogglingly useful cannot have come into existence through the random processes of evolution'

One might think that it is only a matter of time before science will come up with evolutionary explanations for *all* things which evolve. There *has to be* a scientific explanation. If we think so, then we would have no need for a God to explain the existence of *any* living thing. Under this thinking, one would reject this premise. But such a thought begs the question, that is, it uses circular reasoning.[4] What we are entitled to say is that *in the end* we might not need to postulate a God because science has, fortuitously, come up with explanations for all living creatures.

2.3   Step 3: 'We have a proof that God exists'

This bit of argumentation – namely, the inference from step 2 to step 3 – needs a bit more spelling out. Bear with me.

   I. Living things come into existence either through normal evolution **or** by the hand of God.[5]
  II. **If** evolutionary theory cannot account for the existence of the Babel fish, **then** God must have created the Babel fish.
III. **If** God created something, **then** He must exist.

Notice the words in bold. These are called 'logical connectives'. When highlighted, they show the *logical* structure of an argument. Step 'I' is what we call 'a disjunction'. We can spot a disjunction by the use of the word 'or'. An 'or' statement gives us two options. We infer II from I, by using a rule of logic called 'disjunctive syllogism'.[6] The idea of the rule is that if we have a disjunction, and we are told that one of the options is out, then only the other option is left.

This piece of argumentation is a version of the famous 'design argument'[7] for the existence of God – although, *later* in the Babel fish argument, the design argument will be used for the *non*-existence of God; but we'll get to that. Right now, let us just consider the normal (non-*Hitchhikery*) version of the design argument *for* God's existence.

The design argument proceeds by invoking something which is very beautiful, or ordered or remarkable in some way. Then one is asked to *wonder* how such a thing could have come into being. We consider some options, such as God created the object, it came about naturally, it was placed here by aliens and so on. These options are presented in the logical form of a disjunction. Either God created the Babel fish, **or** the Babel fish came about by evolution **or** it was placed here by aliens. In our case, we do not consider aliens, so we have a disjunction with only two options: God created the Babel fish, **or** the Babel fish came about by evolution. One disjunct is ruled out because of our wonder![8] The conclusion one is supposed to draw from the design argument is that only a very powerful and great godlike being could have created the thing in question, by *disjunctive* syllogism. Therefore, God exists, and, by the way, this is meant to be the Christian God, since the design argument is used to argue for Him and (in the Babel fish version) for Adams's *Hitchhiker* God.

It is interesting that the design argument is not all that convincing, especially to those who are not already 'of the faith'. Aside from the problem identified in the previous subsection – the problem that, *in the end*, we might *not* need to postulate a designer – there are two weaknesses. Both concern the sort of God we get from the design argument.

The first weakness is that, if we were convinced by the argument, then it would give us no information about the *number* of gods. There might have been a community of gods, such as the Hindu gods, the Roman or Greek gods, the gods of the Sagas, etc.

The second weakness is that even if one *single* God were the designer, we have no information about *which* of the gods worshipped by man is that sole designer. The designer could have been Allah, the Christian God, Jehovah, or any other God of a monotheistic religion, where one of God's attributes is that He created the world we occupy.

So: even if we accept that some object is *so* remarkable that it has to be created by something outside nature (and other than us), all that the argument shows is that there has to be *something* outside/besides nature or us. We have no idea what – save that He, or some of him, or one of them – created a wondrous object. On the basis of the design argument, the only characteristic we can attribute to the supernatural cause is that He or they are *creators of living creatures*. We cannot conclude that He or they is, or are, all-powerful, all-knowing, omnipresent, all-loving, angry, fond of cricket or what have you. So we do not get the whole package of the Christian God at once from the design argument. Indeed – and we could count this as a third problem – the so-called *'Argument from Evil'* tells against (at least) one of the traditional characteristics attributed to the Christian God.

The Argument from Evil is this:

I. There are some pretty awful things which happen in the world.
II. The Christian God is supposed to be: omnipotent (i.e. all-powerful) **and** omniscient (all-seeing, or all-knowing) **and** omnibenevolent (i.e. all- good or all-loving).
III. By *definition*, a God that is omnipotent, omniscient and omnibenevolent is *able* to remedy any evil that He knows about; knows about *all* evil; and *wants* to remedy it. So, were there such a God, there would be no evil.
IV. Therefore, since there *is* evil (i.e. given I), God *cannot* have all of the characteristics attributed to Him in II).

The 'and' (which is used in step II) is another logical connective – the connective indicates what we call a 'conjunction'. A conjunction is quite fussy. For a conjunction to be true each conjunct has to be true (all the parts conjoined together have to be true separately). Therefore, a conjunction (as a whole) is false if even just one of the conjuncts is false. Steps I and III together tell us that we have to rule out one of those conjuncts. Therefore, God cannot have all of the attributes of II. But we don't know which one to rule out, or whether we should rule out several!

To *counter* the Argument from Evil, theologians and philosophers look to what are referred to as 'theodicies' – which are explanations of 'the ways of God'. The important ones deal with the Argument from Evil. The most famous of these theodicies is owed to Leibniz, who proposed that while there is indeed *some* evil in the world, nevertheless it remains the case that the world *overall* is good. Leibniz argues that, *on balance*, the world we live in is the 'best of all possible worlds*'. God had several options, and He is good because He chose the best. Voltaire lampoons Leibniz in his novel *Candide*.[9]

A different counter-argument to the Argument from Evil is more sophisticated. The sophisticated thinking goes like this. There has to be *some* evil, and here (on this earth) is the least evil possible. Why does there have to be *some* evil? The argument continues: it is good that there should be some evil, for, it is the presence of evil which ensures our free will. Evil is present in order to test our faith. If the world were all good and pleasant and nothing ever nasty ever happened, then our faith in God would be too easy. Therefore, it is necessary that there be some evil in the world. This might, or might not, be convincing.[10] But, as we shall see in the next section, it is this sort of argument that Adams has in mind. Nevertheless, the design argument, by itself, is not enough to prove the existence of the Christian God.

2.4 Step 4: God says: 'Proof denies faith, and without faith I am nothing'

We shall see that, in this case, God's pronouncement is unfortunate. Nevertheless, the pronouncement lies in a well-rehearsed tradition. Let me explain.

The idea is that *if there were* a knock-down proof of God's existence, then that would be too easy. It would simply be *rational* to believe in God. It would suffice to show non-believers an argument, and if they could follow it, they would instantly convert.[11] The God of the *Hitchhiker's Galaxy* is like the gods of this tradition. He does not want this. The *Hitchhiker's* God wants us to believe in Him of our own free will and choice, *not* because we have gone through a process of thought and reasoning. Here, perhaps, we have what the Danish philosopher Søren Kierkegaard calls the 'leap of faith'.[12] When we make a leap of faith, we resign ourselves to not having a proof. We no longer look for reason to guide us to a belief in God's existence. Reason will not guide us, and leaves a void. We leap into the void to have God catch us – or not. This is what God – in the *Hitchhiker* argument – wants us to do – leap. We should abandon reason (on the matter of faith in God) and leap into a state of faith and sacrifice, thereby proving our faith! This is the *glory* of free choice and the importance of faith over reason – according to this tradition.

In this tradition, a God believed in by virtue of rational argument, is a *lesser* God; in fact, He would not be a God at all but rather only a perfectly reasonable creature *falling within the reach* of our understanding – whereas the tradition has it that God should be *beyond* our (poor human) understanding. Note that this doctrine also safeguards the 'mysteries' of the Church. But it also leaves us in a bit of a mess. When we find ourselves in a mess, the best remedy is to use some *formal* logic*. We use it to examine the structure of the idea that, if there is a proof of the existence of God, then God does *not* exist. The faint-hearted can skip the excursus.

2.4.1 An excursus into formal logic

The formal logical language I shall be using is called 'first-order logic'. First-order logic is a well-accepted formal logical system, which is taught in a first-year course in logic. The language for the logical system includes symbols for: proper names, predicates, identity (the symbol being =), logical connectives, quantifiers and variables.

Let us begin with names and predicates. The names are proper names, such as 'Marvin' or 'Arthur Dent'. 'Predicates' correspond to properties that an object, or subject of a sentence, might have.[13] For example, we might want to formally express: 'Marvin is a robot'. We would let 'm' stand for the name 'Marvin', and let R stand for the predicate 'is a robot'. (By convention, proper names are represented with a lower- case letter, predicates with an upper-case letter.) To express formally that 'Marvin is a Robot' we write: Rm.[14]

For expressing the *existence* of an object or subject, first-order logic uses what is called an 'existential quantifier', ∃. (This has nothing to do with the philosophy, made popular by Sartre, called 'existentialism'. So don't put on your black turtleneck and light up a Gauloise just yet.) The existential quantifier says that 'there is at least one thing'.[15] We write '∃x[...]' to mean that there is at least one x, that.... The 'that' part is what we would find between the square brackets, and what we put there would give us information about the x thing we think exists, telling us what type of thing exists. Existence is related to counting, hence the word 'quantifier'. We count existent things. (Some formal logics allow us to count non-existent things, and even impossible things, but we reserve that for a more advanced class in logic.) The 'x' is a variable – which is to say – as logicians put it – something that *varies over* a *domain of objects*. A 'domain' is a set of objects about – or 'over' – which we reason. The objects are pretty much anything which can be counted; they are whatever things that can be included as the subject of a subject–predicate sentence. These might be particular robots, cricket matches and can even include God – since God can be the subject in a sentence. These, then, are the sorts of things over which variables range. That is, variables float over the objects ready to pick one out by means of more information such as a proper name – so a variable is a sort of indeterminate name for an object. So when we write ∃x[. . .], what we mean is that there is at least one object in the domain that answers to the description within the brackets.

It should be stressed that in logic, the notion of existence, symbolised by '∃', is a *quantifier and not* a predicate. Now, in *English*, 'God exists' has God as the subject and 'exists' as a predicate. But logical grammar and English grammar are not perfectly matched. In *logic*, 'There is at least one ...', or 'there exists' is *not* considered to be a predicate in a subject–predicate sentence. This is because of the peculiar nature of asserting *the existence* of an object. Presumably, in order to be an object, it must exist – in some sense. (If our domain contains fictional objects, then the object could be one of those. In that case 'exist' would mean 'exists in the fiction'.)[16] And existence is *logically* different from properties such as 'is a robot'. Therefore, in logic we cope with the notion of existence in an indirect way, by means of the quantifier ∃.

How do we say, in logic, that some one entity, say Marvin, exists? We write: ∃x[x = m]. That means: there is an object in the domain and it is identical to the object picked out by the proper name 'Marvin'. To write that there is at least one *robot* called Marvin we write: ∃x[Rx & x = m]. That is, there is something that is a robot, and it is identical to an object (or subject of a sentence) called Marvin. The '&', then, stands for the aforementioned logical connective 'and'.

Above, I wrote that 'names pick out an object in the domain'. The astute reader will be asking herself 'but what about saying something about non-existent objects? Can't I reason logically about unicorns for example?' To write that there does *not* exist a robot called 'Marvin', we would write: ~∃x[Rx & x = m]. '~' stands for negation. It too is a logical connective. It means 'it is not the case that ...'. So the formal expression ~∃x[Rx & x = m] means: 'it is not the case that there is at least one entity that is a robot and is identical to the object called Marvin'. Note that formal expressions can be true or false. Whether or not they are true depends on the domain. In our real world – where the domain is only the real objects in our world – it is true that ~∃x[Rx & x = m].

Let us now leave Marvin and return to God. 'God' is a proper name. We can symbolically represent the name with 'g'. However: to express the idea that God exists, we may *not* write ∃g. For, that would count as bad grammar in formal logic. So we might ask: how do we express that a particular named entity in the domain of objects exists? Remember the trick? We write: ∃x[x = g]. That is, there is at least one object identical to God.

We are now getting close to being able to express in formal logic: 'if there is a proof of the existence of God, then God does not exist'.

Let M be the predicate 'is a man', in the generic sense (i.e., is a man or woman) and F be the *relation* '... has faith in ...'. *Relations* bear between (at least two) objects. They compare objects to one another. To formally represent the thought that at least one man has faith in Snow White, where s stands for Snow White, and F stands for the relation 'has faith in', we would write: ∃x[Mx & xFs]. Expressed explicitly: there is something in the domain, it is a man and it has faith in Snow White.[17] God says that if there is proof of his existence, then there is no faith in Him. The arrow: '→' is another logical connective and stands for 'if ... then ...', and in a formal logical expression we place it where we would write the word 'then'. Let P be the predicate 'is a proof of God's existence'. ∃x[Px] represents the thought that there is at least one proof in the existence of God.[18] So to write that 'if there is a proof of God then ...' we write: '∃x[Px] →'. Test question: what does the following formal expression mean? ∃x[Px] → ~∃x[Mx & xFg]. Answer: if there is a proof of the existence of God, then there is no one who has faith in God.

Still with me? Then let's continue. Recall step 4: God says: 'Proof denies faith, and without faith I [God] am nothing.' We can give formal expression to God's pronouncement if we reword it a bit, thus: 'If no one has faith in God, then God does not exist.' We prefer this formulation because it is closer to that of the formal language translation: ~∃x[Mx & xFg] → ~∃x[x = g]. Retranslating this back into English we would say, 'If there is no one in the domain (~∃x) who is a man (Mx) and (&) who has faith in God (xFg), then (→) there is no object in the domain (~∃x) identical to God (x = g). The domain, in *Hitchhiker's* is, presumably, 'the WSOGMM, or Whole Sort of General Mish Mash'![19]

We can now assemble two formal expressions. The first is:

$$(1) \ \exists x[Px] \rightarrow \sim\exists x[Mx \ \& \ xFg]$$

That means: if there is at least one proof of the existence of God, then there is no one who has faith in God.

The second expression is:

$$(2) \ \sim\exists x[Mx \ \& \ xFg] \rightarrow \sim\exists x[x = g]$$

That means: if no one has faith in God, then God does not exist.

Notice that the sub-formula ~∃x[Mx & xFg] is common to the two expressions. Since ~∃x[Mx & xFg] comes *after* the arrow in the first expression and *before* the arrow in the second, we can apply what is sometimes called the 'chain rule' and cut it out to form a new expression. The 'chain rule' applies to formal expressions with the arrow. It says that if we have an expression of the form A → B, and another of the form B → C, then we may cut out the middleman 'B' and infer A → C, where A, B and C are grammatical (sub-formulas) in the language. Applying the chain rule to (1) and (2), we may then logically infer the new formula: ∃x[Px] → ~∃x[x = g]. Miraculously, or really, logically, this just says: if there is a proof of the existence of God then God does not exist.

How does this help? We note, first, that the proof for the non-existence of God depends on a loyal translation from English into the language of first-order logic. Once translated, then the *only* logical move in the argument is to use the chain rule! So, the argument seems pretty tight. Unfortunately, it is not that tight.

The chain rule is not accepted by all logicians, and this is because of the nature of 'if … then …' statements.[20] So this is a further weakness in the Babel fish argument. The rejection is quite technical, and requires quite a lot of knowledge of 'alternative' logical systems to really bring out the weakness. There are whole books written on the subject of 'if … then …' statements. These will provide you with ammunition for frightening people at cocktail parties. However, if there is a logician at the party, beware. You risk being subjected to a very long lecture about conditionals, inferences, implications and logical consequence, and all the subclassifications thereof. Advice: bring at least two quite different 'means of escape' to cocktail parties. Logical vocabulary can be used as one (because it usually chases people away). If you suspect there will be logicians present, then you'll have to look for the other 'means of escape' elsewhere.

End of excursus.

We made it! Let us now turn to step 5.

2.5   Step 5: God tells the truth and abides by his own pronouncements

This is an implicit premise. I added this to fill in one of the background assumptions of the argument, namely, the assumption that God is not lying, joking or making a mistake which he could later correct.

In premise 4, God himself expresses the idea that if we have a proof of the existence of God, then man has no need for faith; and if man does not have faith in God, then He is nothing. We looked at this in logically gory detail in the excursus. Premise 5 ensures that we take seriously the words of premise 4. God cannot revise his pronouncements. He is committed to the consequences of what He says. What are those consequences?

2.6   Step 6: God is *nothing* – according to principles He endorses! He vanishes in a puff of logic

The reasoning by which we reach this step is as follows. If there is a proof of God's existence, then God does not exist. The Babel fish *is* (we are taking it) proof of God's existence. But, according to God himself, with proof – which precludes faith by making it redundant – he is nothing; and (we are taking it) God is right about that. Hence God is nothing.

God's 'being nothing' means that He no longer exists, or He never did exist. Since the God of the *Hitchhiker's Guide to the Galaxy* talks to man, He presumably exists while he talks, and presumably before, also. So, we really are talking about God *ceasing* to exist. This very idea is unusual in religion. In some religions gods can be defeated by other gods, or temporarily tricked by man, but the idea of a God ceasing to exist altogether is rare. One exception is in Norse mythology where the gods and the giants fight a great battle and some of the gods are killed and, so, cease to exist. Some survive. In the Christian religion, Christ (who is a part of God) dies at the hand of man, on the cross. But He does not vanish or cease to exist, for He is reborn in the kingdom of heaven. In *Hitchhiker's*, God vanishes in a puff of logic – He becomes 'no thing'. He is no longer in the domain of objects.

It is not easy to grasp what all this means. But the analysis of the final step in the argument (step 7) should cast some light. Moreover, we can consider, right now, one thing that is remarkable about the idea of God vanishing in a puff of logic. To wit: it makes God *less powerful* than logic! For, the step asserts or presumes that God is subject to logical reasoning. There was a long debate about this in the Middle Ages.

The debate was about this question: is logic more powerful and fundamental than God, or is God more powerful and fundamental than logic?[21] If God is all-powerful, then surely He has the power to break the rules of logic. After all, He breaks the rules of biology when performing miraculous healings through saints and holy relics, He even sometimes breaks other laws of nature, as when he has Jesus walk on water. Transubstantiation (the process whereby bread and wine are transformed into the body and blood of Christ) is also unnatural and miraculous in that sense. So: on this view, God can break the laws of nature. Why not, then, the laws of *logic*? After all, God is supposed to be all-powerful.

Taking the other side of the debate, we might be swayed by the idea that logical laws seem to be pretty inviolable.

They are absolutely basic. They are more basic than physics because we can imagine the laws of physics being broken – we do this a lot in science-fiction writing, but not the laws of logic. Logical laws are not only more basic than physics, they are more basic than speaking, writing and thinking. They are basic in the sense that logical laws are *preconditions* for reasoning, thought and language. To see this, try to imagine reasoning, thinking, etc. with no rules – even the most basic. You end up sputtering gobbledygook. So, if *God* is to think (as opposed to His simply 'being'), then He has to be subject to logical laws. The *Hitchhiker* God does think, since he speaks to man and He does not speak gobbledygook.

Quite separately, on this side of the debate, we can point out that it would show an *imperfection* in God, if He were to have to occasionally break a law of logic. By changing or breaking a law of logic, God would be reasoning poorly, in the same way as *we* sometimes make a mistake in reasoning!

To expand on that last point: if there is a God, or if there are many gods, then what else *but* logic could be more powerful?[22] This is a completely general point, not restricted to a particular religion. If God has a purpose, then He has to reason to achieve His purpose. If He created something, then He has to reason to create – to come up with the best design. Even to love, God has to reason! He has to decide what He loves, how much, when, and how He will show this.

2.7 Step 7: Therefore, God does not exist

A vanished God is a non-existent God, so God does not exist. Does this mean He *never* existed? After all, as we noted in section 2.4, it is not common to religions that they have a God vanish.

Because the idea of a vanishing God is so unusual, we might be tempted to think of the argument in *Hitchhiker's* as a *reductio ad absurdum* ('reduction to absurdity') argument to the effect that God never existed in the first place. If we think this, then the standard form of the original *Hitchhiker* argument would be written differently from the standard form I gave above. A *reductio ad absurdum* argument[23] has the following form. Suppose (for the sake of the argument) that X. 'X' is some fact or claim, such as 'God exists'. We then reason to an absurd conclusion: something quite distasteful, something ridiculous, or better (or, depending on how one looks at it, worse), a contradiction. We then reject our starting hypothesis X, and conclude: '*not* X', which is to say, here: 'God does *not* exist'.[24] In our new standard form of the *Hitchhiker* argument, we would start with the *assumption* or *hypothesis* that God exists, then do our reasoning to show that this ends in quite an impossible muddle, and then conclude that God *does not* exist. Nice though this form of argument is, I'm not convinced that it is the form we find in *Hitchhiker's*, since God's existence is not *first* brought forward *as* a hypothesis. If the argument is not best represented as a *reductio ad absurdum* argument, then we must put up with the idea that, first of all, God exists, but that subsequently – at the end of the reported conversation with man – he vanishes.[25]

3   Musings on logic, God and the universe

What is delightful in discovering the *Hitchhiker's* universe is that it contains such interesting creatures as the Babel fish and that within that universe one can engage God in conversation. Best of all, one can use a logical argument to have God vanish. The image of God vanishing after working through an argument is one of the most conceptually daring and playful images in literature. I suppose that this is because many of us have the fantasy that we should like to engage God is a discussion. Would it not be a coup to reason with him in debate, and moreover win! Since I teach logic to university students, I have a particular penchant for the idea that God is subject to logic. (Recall section 2.6 above.) Logic is then not just useful; mastery of it makes us very powerful and frightening! It places us on a level with God. God is beyond life and death – and logic is beyond/underlies/is presupposed by everything, including God. For this reason learning logic and learning *about* logic gives us a type of power: a power of thought. In logical thoughts we join God, or ascend to a higher plane. We do that in this sense: when using logic, we engage in a pure form of thought that is universal, thereby transcending time and space and applying even to God!

Still: what of the idea that, according to the Guide (the Guide within the *Hitchhiker's Guide*, as it were), a lot of theologians think that the Babel-fish-so-no-God argument 'is a load of dingo's kidneys'?[26] Well, we might remind ourselves that theologians have a vested interest! (Compare the worries Majikthise and Vroomfondel have about Deep Thought putting them out of a job.) Theologians want God to exist so that their work is about something that exists, not something that existed in the past, or never existed at all. So: if theologians dismiss the Babel fish argument, can we, in turn, dismiss that dismissal – on the grounds that the theologians are biased?

No. For, as good logicians, we should avoid the *fallacy* of reasoning called the ad hominem fallacy. 'Ad hominem' means 'to the man'. Ad hominem *reasoning* goes:

- X (where X is some fact) is true.
- But person y said X; and person y is wonderful, generous, trustworthy (or alternatively: mean, deceitful, nasty, has a vested interest).
- Therefore X is true (or alternatively, false).

The reasoning is fallacious. Just because some person or persons – Majikthise and Vroomfondel, or other religiously minded members of the 'Amalgamated Union of Philosophers, Sages, Luminaries and Other Thinking Persons'[27] – have a vested interest in arguing X, it does not follow that X is false. As good logicians we separate the proponent of the argument from the raw, reasoned argument itself. We must assess the Babel fish argument on its own merits. (So, logic not only has power over God, but constrains *our* reasoning too. There is a price to pay for learning logic!)

Let us just summarise our findings about that argument. We found weaknesses in that part of the argument which, remarkably, would operate – were it taken independently – as an argument *for* God's existence. For, as seen (sections 2.1–2.3), there are weaknesses in the general idea of an Argument from Design. Moreover, there is something a bit fishy about God vanishing after talking to man. 'Fishiness' is not a logical ground for complete rejection, but it is a ground for careful examination of an argument. This is why we investigated the argument in such detail. Still: the *failure* of any particular argument for God's existence does not establish that God does not exist, since there could be other stronger arguments for God existing. Nor does the failure of any particular argument *against* God's existence establish that God *does* exist. For, again, there could be other arguments. So, we cannot conclude that the God of Adams's *Hitchhiker's* galaxy exists (within the fiction) nor that He does not exist (within the fiction). Moreover it would be a grievous logical mistake to extrapolate from the logical underdetermination of the argument (that we don't know if God exists or not) in *Hitchhiker's*, to the existence or non-existence of one of the more respectable gods outside the fiction. In this respect, logic tells us very little. But it can tell us *that* we don't know, and when we know that we don't know something, we are better off than when we mistakenly thought we did!

For deeper thought

- On arguments for and against the existence of God, see J. L. Mackie's *The Miracle of Theism*. Mackie's book includes a treatment of Hume's influential criticisms of the Design Argument. For Kierkegaard and the 'leap of faith', see Kierkegaard's striking and fairly accessible *Fear and Trembling*.
- Interesting *fictional* perspectives on religion include José Saramago, *The Gospel According to Jesus Christ* and Milorad Pavić, *Dictionary of the Khazars: a Lexicon Novel in 100,000 Words*.
- On formal logic* see Paul Tomassi, *Logic*. This is a well-written book that presupposes no background in logic. For more on logic, and indeed on the *philosophy* of logic (i.e. the deeper questions about logic), see Stephen Read's *Thinking about Logic*. That latter book is best approached once one already has some knowledge of formal logic under one's belt.

Notes

1. We should understand that throughout this text we are not referring to a God of any particular religion. No such God is directly under attack. The God we write about here is a fictional God, a *construct* of Adams. So He is a fictional God, or a possible God. Nevertheless, Adams's God does bear some resemblance to the Christian God. The reason the God of Christianity, or any other religion, is not threatened by these arguments, is that a God constructed by Adams is not *identical* to the Christian God. He is only similar in some respects. Therefore attacking the God constructed by Adams is not the same as attacking the Christian God. See if you can spot the differences between Adams's God and the Christian God for yourselves. There are several hints in this chapter.

2. The numbering system for my sections comes from mathematical practice, and is quite useful. Wittgenstein also uses it in his famous *Tractatus Logico-Philosophicus*. The idea is that the first number is the number of the section. A subsection to that, is indicated by a period followed by a number for that subsection. A subsection to the subsection is announced by a period followed by a number. For example: section 1 is labelled '1'. The first subsection of section 1 will be labelled '1.1'. The third subsection of the second subsection of the first section will be labelled: '1.2.3'. The system can be quite handy when making tangled arguments.

3. Logic handbook throwing competitions have the same rules as haggis throwing competitions.

4. 'Begging the question' is a phrase which is used differently by laypersons and logicians. For laypersons it means: begging for a question to be asked, or inviting a question. For a logician it means sticking the conclusion of an argument into the premises, so that the conclusion is unavoidable. The idea dates back to Ancient Greece, where, for entertainment, the crowd would gather to watch two philosophers debate some hot question such as whether morals can be taught, or if they are inherent in us already. Before the debate started, the philosophers were allowed to beg the audience to accept their premises. If the debaters were sneaky, they would state premises in such a way as to make their conclusion unavoidable. This is a trick, and is called 'begging the question', i.e., begging in advance the answer to the very question at issue. It is a debating fault. In the case of the evolution question, if we think (as a premise, or background assumption) that evolutionary theory *will* come up with explanations of all things, then we have ruled out the possibility of God directly creating a living creature, since we would not accept that sort of explanation. For this reason, we cannot rule out the God hypothesis in advance.

5. The justification for this is: if all living things come about by evolution then we don't need God to account for their existence. (We might need Him for other things, such as to account for the creation of the whole universe or for starting the evolutionary process. But that is another matter.)

6. In logic classes we learn a lot of new words for rather mundane and ordinary things. One advantage of the vocabulary is that one can sound quite erudite while talking of quite simple matters. Another advantage is that one can use the vocabulary to frighten people away. Exercise: next time you are at a cocktail party, and don't want to engage in conversation with a particular person, start to introduce some logical vocabulary. Then time how long it takes before they flee. This is a practical application of logic!

7. Sometimes this is confused with the 'teleological argument' for the existence of God. The confusion arises because we associate design with a purpose. For example, a bridge can be well designed for the purpose of allowing traffic across a river. It can also be well designed from an aesthetic* point of view, or for purposes of longevity, or for maximising the investment in building the bridge, only within a short period of time. *Telos* has to do with end or goal. There is one, not many. It is an ultimate end. A bridge has no ultimate end, except destruction. *Telos* is one measure of design. In the case of God, design and *telos* should also be considered separately. God designed the world as an act of creation. According to some religions and interpretations of religions, we should not speculate as to the motivation for designing the world as He (supposedly) did, and if we do, we might consider several design considerations. Similarly, depending on the religion and the interpretation of the religion, there is, presumably, one *telos* or one ultimate end to the creation of the world. Judging whether the world is well designed for that, depends on what we think the end is. But it remains that there is one end and several design considerations. The design argument for the existence of God argues for a designer (of wondrous things), not for a design which answers to an ultimate end.

8. A disjunct is an option in an 'or' statement. 'Either God created the Babel fish, **or** the Babel fish came about by evolution' has two disjuncts: (1) 'God created the Babel fish' and (2) 'the Babel fish came about by evolution'.

9. On this, see chapter 9 below.

10. It should not be convincing, because the argument uses circular reasoning. Can you spot the circle?

11. Raymond Lull tried to convert a number of Muslims to Christianity by using syllogistic* reasoning. In fact, he went further. He tried to set up a *system* of choosing and deploying syllogistic reasoning for the purposes of converting Muslims.

12. Apparently, Kierkegaard himself does not actually use the term 'leap of faith'. However, it is attributed to him by some of his interpreters. It is an apt and pithy phrase, which is useful here.

13. We can also think about this in terms of a 'subject–predicate' sentence in English. Declarative sentences have a subject–predicate form. Confusingly, the subject is what logicians call an 'object', and the predicate part of such a sentence attributes a property to the subject/object.

14. A natural language is one we use for everyday communication. A *formal* language is artificial and is developed in order to highlight logical form over content. We write mathematical formulas in a formal language. The order in the formula is not the same as in English.

In English the name comes *before* the predicate. The reason logical grammar insists on this order has to do with conventions in mathematics rather than conventions in English or in many other natural languages.

15. We normally think of 'quantities' as definite numbers, such as, say, 8 or 42. However, logicians discovered that they can get away with just having one quantifier and negation. When I say that 'we can get away with this' what I mean is that we can express all of the definite quantities using the existential quantifier, and the rest of the language, so there was no reason – besides convenience and shortening sentences – for introducing more quantifiers. This finding (that we can get away with only one quantifier) is philosophically important, since it (controversially) reveals to us that the logical notion of quantity is reducible to this one vague quantity: 'there is at least one'. In first-order logic we usually also include one *further* logical quantifier, the quantifier 'for all' that is called 'the universal quantifier' and is symbolised $\forall$. Again this is a vague sort of quantity. How many 'all' is, depends on the context. 'All the things in the universe' gives us a very different definite number from 'all the dishes on the table'. Definite quantities such as 'exactly 8' can be given a special symbol: $\exists!_8$. The '!' stands for 'exactly', and we can put whatever subscripted number we wish. As noted, these quantifiers are strictly redundant. That is, they are only a shorthand for a longer expression using the existential and the universal quantifier and other parts of the logical language. Logicians, being purists, prefer to use as few quantifiers as possible.

16. Another way of thinking about this is that logic alone cannot tell us whether a common-sense object exists or not. Only our common sense or experience can tell us. Logic 'does not care' whether your favourite chesterfield exists or not, for, it is logically possible* for it to have never existed. The only thing logic can tell us exists are *logical objects*, if there are any. Indeed, 'first-order logic' cannot prove the existence of *any* such objects. Whether or not there are any, and what they are like, depends on further features we can add to the formal logic. And we *choose* which extra formal features to add on. An example of a formal object needing a more sophisticated formal system is a natural number. In some 'higher-order' formal logical systems we can prove the existence of the number 2, or 46 as a matter of our chosen logic. If we accept that our sophisticated logical system is a *logical* system, then it is logically necessary for these numbers to exist as objects. They are then considered to be logical objects.

17. This is an ambiguous sentence. It is ambiguous between *man has faith that Snow White exists* and *man has faith in what Snow White says or does*. But that ambiguity does not matter here. In fact, we want to preserve it, since it is present in the argument in *Hitchhikers*.

18. Note that 'x' is a proof, so there are proofs (considered to be objects) in the domain over which we are reasoning.
19. *Mostly Harmless*, chapter 3.
20. Here is one example way to reject the chain rule. On the left side of the → we could have a contradiction. There is nothing in logic to prevent this – only the real world (if it contains no contradictions) can prevent this. We would then be starting a chain of reasoning *from* a contradiction, and, according to some logicians, implementing the chain rule is absurd. Therefore, the chain rule is not universally applicable (since not applicable in the presence of contradictory sentences). Therefore, the chain rule is not a logical rule.
21. This question is related to another one with which medieval thinkers wrestled: 'Could God have created something so heavy that He could not lift it?' These arguments are useful if you are surrounded by theologians, especially if they are being tiresome. Next party trick: innocently ask the question, and time how long it takes before there is a physical sign of frustration: thumping the table, rising from a seat, raising the voice, storming out of the room or a fist fight!
22 Nothing in the physical world will do, since He created it, and can destroy it too. One alternative might be emotions and faith. However, it is far from clear what it would mean for emotions or faith to be 'more powerful' than God. It is a nice exercise to think about this question.
23. A contradiction is better (or worse) in the sense of making a more conclusive logical argument. If a temporary hypothesis leads to a contradiction, then we are logically forced to reject the hypothesis. By contrast, if a hypothesis leads to a conclusion that is simply *distasteful*, then we might decide to put up with the distastefulness, and keep the hypothesis.
24. I used this form of argument in note 16, but I did not spell it out.
25. This relies on a shortened version of *reductio ad absurdum*. It is called 'counter-position'. The idea is that if we have a conditional, then its counterposed version follows logically. Recall that a conditional is an 'if ... then ...' sentence. The counter-position switches the positions of the antecedent (the 'if' part) and consequent (the 'then' part) and negates both (or gives the opposite of both). For example, take the conditional sentence: '**if** God vanishing is unpalatable, **then** the *Hitchhiker* argument should be represented as a *reductio ad absurdum* argument'. The counter-position of the conditional, which logically follows, is: '**if** the *Hitchhiker* argument is **not** best represented as a *reductio ad absurdum* argument, **then** God vanishing *is* palatable'. Counter-posing is a useful tool in debates and arguments. Try it next time someone argues for a conditional statement. Counter-pose it. Do this in your head before you say anything out loud. Quite often the

counter-posed version (which logically follows from the conditional statement) does not sound quite right. If it sounds a bit odd, then you can use it to throw the opponent into a muddle. And all you did was use a little logic.

26. *Restaurant*, chapter 6. This epithet/insult is surprisingly common in *Hitchhiker's*!
27. *The Hitchhiker's Guide to the Galaxy*, chapter 25.

8
The Judo Principle, Philosophical Method and the Logic of Jokes

Andrew Aberdein

1 The Judo Principle

As early as the second episode of the original radio series of *Hitchhiker's*, Douglas Adams wrote himself into a corner. He had arranged for Arthur and Ford to escape the destruction of the Earth on board one of the Vogon ships responsible for that destruction. There they were 'safe', as Arthur observes, only in a usage of that word he 'wasn't previously aware of' (*The Hitchhiker's Guide to the Galaxy*, chapter 5). They are duly expelled from the Vogon ship into the vacuum of space with no form of life support, a predicament from which any escape seems utterly improbable. That left Adams in a bind: all the solutions he could come up with seemed like cheating, and, as he wrote in notes accompanying the published radio scripts, '[t]here's no point making a big song and dance about what a terrible predicament your characters are in if you just cheat your way out of it'. But, watching a documentary on judo, he had a breakthrough: 'If you have a problem ... the trick is to use this problem to solve itself' (Adams, *The Hitch-Hiker's*

Guide to the Galaxy: The Original Radio Scripts, p. 51). Let us call this trick the *Judo Principle*. In accordance with the Judo Principle, Adams used the problem of improbability against itself, by making the improbability of Arthur and Ford's rescue the means of their rescue.

The Infinite Improbability Drive did not just get Adams out of this particular bind. It licensed all the coincidences that litter the rest of the complex and divergent narratives of the *Hitchhiker's* sequence. The Judo Principle is also, naturally enough, echoed in his description of how the drive was invented. Apparently, physicists had long since cracked the problem of generating finite amounts of improbability from a 'strong Brownian motion producer (say a nice hot cup of tea)' (*Hitchhiker's*, chapter 10), but have little success in scaling up this work to produce an Infinite Improbability Drive capable of interstellar travel until one student has a breakthrough: 'such a machine is a *virtual* impossibility, [so] it must logically be a *finite* improbability. So all I have to do in order to make one is to work out exactly how improbable it is, feed that figure into the finite improbability generator, give it a fresh cup of really hot tea … and turn it on!' (*Hitchhiker's*, chapter 10). The Infinite Improbability Drive then pops into existence, as if by magic. Indeed, the drive is essentially magical: it bears little relationship to anything we know about infinity, improbability, Brownian motion, or indeed, tea. However, the Judo Principle which led to its discovery, the use of problems to solve themselves, turns out to have a very important place in philosophical methodology. This chapter will explore how the Judo Principle works through discussion of some of the specific uses philosophers have made of it, each of which also attracted Adams's attention: the definition of infinity, the foundations of knowledge, artificial intelligence and parallel worlds. I will discuss each of these ideas in turn, and then examine the principle itself and a problem it raises.

2 Defining infinity

The *Guide* rather struggles to define infinity:

Infinite: Bigger than the biggest thing ever and then some. Much bigger than that in fact, really amazingly immense, a totally stunning size, real 'wow, that's big', time. Infinity is just so big that by comparison, bigness itself looks really titchy. Gigantic multiplied by colossal multiplied by staggeringly huge is the sort of concept we are trying to get across here.

(*The Restaurant at the End of the Universe*, chapter 19).

Scientists and philosophers have not always done much better than this. It was already clear to Aristotle (384–322 BC) that a distinction may be drawn between potential infinity and actual infinity.[1] Something is potentially infinite if its size may be increased without limit. For example, there are potentially infinitely many natural numbers: '1, 2, 3, …'. The '…' indicates that we may continue to add numbers to this sequence without it ever coming to an end. Thus it is infinite, in the sense of being unbounded, but we cannot assign a specific quantity to it unless we treat it as completed, that is as an actual infinity. This is where the trouble begins: actual infinity is hard to define, and philosophers and mathematicians from Aristotle onwards generally tried to avoid it altogether.

Galileo Galilei (1564–1642) brought the problem into sharp focus. He made the insightful observation that two sets of objects may normally be understood to have the same number (there will be the same number of objects in the first set as in the second) when they may be placed in one-to-one correspondence, that is when each of the members of one set may be paired off with one of the members of the other set.[2] This has come to be known as *Hume's Principle*, because, a century later, the Scottish philosopher David Hume (1711–76) made a similar observation somewhat more explicitly.[3] However, as Galileo appreciated, Hume's Principle seems to run into difficulties when applied to sets which are infinite in number. For, as he observes, the natural numbers may be placed in one-to-one correspondence with their squares:

$$
\begin{array}{cccccc}
1 & 2 & 3 & 4 & 5 & \ldots \\
\updownarrow & \updownarrow & \updownarrow & \updownarrow & \updownarrow & \ldots \\
1 & 4 & 9 & 16 & 25 & \ldots
\end{array}
$$

And yet there are clearly lots of natural numbers missing from the second set, the square numbers, because most natural numbers aren't square. So, intuitively, it seems obvious that there must be more natural numbers than square numbers, contradicting the assumption that sets in one-to-one correspondence have the same number. That is to say, adherence to Hume's Principle violates an even more entrenched mathematical axiom, Euclid's fifth 'Common Notion', which states that the 'whole is greater than the part'.[4] To explain: the set of square numbers is only a part of the set of natural numbers but, according to Hume's Principle, these sets have the same number, since they are in one-to-one correspondence. Galileo concludes that 'the attributes "equal", "greater", and "less", are not applicable to infinite, but only to finite, quantities',[5] or in other words: we just cannot make meaningful comparisons between actual infinite quantities; so we should avoid them altogether or we will get bogged down in paradox*.

However, later mathematicians were able to rescue actual infinity from Galileo's paradox, by application of the Judo Principle. The apparent obstacle to the mathematical respectability of actual infinity is that such quantities would be at odds with Euclid's Common Notion Five, by dint of having the same number as a 'proper part' (that is, a subset smaller than the whole set). The solution adopted by the German mathematicians Georg Cantor (1845–1918) and Richard Dedekind (1831–1916) was to *use this problem (or paradox) against itself,* by making 'has the same number as a proper part' the *definition* of actual infinities. Galileo was right that Common Notion Five cannot be consistently applied to the actually infinite, but he did not see that a consistent account can be developed by dropping it. That account is foundational to subsequent work on infinity and, indeed, much of modern mathematics.

3 Foundations for knowledge

Since ancient Greece, philosophers have been much concerned with the nature of knowledge. In ordinary talk we often claim to know things, but we also often discover that we are wrong, and therefore that we don't really know what we thought we knew. But what is it that distinguishes real knowledge from false knowledge claims? This turns out to be a difficult question to answer satisfactorily, but the Judo Principle has given rise to two very different solutions.

Some philosophers turned the difficulty of identifying knowledge against itself in a simple way, concluding that knowledge can't be had, and that we should just learn to be happy with our ignorance. These were the original sceptics, a school inspired by Pyrrho of Elis (*c.*365–*c.*275 BC); due to his influence, scepticism* of this uncompromising nature is called Pyrrhonian scepticism. Adams gives us a textbook Pyrrhonian sceptic in the person of the Man in the Shack, who provides the anticlimax to Zaphod and Zarniwoop's protracted quest to discover who really rules the Universe. We never learn any other name for the Man in the Shack. Indeed, he is so committed to scepticism that he is uncertain whether he has or needs a name: 'I don't know. Why, do you think I should have one? It seems very odd to give a bundle of vague sensory perceptions a name' (*Restaurant*, chapter 29). Just as Pyrrho predicted, however, this radical scepticism seems to have made the Man in the Shack happy: despite his meagre circumstances and great responsibilities, he exudes 'ataraxia', or freedom from care, the peace of mind which Pyrrho and his school claimed to follow from the determined avoidance of having an opinion about anything.[6] This radical disinterestedness also makes him the perfect solution to a political paradox which Adams observes: 'those people who most *want* to rule people are, ipso facto*, those least suited to do it' (*Restaurant*, chapter 28). The Man in the Shack so little wants to rule people that he's not even convinced that he actually *does* rule people. Zaphod and Trillian conclude that 'the Universe is in pretty good hands' (*Restaurant*, chapter 29). This passage has lent itself to some tenuous interpretation: some have seen it as evidence of Adams's implicit commitment to political libertarianism*;[7] others assume that the Man in the Shack is a representation of God.[8]

Nonetheless, for ordinary mortals with no Universe to rule, Pyrrhonian scepticism is not a very attractive position. Understandably, many philosophers have sought more definite answers. René Descartes's (1596–1650) answer to the problem of making knowledge secure took the form of a new, more sophisticated application of the Judo Principle. His argument is famously known as the Cogito, from its formulation in Latin: Cogito ergo sum, I think therefore I am.[9] Descartes concludes that, whatever else he may be wrong about, he cannot deny his own existence, so that is one thing of which he can be certain.[10] That much was not original: Aristotle and Augustine had reasoned in a similar fashion many centuries earlier.[11] But Descartes didn't stop there; he proceeded to argue that the whole structure of knowledge could be re-established on this indubitable foundation. Scepticism is thus a procedure to 'demolish everything completely and start again right from the foundations' (*Meditations on First Philosophy*, p. 76); but rather than content himself with a shack Descartes believes he can construct a palace: a prodigious rational edifice ultimately encompassing all of science.

The Cogito finds a place in *Hitchhiker's* too – in the ruminations of the supercomputer Deep Thought, which 'was so amazingly intelligent that even before its databanks had been connected up it had started from *I think therefore I am* and got as far as deducing the existence of rice pudding and income tax before anyone managed to turn it off' (*Hitchhiker's*, chapter 25). Descartes was particularly concerned with the reliability of ideas that he owed to his senses, ideas which would come to be known as 'a posteriori'*, and contrasted with 'a priori'* ideas, which may be known independently of the senses. He eventually concluded that his a posteriori knowledge was by and large reliable by appealing to the existence of God (something he believed he could deduce a priori), since God would not permit him to be systematically deceived by his senses. Since Deep Thought's databanks have not been connected, a priori reasoning would be the only variety available to it.[12] Hence Deep Thought goes one better than Descartes by deducing the existence of such ostensibly a posteriori phenomena as rice pudding and income tax from wholly a priori grounds.[13]

Intriguingly, Douglas Adams was not the only philosophically minded English satirist to speculate in the 1970s about computers imitating Descartes.[14] Shortly before *Hitchhiker's* first appeared, Michael Frayn wrote the following:

> Suppose a computer prints out this: 'I think, therefore I am.'
>
> We smile. But its logic is surely no worse than Descartes's. Seriously! Descartes wasn't making any claims about the quality of his thought. He was claiming that any piece of thought-thinking necessarily implies the existence of a thinker, any piece of statement-making the existence of a statement-maker.
>
> – But the computer couldn't *feel* the force of this necessity!
>
> – Logical necessity doesn't have to be felt.
>
> We don't know now whether to smile or click our tongues in irritation. We rely on computers not to puzzle us like this.[15]

This problem, of whether, or in what sense, machines can think, has been the occasion for another famous application of the Judo Principle.

4   Intelligent machines

Long before computers were capable of anything that might be taken for independent thought, their programmers were already beginning to speculate about whether they ever would be. The most famous answer to the question 'Can machines think?' is that of Alan Turing (1912–54). He pointed out, rather as Deep Thought does to Loonquawl and Phouchg (*Hitchhiker's*, chapter 28), that the problem with this question is that we don't really understand what it means.[16] This is because 'thinking' is formidably hard to pin down in humans, never mind other sorts of entity. So instead of postponing our search for a criterion for machine intelligence until we have solved the stubborn philosophical problem of providing a criterion for human intelligence, he proposes that we play a game. He introduces his game by analogy with a different game: the 'imitation game' is a game played by three humans, an interrogator and two others, one male and one female. The interrogator, communicating with the other two by teleprinter, tries to work out which of them is which, while they both try to present themselves as female. The well-known 'Turing test' results from substituting a computer and a human for the man and the woman respectively. So, instead of asking 'Can machines think?', Turing asks 'Could a machine win this sort of game?' If it does, we would be no closer to solving the hard philosophical question of whether we should characterize its behaviour as conscious thought, but Turing makes a persuasive case that we should treat it *as if* it were intelligent, since it would have shown itself capable of 'passing' as intelligent.[17]

Turing's answer to the question 'Can machines think?' may thus be seen as another application of the Judo Principle. The problem he was confronted with is the same one that puzzled Frayn: that machines might give every appearance of thought, even if we were unable to determine whether their behaviour was evidence of real thought. Turing's solution was to use this problem, the indistinguishability of apparent and real machine intelligence, against itself: accepting as a criterion for intelligence our inability to determine that the machine is not intelligent.

Some prophets of machine intelligence anticipate a rapid acceleration in its abilities if it ever achieves superhuman intelligence. The reasoning behind this is that the super-human intelligence could design an even more intelligent successor, and so on in ever faster and greater leaps: 'a runaway phenomenon of rapidly escalating superintel-ligence'[18] that has come to be known as the Singularity. This process echoes Deep Thought's 'needlessly messianic' predictions of a 'computer whose merest operational parameters I am not worthy to calculate, but which it will be my fate eventually to design' (*Hitchhiker's*, chapter 28). One of the tasks to which such mind-bogglingly intelligent machines could be put is the simulation of specific humans: not just 'Genuine People Personalities' (*Hitchhiker's*, chapter 11), but the personalities of genuine people.[19] The futurist Ray Kurzweil concludes that this possibility of 'backing ourselves up' will lead to practical immortality: the 'eliminati[on] of most causes of death as we know it'.[20] But even if Kurzweil is right about the feasibility of the technology, how would we know if it works? Kurzweil argues that confirmation that Jane Smith, say, has been successfully uploaded 'will be in the form of a ... "Jane Smith" Turing test, in other words convincing a human judge that the uploaded re-creation is indis-tinguishable from the original specific person'.[21] If the regular Turing test is an application of the Judo Principle, then so is Kurzweil's. However, Kurzweil's application of the principle seems more troublesome than Turing's. It is reminiscent of Arthur's exchange with the mice who want to buy his brain. They offer him a simple electronic alternative, which, at least according to Zaphod, would easily pass an 'Arthur Dent' Turing test: 'you'd just have to program it to say *What?* and *I don't understand* and *Where's the tea?* – who'd know the difference?' (*Hitchhiker's*, chapter 31). When Arthur insists *he* would know the difference, the mice reply 'No you wouldn't ... you'd be programmed not to' (*Hitchhiker's*, chapter 31). Arthur's objections seem entirely reasonable, even against a more rigorous test than Zaphod's facetious suggestion, yet it is hard to see how Kurzweil can accommodate them. The best he offers is that the problem wouldn't arise if the replacement process were sufficiently gradual.[22] That's not much help if it isn't, and it doesn't seem to help Arthur either: even if the mice replaced his brain *gradually* he would be in the same predicament. An 'Arthur Dent' Turing test would not be a good enough test for Arthur Dent.

The difficulty here is that the Turing test solved the original problem by shifting the context to one in which the most troublesome part, working out whether the computer was genuinely conscious, could be disregarded.[23] This application of the Judo Principle was successful because it turned out that progress on artificial intelligence could be made without that component: emphasizing the artifice rather than the intelligence, as it were. But in the superficially similar case of the 'Arthur Dent' Turing test Arthur's *consciousness* is absolutely critical. Unless that can be preserved, there would be no more Arthur Dent, only a sort of Arthur Dent zombie.[24] Alternatively, but just as bad from Arthur's point of view, the new electronic brain might have *a* consciousness, just not Arthur's. The 'Arthur Dent' Turing test fails to rule out either of these possibilities. The salutary point of this discussion for present purposes is that it shows that the Judo Principle is not foolproof. It is a fertile source of philosophical problem solving, but it is not guaranteed to work every time. This, however, is exactly what we should expect. The principle is a heuristic, not a panacea. That is to say, it is a device which can be used to find possible solutions to a problem; it is not a cure-all which can be trusted to eliminate every problem.

5 Multiple worlds

As the *Hitchhiker's* sequence develops, references to parallel universes proliferate. In *So Long, and Thanks for All the Fish* (chapter 32) we get an intimation of how the dolphins had averted the Vogon destruction of the Earth, replacing it with 'a shadow Earth in the implications of enfolded time'. The resulting 'plural' nature of the Earth has drastic and unresolved consequences for Fenchurch in the events that occur between this and the final book, which addresses this topic extensively, if not always illuminatingly: 'The first thing to realise about parallel universes, the *Guide* says, is that they are not parallel. It is also important to realise that they are not, strictly speaking, universes either' (*Mostly Harmless*, chapter 3). One might speculate that the multiple, frankly inconsistent, rearrangements of *Hitchhiker's* itself, as it ramified across diverse media (and as Adams struggled to construct a version acceptable to Hollywood producers), led to this fascination with branching time. However, Adams had been contemplating the use of this device to soften the blow of Earth's destruction right from the start. An early draft of the script for the radio pilot gives the following speech to Ford: 'But there are plenty more Earths just like it. ... The universe we exist in is just one of a multiplicity of parallel universes ..., and in millions of them the Earth is still alive and throbbing much as you remember – or very similar at least – because every possible variation of the Earth also exists.'[25] This is an allusion to the many-worlds interpretation of quantum mechanics: a solution to the equations of quantum mechanics that implies the existence of parallel worlds. Their existence poses a problem, since it is so contrary to our intuitions; but attempts to interpret the equations in such a way that only a single world exists throw up hard problems of their own. Eventually, at least

according to the evangelists of the many-worlds interpretation, we come to realize that these problems are best dealt
with by treating parallel worlds not as a problem but as a
means to a solution. As Adams put it, recapitulating a leading many-worlds theorist, 'David Deutsch points out that
if you imagine that our universe is simply one layer and
that there is an infinite multiplicity of universes spreading
out on either side, not only does it solve the problem [of
wave/particle duality], but the problem simply goes away'
(*Salmon of Doubt*, p. 133).[26] This outcome should now be
familiar: on Adams's own account, the many-worlds interpretation is yet another example of the Judo Principle.

The notion of a plurality of worlds is not unique to quantum mechanics: it goes back to Gottfried Leibniz (1646–1716),
and has been proposed on multiple occasions in response
to both scientific and philosophical problems. One such
philosophical problem is *modality** – what do statements
about *possibility* and *necessity* actually mean? The influential
metaphysician* David Lewis (1941–2001) made the following suggestion:

> I believe, and so do you, that things could have been
> different in countless ways. But what does this mean?
> Ordinary language permits the paraphrase: there are
> many ways things could have been besides the way they
> actually are. I believe that things could have been differ-
> ent in countless ways; I believe permissible paraphrases
> of what I believe; taking the paraphrase at its face value,
> I therefore believe in the existence of entities that might
> be called 'ways things could have been'. I prefer to call
> them 'possible worlds'.[27]

These possible worlds are normally understood as distinct
from the parallel worlds invoked by physicists. This is for

several reasons: possible worlds may be physically impossible, and thereby excluded from the physicists' model; possible worlds do not interact with each other, but parallel worlds must do so if they are to explain quantum mechanics; and possible worlds are generally understood by philosophers as an abstraction, whereas parallel worlds are by hypothesis physically real. Lewis's innovation was to drop the last of these points, adopting a position he called 'modal realism': his possible worlds differ from the actual world in which we live only in not being actual. This bold move sacrifices our intuitions as the price for a neat solution to the problem of modality* which, according to Lewis, could not otherwise be solved. Once again, an initial problem, that modal talk sounds like it refers to possible worlds, is exploited to solve itself – and the more general problem of defining modality.

6   Three grades of Judo Principle

We have seen that the Judo Principle has been widely deployed by philosophers in response to many different problems, and in several different ways. It may help to itemize some of the different forms it can take. Firstly, the Judo Principle sometimes amounts to no more than just accepting a problem. Adams's own original application of the principle, the Infinite Improbability Drive, is little more than this. Philosophers often refer to this strategy, of just resolving to put up with (or, as we shall see, *insist upon*) a counter-intuitive or unpalatable conclusion, as 'biting the bullet'. As a solution to a problem, this seems less like a solution than a way of drawing attention to the problem and agreeing not to worry about it. Some creative writers refer to this as 'hanging a lampshade' on the problem;[28] in Adams's terms, we might think of it as erecting a Somebody

Else's Problem field. An SEP field tricks us into treating a problem as 'something that we can't see, or don't see, or our brain doesn't let us see ... The brain just edits it out, it's like a blind spot. If you look directly you won't see it unless you know precisely what it is' (*Life, the Universe and Everything*, chapter 4). On one conception, with a pedigree reaching back at least to Plato, the philosopher's job is precisely to see through such illusions and draw them to the attention of others. So surrendering to an SEP might seem like philosophical failure. However, knowing that something is an illusion doesn't change its appearance; similarly, if the solution to a problem is counter-intuitive, it will confound our intuitions even after we have learnt this. So training ourselves to ignore these intuitions may be the best response, provided that we have excellent reasons for believing that the solution which is bothering us really is the best answer to the problem. It is this positive aspect of the bullet-biting or lampshade-hanging version of the Judo Principle which Lewis uses in defence of his modal realism, noting that 'an incredulous stare is not an argument'.[29]

However, we have seen that the Judo Principle characteristically does more than just reconcile us to our incredulity. It often works by *shifting the frame, or terms of the debate, in which the problem originally arose to one where it isn't a problem*. On this version of the Judo Principle, the problem still solves itself, but it does so indirectly, by provoking the adoption of a whole new way of looking at the situation. If this move works, we find that, once we adopt the new perspective, 'the problem simply goes away' (Adams, *Salmon*, p. 133). The new perspective may well have additional dividends beyond the solution of the original problem that attract support on their own merits, hence this version of the Judo Principle is potentially much more productive than the first. Perhaps for that reason, this is the version that arose most frequently in the examples discussed above. Cantor's definition of infinity led to a new understanding of number broad enough to include infinite totalities. Turing's proposal was quite explicitly to shift from an intractable way of looking at the problem (Can machines think?) to a problem which stood a much better chance of solution (Can machines act as though they think?). Here, however, the original problem remains; however accomplished computers may get at passing for intelligent, we are not necessarily any closer to knowing whether they have experiences that resemble our own. The unsatisfactory outcome of the 'Arthur Dent' Turing test demonstrates that this underlying problem can re-emerge. It also shows that closely related problems need not have closely related solutions.

Lastly, at its most sophisticated, the Judo Principle can do more than eliminate the problem or prompt a new perspective; it can put the problem to work. This interpretation of the Judo Principle does most justice to Adams's original idea of using a problem to solve itself, in that this version of the principle *transforms the problem into a problem-solving technique*. Understandably, perhaps, this is a difficult standard to meet; as we saw above, the Infinite Improbability Drive, Adams's own example, falls short. The one fully fledged example discussed above is Descartes's response to the problem of scepticism. Descartes's development of methodological scepticism not only facilitated his own solution to the problem, it played a central role in his theory of knowledge, and was deeply influential on contemporary and later thinkers.

7   The logic of jokes

The Judo Principle in its various forms has been a powerful and successful way of dealing with philosophical problems. Its applications are widely distributed and include some profound intellectual turning points, many of which find echoes in *Hitchhiker's*. However, Adams is on record as saying that his ideas 'come from the logic of jokes, and any relation they bear to anything in the real world is usually completely coincidental'.[30] That looks like a more appropriate answer for Adams, who made his living as a humorist, than for philosophers: if the Judo Principle also comes from the logic of jokes, its philosophical ubiquity starts to look like an embarrassment for philosophy, not a strength. The indebtedness of the Judo Principle to the logic of jokes is a tough problem. But the Judo Principle is a method for dealing with tough problems: the method of using them to solve themselves. Let's see how well this method fares with the problem of its own seriousness.

The first step in applying this problem to itself – of trying to show how it is not problematic that much philosophy has the logic of jokes – is to take the logic of jokes seriously. In coining this term, 'the logic of jokes', Adams may merely have intended to deter an importunate student from writing a thesis on his work. However, not only does his phrase provide an insightful account of his own thought; it also points to an overlooked feature of philosophical methodology in general. To wit: the logic of jokes is not just a legitimate source of philosophical inspiration but a uniquely valuable one. 'Quite often there are things that you can only say as jokes,' as Philip Larkin once observed in defence of his fellow poet John Betjeman, who was sometimes underestimated because of the laughter his verse elicited.[31] The cognitive scientist Marvin Minsky has given this observation a sharper focus, arguing that jokes (and especially those, like many in *Hitchhiker's*, which trade in apparent nonsense) play an indispensable role in the function of human reason:

> Common sense logic is too unreliable for practical use.
> It cannot be repaired, so we must learn to avoid its most

common malfunctions. Humor plays a special role in learning and communicating about such matters ... Productive thinking depends on knowing how to use Analogy and Metaphor. But analogies are often false, and metaphors misleading. ... This is why humor is so concerned with the nonsensical.[32]

If Minsky is correct, then we should not be surprised when problem-solving heuristics make us laugh. His picture suggests that the logic of jokes is not just something we must put up with, but something we should embrace. Thus, not only does the Judo Principle work in defence of the logic of jokes, it works at its most sophisticated level, by revealing the logic of jokes to be a powerful problem-solving technique.

Indeed, some philosophers have acknowledged the potential of the logic of jokes. In particular, Ludwig Wittgenstein is reported to have averred that 'a serious and philosophical work could be written that would consist entirely of jokes'.[33] In recent years, there have been several attempts at composing such a work; the authors of one of the latest explain the structural similarities between philosophy and jokes that underpin their project:

The construction and payoff of jokes and the construction and payoff of philosophical concepts are made out of the same stuff. They tease the mind in similar ways. That is because philosophy and jokes proceed from the same impulse: to confound our sense of the way things are, to flip our worlds upside down, and to ferret out hidden, often uncomfortable, truths about life.[34]

Careful readers of Adams have long since observed this impulse in his work. As one of his biographers puts it,

'Douglas's genius was to sneak [philosophical notions] into the reader's brain camouflaged as a series of extremely good jokes. It is this serious underpinning of dazzling notions and intellect that made *Hitchhiker's* so extraordinary.'[35] Indeed *Hitchhiker's* comes closer to Wittgenstein's 'serious and philosophical work ... consist[ing] entirely of jokes' than anything else, before or since.

For deeper thought

This chapter touches on many philosophical topics, all of which have been written on at great length; this section lists some of the most approachable works.

There has been a spate of popular treatments of infinity. Maor, *To Infinity and Beyond* is an excellent historical survey. Wallace, *Everything and More: A Compact History of ∞*, is one of the most surprising works to have been commissioned from a famous novelist. David Foster Wallace applies his distinctive style to a deft treatment of the central philosophical and mathematical questions concerning infinity, although purists have found some errors of exposition. Perhaps the best such work is Rucker's *Infinity and the Mind*, which is mathematically accurate, philosophically original, and pursues its subject to greater depth than many less readable works. Uncoincidentally, its author is both a mathematician and a science fiction novelist!

A key part of Descartes's philosophical project was to bring a new level of clarity to the discipline and, to a large degree, he succeeded. His *Meditations* in particular is an accessible and enjoyable read. As a staple of the philosophy syllabus, it has attracted any number of glosses and handbooks. One of the best, by a great twentieth-century philosopher, is Williams, *Descartes: The Project of Pure Enquiry*; but a more accessible introduction is Sorell's *Descartes: A Very Short Introduction*.

Turing is well served by both a readable biography (Leavitt, *The Man Who Knew Too Much*) and a handy compendium of his principal writings which also contains valuable explanatory notes and supplementary material (Copeland, *The Essential Turing*). The Turing test has an extensive literature of its own, and is the subject of an annual competition with an as yet unclaimed lump sum awaiting the first successful program: the Loebner Prize. A recent work (Christian, *The Most Human Human: What Talking with Computers Teaches Us about What It Means to Be Alive*) is written from the unusual perspective of a 'confederate' in this competition – one of the humans against which the competing programs are tested.

There are many popularizations of the many-worlds model of quantum mechanics, but for the readers of this book the best choice must be the one endorsed by Adams himself: Deutsch's *The Fabric of Reality*. Lewis's work, such as his book *Counterfactuals*, is highly technical, but always written with clarity and often with wit.

The central discussion in this chapter is related to a broader question, whether there really are philosophical problems, or merely puzzles: for further context, see Joll, 'Contemporary Metaphilosophy', especially section 2.c. This question lay behind the famous confrontation between Wittgenstein and Karl Popper, described in *Wittgenstein's Poker* by Edmonds and Eidinow, which is a fine historical introduction to the work of both men. One of the most penetrating studies of problem solving, focused on a mathematical problem, but of much broader application, is Lakatos, *Proofs and Refutations*.

The intersection of philosophy and humour has been explored in several recent books, notably *I Think, Therefore I Laugh* by Paulos and *Plato and a Platypus Walk Into a Bar* by

Cathcart and Klein. In relation to Adams in particular, it is the focus of an excellent essay, entitled '42', by Adam Roberts.

Notes

1. Maor, *To Infinity and Beyond*, p. 55.
2. Galilei, *Dialogues Concerning Two New Sciences*, p. 32.
3. Hume, *A Treatise of Human Nature*, book I, part III, section 1, p. 71.
4. Heath, *The Thirteen Books of Euclid's Elements*, p. 80.
5. Galilei, *Dialogues Concerning Two New Sciences*, p. 33.
6. Bett, 'Pyrrho'.
7. Day, 'The Subversive Dismal Scientist', p. 123.
8. Webb, *Wish You Were Here*, p. 123. Adams certainly saw through the pretensions of centralized government planning, a frequent target of satire in *Hitchhiker's* and more direct comments elsewhere (see, for example, *Salmon of Doubt*, pp. 143–4). But that is a slim basis from which to extrapolate a political philosophy*. The second proposal is more intriguing. Despite being an avowed atheist, Adams was fascinated by religion, and as he himself commented, 'I've thought about it so much over the years that that fascination is bound to spill over into my writing' (*Salmon*, p. 101).
9. Descartes, *Principles of Philosophy*, section 7, p. 162 ('*I am thinking, therefore I exist*'). For a more accessible presentation of the idea, see Descartes, *Meditations on First Philosophy* (specifically, 'Second Meditation', p. 80). Compare also p. 36 of his *Discourse on the Method*.
10. Truly determined Pyrrhonian sceptics would not be satisfied with this conclusion. They would agree with the Man in the Shack that it 'seems very odd to give a bundle of vague sensory perceptions a name' (*Restaurant*, ch. 29) – even if that name is 'me'. That is, just because thinking is occurring, that's no basis for identifying the thinker as any particular person.
11. Katz, *Cogitations*, p. 11.
12. Unless Deep Thought had access to its perceptual apparatus before its databanks were connected.
13. This is, of course, impossible. It should be said, however, that rice pudding would seem to pose the greater challenge: with no knowledge of the external world, how could one even suspect the existence of rice, or puddings, let alone that one may be made from the other? Income tax has a more baleful inevitability; it must be at least conceivable, given some very rudimentary, although still a posteriori, assumptions about economics.
14. For more on *Hitchhiker's* as satire, see chapter 9 of this book.

15. Frayn, *Constructions*, section 61.
16. Turing, 'Computing Machinery and Intelligence', p. 441.
17. In the light of what we now know of Turing's sexuality, it is perhaps irresistible to see in the computer's attempts to pass as human his own, ultimately tragically unsuccessful, attempts to pass as straight at a time when homosexual acts were punishable at law (Leavitt, *The Man Who Knew Too Much*, p. 244).
18. Kurzweil, *The Singularity is Near*, p. 262.
19. The possibilities that have been envisaged for superhuman AI reach far beyond the simulation of individual personalities to the simulation of whole worlds. Some philosophers have argued that it is more than likely that we are living in a computer simulation. (See for example Bostrom, 'Are You Living in a Computer Simulation?') Arthur, of course, actually was living in a computer simulation. When he discovers this, he sees it as confirmation of his long-held suspicions that the world had some vast plan that he could never get a grip on. Slartibartfast tells him that 'that's just perfectly normal paranoia. Everyone in the Universe has that' (*Hitchhiker's*, ch. 30). Arthur swiftly leaps to the further inference* that the Universe itself could be a computer, before Slartibartfast pours cold water on his enthusiasm. Nonetheless, some physicists have come to share Arthur's suspicions that the Universe is intrinsically computational. 'We arrive at a point when the question "Is the Universe a computer?" becomes inevitable. Maybe Douglas Adams's story is not so science fiction[al]' (Calude, *Information and Randomness*, p. 207). On these matters, see further the chapter in this volume by Barry Dainton.
20. Kurzweil, *The Singularity is Near*, p. 323. On immortality, see, in this volume, the chapter by Tim Chappell.
21. Kurzweil, *The Singularity is Near*, p. 200.
22. Kurzweil, *The Singularity is Near*, p. 384.
23. As Adams observes, 'Some of the most revolutionary new ideas come from spotting something old to leave out rather than thinking of something new to put in ... A well-made dry martini works by the brilliant, life-enhancing principle of leaving out the martini. You also get dramatic advances when you spot that you can leave out part of the *problem*' (*Salmon*, pp. 115–16).
24. Arthur would be a zombie in the *philosophical* sense: he would not be shambling around calling for brains (even his own); he would be behaviourally indistinguishable from his old self, but would lack consciousness. The conceptual possibility of a philosophical zombie has been a major focus of recent debate in the philosophy of mind (Kirk, *Zombies and Consciousness*).
25. Quoted in Gaiman, *Don't Panic*, p. 41.

26. Many physicists reject this solution. For several decades, the standard interpretation of quantum mechanics was the so-called 'Copenhagen interpretation', which makes 'complementarity' a fundamental feature of reality. That is, some objects have ostensibly mutually contradictory properties which coexist but cannot be observed simultaneously. For example, on this interpretation, all particles are also waves, and vice versa. The many-worlds interpretation does not require the assumption of complementarity. In recent years, the many-worlds interpretation has grown considerably in popularity at the expense of the Copenhagen interpretation, and may even have overtaken it as the dominant approach.
27. Lewis, *Counterfactuals*, p. 84.
28. TV Tropes, http://tvtropes.org/pmwiki/pmwiki.php/Main/Lampshade Hanging.
29. Lewis, *Counterfactuals*, p. 86.
30. Gaiman, *Don't Panic*, p. 158.
31. Larkin and Thwaite, *Further Requirements*, p. 29.
32. Minsky, 'Jokes and their Relation to the Cognitive Unconscious', pp. 172–3.
33. Malcolm, *Ludwig Wittgenstein: A Memoir*, p. 29.
34. Cathcart and Klein, *Plato and a Platypus Walk into a Bar*, p. 2.
35. Webb, *Wish You Were Here*, p. 123.

9
The Funniest of All Improbable Worlds – *Hitchhiker's* as Philosophical Satire

Alexander Pawlak and Nicholas Joll

If the other parts of this book establish anything, it is that *Hitchhiker's* is not only a 'Rollercoaster of Ideas' (as ex-Python Terry Jones has called it) but a ride in which many of the ideas are *philosophical. This* chapter argues that one way in which *Hitchhiker's* is philosophical is by being – up to a considerable point, anyway – a *philosophical satire.*[1]

We start by getting some definitional stuff out the way, thereby keeping areas of doubt and uncertainty within professional limits. After that, we discuss satire and science fiction. Subsequent sections treat all sorts of funky stuff including Swift, Voltaire, Vroomfondel and Majikthise, perspective shifts, German philosophy, a bit of science, and the Ultimate Answer and the Ultimate Question. By the end of all this, it should be clear just how *Hitchhiker's* is philosophical satire. We hope that our argument won't be widely criticised as being extremely stupid.[2]

1   Defining terms: 'satire' and 'philosophical satire'

The term 'satire' originated in ancient Rome, a *lanx saturna* being 'a platter or a bowl [of] mixed fruits or food dishes'. Later on, but still in Roman times, the word came to mean, also, a kind of *verse*, namely verse that was something of a medley or hotchpotch and which 'denounce[d] various kinds of vice and folly'. The famous Roman satirist Juvenal (born in the first century CE) described his work thus:

> All the doings of mankind, their vows, their fears, their angers, their lusts, their pleasures, and their goings to and fro, these shall form the motley subject of my page.

Crucially, though, this sort of denunciatory verse intends to be *funny*. The same goes for the wider notion of satire that came to replace the Roman one. According to that wider and more recent notion, satire is any form of literature, or – on the widest use of the notion – anything at all, *which attacks by ridicule*.[3]

We are now in a position to appreciate why various satires get classified *as* satires. *Don Quixote* by Cervantes, *A Modest Proposal* by Swift, Bierce's *The Devil's Dictionary*, Orwell's *Animal Farm*, *Spitting Image*, or *The Simpsons* – all these (to take examples more or less at random) attack by ridicule. Or at least they ridicule by attack. (It's a matter of priorities. To *attack by ridicule* is for the humour to be mostly just a means of attack, whereas something that *ridicules by attack* has humour as its main goal.) *However*: it seems that satire must involve, further, *some sort of transfiguration*.[4] That transfiguration comes in many forms. One is caricature, which is itself, often, a mode of ridicule. *Spitting Image* is an example. A further form of

238 *Philosophy and* The Hitchhiker's Guide to the Galaxy

transfiguration used by satire is a kind of *co-option of a format or genre*. One sees this in Bierce's *Devil's Dictionary* – which doesn't actually pretend to be written by a devil (unlike *The Screwtape Letters* by C. S. Lewis) but does steal the diction-ary away from the pious and give it to the cynical. Another example is Mark Twain's *A Connecticut Yankee in King Arthur's Court*, which uses the form of the early medieval heroic saga in order to satirise nineteenth-century civilisation. There's also the form of satirical transfiguration that consists in *fantasy* (or the kind of fantasticalness that one gets in Science Fiction). One comes close to such fantasy in, say, Swift's *Modest Proposal* (wherein the proposal is that impoverished Irish people might ease their plight by selling their children as food for rich gen-tlemen) and actually *reaches* it in, say, Swift's *Gulliver's Travels* (on which more later) and – we will maintain – *Hitchhiker's*.

We conclude that satire is *attack by transfiguring ridicule*. But what of *philosophical* satire?

It could be various things. That is because 'philosophical satire' is a phrase that incorporates a so-called ambiguous genitive. We can compare the phrase 'stories of the Bugblat-ter Beast', which could mean stories *told by* the Bugblatter Beast or stories *about* the Bugblatter Beast. Indeed conceiv-ably it could mean *both* things, i.e. stories both told by and about the Bugblatter Beast. The same points hold for 'phil-osophical satire' (even though that phrase lacks the word 'of'). Philosophical satire could be (1) *satire of philosophy* in the sense of a satire that targets – satirises – philosophy. Alternatively, it could be (2) *philosophy as satire*: satire that does not target philosophy, but which is somehow phil-osophical in its own character. And, again, some single thing can be philosophical satire in *both* senses.[5]

Into which of these categories does *Hitchhiker's* fall, if any? Well, we will start by putting aside philosophy, and considering, first of all, the various ways in which *Hitchhiker's* is satirical. After that, we'll bring philosophy – *philosophical satire* – in.

2 *Hitchhiker's* as satire of science fiction

One way in which *Hitchhiker's* is satirical is by satirising science fiction, even though it itself has at least one foot in that genre. *Hitchhiker's* does that by flagrantly disregarding the conventions of science fiction and sometimes even turning them on their heads. *Hitchhiker's* targets at least four 'SF' conventions, themes or staples. (And here we build upon Kropf's fine article 'Douglas Adams's "Hitchhiker" Novels as Mock Science Fiction'.)

(1) *The last of their kind*. There's an SF and indeed fantasy norm for situations in which only two individuals of a species survive: they get together and, typically, proceed to procreate, thereby recreating the race. In *Hitchhiker's*, Arthur and Trillian come to be the only remaining humans. *But* they don't become romantically involved (despite an early attempt by Arthur) and they do not procreate. Well, they *do* procreate, but – and this adds to the satire – they do it without being sexually involved with each other. (See chapter 2, section 3, above.)

(2) *Space opera*. *Hitchhiker's* sends up pretensions of the SF 'space opera' subgenre. Witness this description of 'the great and glorious days of the former Galactic Empire', when 'life was wild, rich and largely tax free':

> Mighty starships plied their way between exotic suns, seeking adventure and reward amongst the furthest reaches of Galactic space. In those days spirits were brave, the stakes were high, men were real men, women

were real women, and small furry creatures from Alpha
Centauri were real small furry creatures from Alpha
Centauri. And all dared to brave unknown terrors, to do
mighty deeds, to boldly split infinitives that no man had
split before – and thus was the Empire forged.

(*Hitchhiker's Guide*, chapter 15)

Note also the treatment in *Hitchhiker* of the *Encyclopaedia
Galactica*, which might well be a parody of the thing that
goes by that name in Isaac Asimov's epoch-spanning *Foundation Trilogy*.

(3) *Robots*. The robots in *Hitchhiker's* are not at all the SF
norm. SF robots tend to be either emotionless or hostile or
mindlessly cheery. *Hitchhiker's* robots tend be to be neurotic.
See further Jerry Goodenough's chapter.

(4) *Explanations*. As a rule, SF deals in explicable things
(well, broadly; obviously, full explanation of the work-
ings of the matter transference beam, or whatever, is not
forthcoming). And it likes to offer grand explanations. An
example is Isaac Asimov's idea of psychohistory, described
in his novel *Foundation* as 'that branch of mathematics
which deals with the reactions of human conglomerates
to fixed social and economic stimuli'. Another example:
in Charles Harness's short story *The New Reality* (1950), the
secrets of the Universe are discovered by removing 'lamb-
das' from photons. One might instance, too, some of the
grander bits of technobabble in *Star Trek*. *Hitchhiker's* parodies technological explanation. Think of the Improbability
and Bistromathic drives. Moreover, it stomps upon the idea
that the wider scheme of things could make much sense.
That last point extends to the *Hitchhiker's* plot (if you can
call it a plot – which is the point): *Hitchhiker's* jumps from

one improbable situation, one bit of space and time, to another, and, where it creates the expectation of a climax, it subverts it. Want to know the meaning of life? It is, er, 42. Want to know, now, what that answer means? Happily, a computer has been built to find out. *Unhappily*, it gets destroyed five minutes before it was due to give its explanation. Then there's 'God's Final Message to his Creation', which, though written in massive letters of fire, turns out to be rather underwhelming. (We'll return to it, though.)[6]

Now, one might think that any satire of *science fiction* must itself be anticlimactic. Given its subject matter, isn't there a limit to how serious, or telling, or deep, satire of SF can be?[7] But two points mitigate – limit or tell against – this worry.

First, one can satirise various things *via* satire of SF. Here we have in mind something we've touched on already: technology. SF tends to glory in technology. Here on contemporary Earth, though, those fortunate (or 'fortunate') enough to have access to new technologies often find them troublesome. Adams was very much alive to this (despite his love of gadgets). Hence such things as: the 'please do not press this button again' button; the Heart of Gold's unusable radio; the Nutri-Matic machines (whose 'fundamental design flaws are completely hidden by their superficial design flaws'); the 'Ident-i-Eeze' ('technology's greatest triumph to date over both itself and plain common sense'); and 'the Great Ventilation and Telephone Riots'. All of this has a serious edge, part of which is this: small annoyances can mount up into a significant feature of life; and (in)ability to understand how things work is quite an important feature of life.[8] Second, SF can treat grand themes. As Stanislaw Lem has argued, some SF 'reports on mankind's destiny, on the meaning of life in the cosmos, on the rise and fall of thousand-year old civilizations: it brings forth a deluge of answers for the key questions of every reasoning being'. So, if *Hitchhiker's* satirises or parodies that sort of thing, then it might itself be saying something fairly serious. We will return to this when we discuss the meaning of life. For the moment, we consider how *Hitchhiker's* satirises – *directly* satirises – something other than SF (and other than technology).[9]

3   *Hitchhiker's* as broader satire

When I thought of my family, my friends, my country-men, or the human race in general, I considered them, as they really were, *Yahoos* in shape and disposition [. .]

(Swift, *Gulliver's Travels*, chapter X)

'Mean?' said Arthur, 'Mean? You know perfectly well what it means. It means that this planet is the Earth!'

(*The Restaurant at the End of the Universe*, chapter 33)

The earliest synopsis of the *Hitchhiker's* story refers to *Gulliver's Travels* by Jonathan Swift. Ford and Arthur, Adams wrote, are to

find that many of the eccentric alien races they encoun-ter epitomise some particular human folly such as greed, pretentiousness etc., rather in the manner of Gulliver's Travels.

(Original plot synopsis for *Hitchhiker's*, reproduced in Gaiman, *Don't Panic*, p. 194)

And so it came to pass – in the form of bureaucratic Vogons, greedy and decadent Magratheans, high-handed mice, and the hyper-aggressive and rather stupid 'Silastic Armorfiends', who get Hactar to build the Universe-destroying supernova bomb (and then try to use it to blow up a munitions dump), not to mention the childish 'teasers' (who, admittedly, aren't a race, but rather a bunch of rich kids). Then there are the Golgafrinchams of the 'B Ark'. This last lot can be feckless, greedy and destructive; and their captain can't get out of his bath. Moreover: the Golgafrinchams are *us*. Actually, the identity between us and the Golgafrinchams is more thoroughgoing than the identity, in *Gulliver's Travels*, between us and the 'Yahoos'. Ford to Arthur: 'Face it [. .] those zeebs over there are your ancestors' (*Restaurant*, chapter 33).

Like Swift, then, *Hitchhiker's* sends up our flaws, folly and vices. Indeed, like Swift, *Hitchhiker's* tends to do that via the device we might call the fantastical mirror. We say 'tends' because *Hitchhiker's* contains some satire of a more immediate type – i.e. satire that's independent of the Golgafrincham back-story and of the various alien races. Some of that further satire concerns bureaucracy and marketing and advertising. There is also Arthur himself, who represents a satire, though a gentle and even loving one, of Englishness. Further yet, there is *Hitchhiker's* mice-and-men conceit, which echoes Swift's role reversal of men and horses. A yet further parallel between Swift and Adams is that both make fun of science and philosophy. We consider that next.

4   *Hitchhiker's* as satire of philosophy

On the floating island of Laputa, Swift's Gulliver encounters research all of which is more or less nuts, and yet which is meant to recall actual research. One professor at an academy there 'has been eight years upon a project for extracting sunbeams out of cucumbers'. Another has a machine that conjoins words almost randomly and aims thereby to create 'books in philosophy, poetry, politics, laws, mathematics, and theology, without the least assistance from genius or study'. A third scholar proposes to relieve us of the burden of speaking, by having us carry objects the exhibition of which can serve, wordlessly, to convey thoughts. This last idea requires 'two strong servants' to cart all the labour-saving stuff around.[10]

Compare the cheeky portrait of the 'respectable physicists' in the *Hitchhiker's Guide to the Galaxy* (chapter 10) that describes the invention of the Infinite Improbability Drive. Recall also the scientists who 'discover' various well-known emotions via an experiment involving a robot and a herring sandwich. Still: Adams was, like Slartibartfast, a 'great fan of science' (*Hitchhiker's*, chapter 22; see also this book's Introduction). Consequently, Adams is not as rude about science as Swift can seem to be. The satirical drive of *Hitchhiker's* is more evident when dealing with *philosophy*. Witness the depiction of the bestselling author Oolon Colluphid. Note also the distinctly unflattering portraits of the philosophers Vroomfondel and Majikthise. Vroomfondel demands that he may or may not be Vroomfondel. Majikthise says, 'You just let the machines get on with the adding up [. .] and we'll take care of the eternal verities, thank you very much.' These two 'professional thinkers' even make the terrible threat of a national philosophers' strike. But Deep Thought calms them down – and reveals their real colours:

> 'So long as you can keep disagreeing with each other violently enough and slagging each other off in the popular press, and so long as you have clever agents, you can keep yourself on the gravy train for life. How does that sound?'

The two philosophers gaped at it [at Deep Thought].

'Bloody hell,' said Majikthise, 'now that is what I call thinking. Here, Vroomfondel, why do we never think of things like that?'

'Dunno,' said Vroomfondel in an awed whisper, 'think our brains must be too highly trained, Majikthise.'[11]

Also, of course, the names 'Vroomfondel' and 'Majikthise' teeter on the edge of extreme naughtiness.[12]

So: one way in which *Hitchhiker's* is philosophical satire is that it is satire *of* philosophy. But is there more? Might *Hitchhiker's* contain, despite the satire of philosophy, some philosophy *as* satire?

5   From satire of philosophy to philosophy as satire

We start here with some further satire *of* philosophy in *Hitchhiker's*. We do so because that satire of philosophy itself amounts to some satire *as* philosophy. Take, first, the 'qualified poet' who testified at a trial that 'beauty was truth, truth beauty and hoped thereby to prove that the guilty party was Life itself for failing to be either beautiful or true'. Consider also what 'Man' does once he has used the Babel fish to establish to his satisfaction that there's no God. Excited by this result, Man goes on, 'for an encore', 'to prove that black is white and gets himself killed on the next zebra crossing'. These two passages suggest a philo-sophical view in its own right. That view is an aversion to philosophies that lose their grasp on reality by being too simplistic or too complacent. And that view reflects – at least a bit – the attacks upon philosophical systems, or at least upon a kind of philosophical patness, that one finds in philosophers as diverse as Nietzsche, William James, Theodor Adorno, Ludwig Wittgenstein and Jacques Derrida.[13]

But there is more – as we can see by returning briefly to Swift. Swift said that he wrote to 'vex the world rather than to divert it'.[14] To cast that in the terms of a distinction introduced above: Swift meant to *attack* by ridicule at least as much as he meant merely to make fun. Indeed, and though truncated children's versions of the book obscure this fact, *Gulliver's Travels* presents deep and complex (if contestable) views on the politics, religion, science and philosophy of eighteenth-century England. Now, does the satire in *Hitchhiker's* extend to anything like that? That is, does it extend to philosophy as satire wherein the philosophy – the philosophy presented via satire – is ethics* and/or political philosophy*? We think it does. For the satire of/via the Vogons, Magratheans, Armorfiends, Golgafrinchams, etc. takes us into the foothills of ethical and political matters. Occasionally, indeed, *Hitchhiker's* gets a bit beyond the foothills. The second chapter of this book provides some support for that assertion.

Is there more yet? Is *Hitchhiker's* philosophy as satire in any further way? Quite possibly. Here's Adams in an interview:

> I like the aspects of [science fiction] which turn the telescope round, by letting you stand so far outside things and see them from a totally different perspective. That's what I try to do in *Hitchhiker's*, and that's what I think the best science fiction does. Science fiction that's just about people wandering around in space ships shooting each other with ray guns is very dull. I like it when it enables you to do fairly radical reinterpretations of human experience, just to show all the different interpretations that

can be put on apparently fairly simple and commonplace events. That I find fun.

(Adams with Shircore, 'Douglas Adams: the First and Last Tapes')

This viewing of events from a new and strange perspective is something, then, that unites Adams's fiction with traditional, or traditional-but-interesting, SF. But such perspective shifts are common in *philosophy*, too. (We take the term 'perspective shifts' from Webb's biography of Adams: *Wish You Were Here*, pp. 20–1.) Here are some examples.

David Hume (1711–76) admitted that the perspective he had achieved – according to which, for one thing, we can never know that anything causes anything else – was unnatural. For he confessed that, when he returned to his philosophy after taking some time off, his cogitations struck him as 'cold, and strain'd, and ridiculous'. Consider next Immanuel Kant (1724–1804). Much of Kant's philosophical project turned on the following idea. Rather than thinking that 'objects must conform to our knowledge', i.e. that to know an object is to have an accurate representation of it as a mind-independent thing, we should think as follows. Humans can grasp objects only by imposing a particular form upon them, such that (although here is where it gets tricky) objects are what they are – at least up to an important point – through the way we represent them. Then there's Edmund Husserl (1859–1938), who made a procedure he called 'bracketing' central to his philosophy. The procedure meant to shift one's perspective away from what Husserl called 'the natural attitude' and towards a distinctively unnatural perspective (which Husserl called 'phenomenological') whereby one perceives things solely *in the manner in which they appear* – and thus in an entirely presuppositionless way. For example: to perceive a cloud (or a tree, or a computer, or what have you) in that 'phenomenological' way is to make no assumptions about the kind of being it is, about what causes it, and even about whether or not it really exists. A final example of a philosophical perspective shift: some so-called Pragmatist philosophers have proposed that truths are true because they are useful, not useful because they are true.[15]

Return now to Adams. A large part of Adams's writerly brilliance was his ability to produce a great quantity of funny and arresting perspective shifts. One such shift features the Golgafrinchams and, specifically, the 'imaginative solution' to the problem of how to get rid of the 'useless third' of their planet's population (*Restaurant*, chapter 25). That idea affords a new perspective upon a whole slice of society, if only momentarily or somewhat jokily. Another example is the inverted house, named 'The Outside of the Asylum' and built by someone who has dropped the name 'John Watson' in favour of the tremendous moniker 'Wonko the Sane'. This amazing notion, *of building an asylum inside out, so that everyone else in the world becomes an inmate*, invites us to invert normal ideas about who is sane.[16]

Now, perspective shifts serve *satire* when, as in the Hitchhikery examples, they make something look ridiculous or doubtful. 'You organise your society like *that*?' 'You call *that* sanity?' And often such shifts have something philosophical about them. For they call into question some very deep assumptions.

An interim summary would be nice at this point. So:

- *Hitchhiker's* is satire in that it satirises SF, technology and, in Swiftian style, a range of human follies.
- *Hitchhiker's* is *philosophical* satire in that it is satire *of* philosophy.

- *Hitchhiker's* is philosophical satire in the further sense that it contains philosophy *as* satire. For it ventures, in its satire, into ethics and politics; and it contains some satirical shifts of perspective that have something philosophical about them.

We consider next a further, final and important way in which *Hitchhiker's* is philosophy as satire. It is here that we reach – work via – Voltaire and his famous satire *Candide*. (We do realise that this chapter is getting a bit long. We thank you for your patience.)

6   *Hitchhiker's*, Voltaire and the meaning of life

If this is the best of all possible worlds, what are the others?

(Voltaire, *Candide*, chapter 6)

[I]f that's their sales pitch, what must it be like in the complaints department?

Adams, *The Hitchhiker's Guide to the Galaxy*, 'Fit the Third' (in BBC, *The Hitchhiker's Guide to the Galaxy*)

François-Marie Arouet de Voltaire (1694–1778) was a major figure of the French Enlightenment*. He wrote an enormous range of works, including plays, poetry, novels, and historical and scientific essays and monographs. These works, which express a rebellious nature and a biting wit, criticise the clergy and advocate civil liberties. This brave outspokenness led to Voltaire being imprisoned in the Bastille and eventually to his being expelled from France. (He went to England, where, in fact, he met Swift.) Voltaire's overall philosophical mentality was characterised by scepticism, not so much about common-sense beliefs but principally about metaphysical* and theological dogmas. One of his main targets – and it is this that will take us to *Candide* – was the philosophy propounded by Gottfried Wilhelm Leibniz (1646–1716) and his followers.

What angered Voltaire about Leibnizian philosophy was its special brand of optimism.[17] A central text of that optimism is Leibniz's work *Theodicy** – *Essays on the Goodness of God, the Freedom of Man and the Origin of Evil* of 1710, which tried to solve 'the problem of evil'. That problem is this: the existence of an omnibenevolent (i.e. all-good), omnipotent (all-powerful) and omniscient (all-knowing) God seems incompatible with the existence of suffering, be it man-made or caused by nature. Leibniz's solution was to claim that, despite appearances, this is the 'best of all possible worlds' in that the suffering it contains is the *minimum possible*. One can say that this strategy tries to turn the problem of evil into its own solution. The argument goes something like this: God is good and omnipotent; and He chose our world out of all possibilities; so this world *must* be a good one and in fact the best of all worlds once one has ruled out the impossible ones.[18]

This 'best of all possible worlds' idea came to seem particularly problematic in 1755 – the year in which the great Lisbon earthquake killed tens of thousands and thereby cast doubt upon the idea that the world was in any way providentially arranged. Similar reactions have followed more recent horrific earthquakes such as those in Haiti in 2010 and in Japan in 2011. Can a world in which such enormous disasters happen really be the best possible one? Voltaire expressed that reaction in his *Poem on the Disaster of Lisbon*, written within weeks of the Lisbon earthquake and billed as 'An inquiry into the maxim, "whatever is, is right"'.[19] But it was his 'philosophical tale'[20] *Candide ou l'Optimisme* (translated as *Candide, or Optimism*), published in 1759, that constituted Voltaire's more thoroughgoing assault upon Leibnizian optimism.

Candide begins with a kind of Arcadian idyll set in 'a castle of Westphalia, belonging to the Baron of Thunder-ten-Tronckh'. Here lives Candide, a young man whose 'face was the true index of his mind. He had a solid judgement joined to the most unaffected simplicity; and hence, I presume, he had his name of Candide.'

Other residents include the Baron's wife and their daughter Miss Cunégonde, the latter being 'about seventeen years of age, fresh-coloured, comely, plump, and desirable'. There's also Pangloss, the tutor. Pangloss

> was the oracle of the family, and little Candide listened to his instructions with all the simplicity natural to his age and disposition. Master Pangloss taught the metaphysico–theologico–cosmo-boobie-ology. He could prove to admiration that there is no effect without a cause; and, that in this best of all possible worlds, the Baron's castle was the most magnificent of all castles, and My Lady the best of all possible baronesses.[21]

Now, because of a clinch with Miss Cunégonde, Candide is propelled from the castle – via a kick on the backside from the best of all possible Barons – and into war-torn Germany. From there, he gets jolted across the globe. His journeyings involve a series of shocks, made all the worse by his having internalised the doctrines of Pangloss – who, even in his name, with its connotation of 'total white-wash', is a caricature of a Leibnizian philosopher. (Voltaire and Adams share a gift for funny names.)

One shock that befalls Candide is the Lisbon earthquake. Others are the Inquisition and the atrocities of the Seven

Years' War. Those atrocities extend to Candide's beloved Cunégonde. Candide faints when he hears tell of what has happened to her. 'Her body was ripped open by the Bulgarian soldiers, after they had subjected her to as much cruelty as a damsel could survive; they knocked the Baron, her father, on the head for attempting to defend her'. In such ways – and the book consists mainly of those ways – is Candide's belief in the optimistic world view of Master Pangloss tested.

Hitchhiker's has quite a few parallels with *Candide*. Here are six (!).

(1) *An initiating disaster.* No actual disaster moved Adams to write *Hitchhiker's*. So there is no exact parallel with the Lisbon earthquake prompting Voltaire to write *Candide*. However: Arthur's adventures start with the destruction of the Earth, just as Candide's start with his expulsion from his Eden.

(2) *Loss of security.* Candide's basic security and basic assumptions take a pounding. So do Arthur's. After the initial shock of the destruction of the Earth ('"Look," said Arthur, "I'm a bit upset about that"'), Arthur learns that his planet 'was commissioned, paid for, and run by mice' for a purpose of their own. Gradually, he comes to doubt most things he had held to be true. He is 'blown up ridiculously often, shot at, insulted, regularly disintegrated', not to mention 'deprived of tea'.[22]

(3) *Love lost.* Both Arthur and Candide lose their loves. Candide does regain Cunégonde, but he finds that he no longer loves her. Arthur, too, regains his love (namely Fenchurch); but, later, he seems to lose her forever (in a hyperspace accident).

(4) *Optimists and pessimists.* In *Candide*, Pangloss personifies optimism and the doomy character 'Martin the Manichean' personifies pessimism. In *Hitchhiker's*, Marvin personifies pessimism and optimism is personified by (in various ways and to various degrees): Zaphod; Ford; Eddie

the shipboard computer; and Colin the Happy Robot. The last of this bunch – Colin the robot – is the cheeriest. At one point he reports to his superiors 'that everything was now for the best in this best of all possible worlds' (*Mostly Harmless*, chapter 6). This is an allusion to Leibniz and almost a direct quotation from *Candide*.[23] Note also that Colin is so very happy only because Ford has rewired his pleasure circuits, inducing a cyber-ecstasy trip.

(5) *Quests*. Candide's improbable adventures come to take on the character of a quest – a quest for happiness; and Arthur, too, seems to be seeking happiness.[24] Additionally, Arthur's adventures become, at least somewhat, a quest for something else, namely 'the Ultimate Question'.[25] Which takes us to –

(6) *The meaning of life*. The respective quests of Candide and Arthur bring each character to the view that life lacks any intrinsic meaning. Indeed, Candide comes to think that this world is very far indeed from being the best possible one. Arthur had never thought that this was the best possible world. However, he may have believed some weak English approximation to it, whereby Everything is Basically Not Too Bad. Moreover, not only *Candide* but also *Hitchhiker's* can be said to try to bring their *readers* to the view that life lacks intrinsic meaning. Or so we will argue. For, clearly, it is this last parallel that is the crux for our purposes. For if this parallel holds – if, like *Candide*, *Hitchhiker's* means to satirise an idea about the meaning of life – then it marks a particular and notable way in which *Hitchhiker's* combines satire with a serious philosophical topic. So let's investigate (and that investigation will be the chapter's last section).

7   Satirising the quest for ultimate truth

Amy Kind's chapter (chapter 3 of this book) does sterling work in showing that *Hitchhiker's* derides the idea that life has meaning. Amy makes the following points (among others).

1. *Hitchhiker's* emphasises how life can seem unintelligible and dwells on the seemingly absurd discrepancy between the import we attribute to ourselves, on the one hand, and our cosmic lack of significance, on the other.
2. 42 seems an absurd answer to the Question of Life, the Universe, and Everything (an absurdity that emphasises the absurdity at issue in 1).
3. *Hitchhiker's* denies that human life could gain meaning via either (i) immortality or (ii) our being a part of a plan conceived by other creatures, howsoever grand that plan may be.

We'd like to build upon these points.

We note, first of all, that the very idea of the meaning of life could use some clarification (even though much of the clarification that we will offer is already present, if somewhat implicitly, within Amy's chapter). What is to be clarified here is nothing less than the Ultimate Question of Life, the Universe and Everything. We give that clarification in the diagram on p. 256.

Admittedly, the diagram itself needs some clarification. So here is some commentary to accompany it. The diagram means to show how, in talk about the meaning of life, the meaning at issue could concern either (i) life's *character* or (ii) life's *cause* or (iii) life's *purpose* or (iv) *import*:

- The *character* of life is *the collection of features that comprise life's nature*, at least as that nature presents itself to sentient beings (and where 'life' can mean human life or life in general or the Universe). Is life suffering? Or a test? Is it a comedy, or a tragedy, or a senseless farce?

- The *cause* of life is an answer to the question, *How is it that human life, or life in general, or the Universe, exists?* An answer to that question could be some explanation of the aforementioned character of life. Moreover, *one* way of answering the question about life's cause is via an answer to the *next* version of the Ultimate Question. That next version is:

- What is the meaning of life in the sense of the *purpose* of life? What is life – or my life, or the Universe – *for*? Is there some higher being that has a purpose for us? If *not*, is there some other way in which life or the Universe can be said to have a purpose? Further: if that last scenario obtains – if no higher being has a purpose for us, but life nonetheless has a purpose – we can ask whether that purpose is *found* or whether, alternatively, it is *made*. To say that life has a purpose one can *find* is to say that life has a purpose that is somehow built into it – that is somehow objective or (to employ a term we've already used) intrinsic. To say that life has a purpose that is *made* is to say that, while life does have a purpose, that purpose is something created by us.

- What we are calling the *import* of life is the meaning of life in this sense: what life means (or should mean) for you or us. What should we *make of, do with*, life? How should I/we live?

We can plug Amy's points, or rather the brutal three-point summary that (p. 254) we gave of her points, into the schema we have just given. Take, first, the idea of an absurd discrepancy between the significance we attribute ourselves and our cosmic lack of significance. Or take the related idea that life is unintelligible or farcical. All that (which, in summarising Amy's points, we labelled '1') seems a matter of life's *character*

256

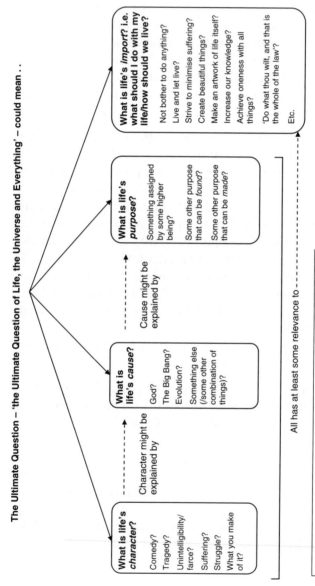

The Ultimate Question – 'the Ultimate Question of Life, the Universe and Everything' – could mean . .

What is life's *character*?

Comedy?
Tragedy?
Unintelligibility/
farce?
Suffering?
Struggle?
What you make
of it?

Character might be explained by

What is life's *cause*?

God?
The Big Bang?
Evolution?
Something else
(/some other
combination of
things)?

Cause might be explained by

What is life's *purpose*?

Something assigned
by some higher
being?
Some other purpose
that can be *found*?
Some other purpose
that can be *made*?

What is life's *import*? i.e. what should I do with my life/how should we live?**

Not bother to do anything?
Live and let live?
Strive to minimise suffering?
Create beautiful things?
Make an artwork of life itself?
Increase our knowledge?
Achieve oneness with all things?
'Do what thou wilt, and that is the whole of the law'?
Etc.

All has at least some relevance to - - - - - - - - - - ►

Note: within this diagram, the word 'life' itself has multiple meanings. It means *either* human life *and/or* life as such *and/or* the Universe/everything.

Figure The meanings of the Ultimate Question

(namely, unintelligibility!) and, perhaps, its *purpose* (or, rather, its *lack* of purpose, or of intrinsic purpose, anyway).[26]

What about the further idea (labelled '3' above) that immortality or being part of a grand plan would not make life meaningful? This is a point about purpose. More specifically, the idea is this. Even if life *did* have a purpose, or at least an intrinsic one, then that purpose would be wholly or largely *irrelevant* to what we are calling life's *import*, i.e. to how we should live our lives.

As to the absurdity of 42 (which is the point we numbered '2'), that seems to be a brilliant two-digit summary of the foregoing points – the points about unintelligibility, lack of purpose, and about how, anyway, some purposes wouldn't help. For '42' makes no sense as a literal answer to the question 'What is life's character?', or to the question 'What is life's purpose?', or to the question 'How should one live?'

42 is crucial for the connection with satire. For that absurd non-answer to the Ultimate Question (or, as we've seen, Ultimate Question*s*) doesn't just deny, but also sends up, presents as crazy, caricatures – in a word, *satirises* – the idea that life is intrinsically meaningful. And several aspects of *Hitchhiker's* sharpen that satire. We've noted one such sharpening already. To wit: the Earth was destroyed *five minutes* before it was due to impart the Ultimate Question (the Question which, it was hoped, would enable us to make sense of 42 as an answer) – destroyed, in fact, to make a road.[27] Further: what the Earth was due to impart *would have been wrong anyway*, because the human race is descended, not, as planned, from the planet's original cavemen, but from the less than ideal Golgafrinchams. Hence the 'six by nine' farce in *The Restaurant at the End of the Universe* (chapter 33). Hence too, presumably, the character of life on Earth.[28] Further yet: we learn (at the very start of *Restaurant* and in the epilogue to *Life*) that the Ultimate Question and the Ultimate Answer

might not be knowable in the same universe, or that, if they are, and someone actually learns what both of them are, then they get replaced by an even more inexplicable set-up; and that indeed *this may have happened already.*

It is as if the intelligibility or purpose of the Universe were a clown whom Adams wants to hit not once but multiple times with a custard pie. Indeed we have it on record, sort of, that Adams thought life had no inbuilt purpose. For his long-time friend and colleague John Lloyd has said that Adams 'didn't believe life was meaningful' (Lloyd in Simpson, *Hitchhiker*, p. xvi). Nonetheless, there is some comfort for our bespattered clown. For there *is* a way in which a number can make sense as an Answer. It can make sense as an answer to the question about the *cause* of life (or of the Universe) and so can make sense also, perhaps, as some explanation of the *character* of life (or the Universe). Consider the so-called fundamental constants of physics. These are numbers that, were they to have been just a little different, would have had a huge effect upon the Universe and could well have prevented most things from existing. Actually, *42 itself* is something of a candidate for being a pretty important number, though not quite a fundamental constant. There was a period (though a period *before* Adams cooked up '42') when the Hubble constant, which expresses the rate at which the universe is expanding, was thought to have the value 42. There's also molybdenum, an element with an atomic number of 42 – it has 42 protons in its nucleus – and which is necessary for much life including human life. Apparently, too, molybdenum is . . the forty-second most common element in the Universe! But it remains true that none of this numerical stuff much helps with the 'purpose' and 'how to live' questions.[29]

God's Final Message To His Creation might seem like a further custard pie. The Message is: 'We apologise for the inconvenience' (*So Long*, chapter 40). Life as an inconvenience! (That gets in the way of . . well, what exactly?) *But* this message manages to comfort Marvin; and it seems to be identical in its content to Fenchurch's epiphany – the epiphany she had moments before the Earth was destroyed and which she subsequently forgot. (You might think you wouldn't forget something like that. But you weren't pulled through the WSOGMM in the way that Fenchurch was.) The epiphany was about how 'the world could be made a good and happy place' and Fenchurch finds that this realisation makes everything make sense to her.[30] The idea here – the message of the Message/of the epiphany – seems to be twofold. The Universe has no intrinsic purpose; there's no purpose one can find as against create. And to realise this lack of intrinsic purpose, this lack of 'Ultimate Truth', is reassuring or liberating. Here, then, one has a final and more positive take on the meaning of life, according to which the lack of an intrinsic purpose – together presumably with the farcical nature of the Universe or at least of human affairs – does not entail a 'give up' answer to the question of how one should live.[31]

Adams's more particular view of life – of whether it is worth living, of whether we can give it any decent purpose – seems to have been as follows. The marvels of the world give us a sufficient reason to hang around (although this will apply, of course, only to those whose lives allow them to appreciate those marvels). Here's Adams in Channel 4's *Break the Science Barrier*:

The world is a thing of utter, inordinate, complexity and richness and strangeness that is absolutely awesome. I mean that the idea that such complexity can arise not only out of such simplicity, but probably absolutely out of nothing, is the most fabulous, extraordinary idea, and once you get some kind of inkling of how that might have happened, it's just wonderful, and I feel that, you know, the opportunity to spend 70–80 years of your life in such a universe is time well spent, as far as I'm concerned.

We will not further explore or defend these views (nor consider their parallels, or further parallels, with *Candide*).[32] What we *have* done, is to explore how the improbable world of *Hitchhiker's* takes in various kinds of satire, including satire of philosophy and – especially in the form of satire of Ultimate Truth – philosophy *as* satire. That's enough to be getting on with, we think.[33]

For deeper thought

- Carl Kropf, 'Douglas Adams's "Hitchhiker" Novels as Mock Science Fiction'.
- Jonathan Swift, *Gulliver's Travels*.
- Voltaire's *Candide*. The Penguin edition of this text (which is the one we've used, and the one in the bibliography) includes a great many explanatory notes and also Voltaire's poem on the Lisbon earthquake. For an overview of Voltaire's life and work, see Gary Gutting, 'Voltaire'.
- Amy Kind's chapter, above. (If you haven't read it already.)
- Adam Roberts, '42'.
- John Wisdom, 'The Meanings of the Questions of Life' – a short article investigating what is at issue with the meaning of life.
- Steven Lukes, *The Curious Enlightenment of Professor Caritat: a Comedy of Ideas*. This 1995 book is very much in the style of *Gulliver's Travels* and satirises various political philosophies*.

Notes

1. The quotation is from the foreword by Terry Jones to the thirtieth anniversary edition of *The Restaurant at the End of the Universe*. Also: we'd like to put readers on notice that sometimes in this chapter we shove all the notes pertaining to a paragraph – all the references and other gubbins – into a single note at the end of the paragraph.

2. On professional limits, one can hear Thomas Hobbes (1588–1679): 'The first cause of Absurd conclusions I ascribe to the want of Method; in that they begin not their Ratiocination from Definitions' (*Leviathan*, ch. 5, p. 20). But contrast Nietzsche, who was never one to toe the line: 'only something that has no history can be defined' (*On the Genealogy of Morality*, essay 2, section 13, p. 57). As to the criticisability (as it were) of our argument: our case does have precursors. Others have characterised *Hitchhiker's* as satirical, among them several contributors to Yeffeth's *Anthology at the End of the Universe*. Indeed, some essays therein compare *Hitchhiker's* – as we will compare it – to *Gulliver's Travels* and to *Candide*. (See the essays by Day and Shirley. See also Hourihan, *Deconstructing the Hero*, p. 211.) Moreover, we haven't invented the term 'philosophical satire'. The term goes back at least to the nineteenth century and is, today, in fairly common currency. Philosophical satire itself – i.e. the thing, not the phrase – dates back to ancient Greece and Rome. Indeed they had a whole genre – which has come to be called 'Menippean satire', after the philosopher Menippus – which often involved philosophical satire. Later, philosophical satire flourished during the Enlightenment*. (By 'philosophical satire' here, we mean either what the next section of the main text will distinguish as 'satire as philosophy' *or* what it will call 'satire of philosophy' *or* a mixture of the two.) Finally here, and as to *Hitchhiker's* as philosophical satire: we've encountered no one who calls it *exactly* that; but it is often described, in a single breath, as philosophical and as satire.

3. 'Platter or a bowl': see Quintero's Introduction to his *A Companion to Satire*, p. 6. (The Latin *satur* means full. *Lanx* is a noun useable for anything flat or broad – and thus can mean dish or platter.) 'Denounced various kinds of vice and folly': Hodgart, *Satire*, p. 132. The quotation from Juvenal is from his *Satires*, I, lines 85–6, as quoted (and seemingly translated) by Hodgart, *Satire*, p. 132. 'Attacks by ridicule' is a close paraphrase from Hodgart's *Satire*, p. 7.

4. Or distortion, or transmutation, or fantasy. Hodgart seems to build a clause to this effect into his definition of satire. Compare also Connery and Combe, *Theorizing Satire*, p. 8.

5. Actually, any piece of philosophical satire is fairly likely to fit both headings. That's because anything that tries to make a philosophical point

via satire – i.e. any 'satire as philosophy' – is liable to do so by satirising some existing philosophy or philosopher. Still, a *thoroughgoing* satire of philosophy could not consistently be philosophical, since one can't attack philosophy *as such* whilst also meaning to be philosophical.

6. The Asimov quotation is from his *Foundation*, p. 16. As to *Star Trek* technobabble, here's an example. 'I'd have to get into the biofilter bus and patch in a molecular matrix reader; that's no problem. But the waveform modulator would be overloaded without the regeneration limiter in the first stage circuit' – Chief O'Brien in *Star Trek: the Next Generation*, Season 2: Unnatural Selection (1988).

7. The mention we've just made of *parody* suggests a related worry. Parody can indeed be, and often is, classified as a type of satire. *But* parody is heavy on imitation (heavier on it than satire need be); and that means that, when the object of parody is something literary, parody concentrates upon *style* or *form*; and that in turn means that parody will tend to be more of a playing for laughs, or an exercise in showing off, than an attempt to make a substantial critical point. In short: parody has a tendency to become mere pastiche. So if *Hitchhiker's* is (only) parody, then it is unlikely to be *real* or *serious* satire.

8. Here are the references. The button: *Hitchhiker's Guide*, ch. 11. Nutri-Matics and flaws thereof: *Life, the Universe and Everything*, ch. 35. Ident-i-Eeze: *Mostly Harmless*, ch. 6. Riots: *Mostly Harmless*, ch. 12. Many of these examples are mentioned by Byrne, 'Beware of the Leopard', p. 3. We add that there is such a thing as 'the philosophy of technology', although we haven't the space to get into that in this chapter. But here, at least, are some sources: Feenberg, *Questioning Technology*; Crawford, *The Case for Working with Your Hands*; Borgmann, *Technology and the Character of Everyday Life*.

9. The Lem quotation is from his *Microworlds*, p. 59 (quoted in Kropf, 'Douglas Adams's "Hitchhiker" Novels . .', p. 67). Now, one might ask whether there is SF other than *Hitchhiker's* that is satirical. There is, but not in any great quantity if we continue to take *humour* – or ridicule, which involves humour – as a necessary condition* of satire. Still: perhaps humour is *not* necessary for satire. For perhaps *wit* suffices to make something – something critical of society (or of ideas or people, etc.) and which involves some sort of transfiguration – into satire. If so, then more SF will count as satire. For much SF uses transfiguration – the transfiguration that is almost inherent in the medium – as a means to social criticism; and that device can be witty. Indeed, it is almost intrinsically witty, because it involves the cleverness of a kind of allegory. If we adopt this 'wit' construal of satire, then we might count as satire such a work as Ray Bradbury's SF novel *Fahrenheit 451*.

10. All quotations in this paragraph are from *Gulliver's Travels*, Part III, ch. V. The particular target of all this, incidentally, was the 'new science' of Francis Bacon (1561–1626). That science was to be resolutely empirical* and free of the shackles of tradition and it would – Bacon hoped – improve the human condition. Swift seems to have been rather sceptical of all this. See Real and Vienken, *Jonathan Swift: 'Gulliver's Travels'*, p. 88 and Simpson, 'Francis Bacon'.

11. All of this is from *Hitchhiker's*, ch. 25. Irvine Welsh's short story 'The Two Philosophers', collected in his book *The Acid House*, tells of two philosophers who make their careers by vehemently disagreeing with each other. They even come to blows.

12. Still: Deep Thought's programmers – the two programmers whose discussion with Deep Thought gets interrupted by the philosophers – have the not-exactly-sensible names of Lunkwill and Fook. Here we begin to see that Adams is pretty much 'an equal-opportunity mocker', in that 'his targets are freely distributed across the spectrum' (Day, 'The Subversive Dismal Scientist', p. 118).

13. The 'qualified poet' makes the argument in *Restaurant*, ch. 6. Actually, that argument (which is a somewhat aesthetic* one, and which repeats the venerable philosophical idea that the good, the true, and the beautiful are somehow one and the same thing) makes some sense. As Albert Camus stressed, frequently life does fail to meet our expectations. But the use to which the judge puts the testimony does *not* make sense. On God and the Babel fish, see *Hitchhiker's*, ch. 6 and also Michèle Friend's chapter. On the Camus point, see the chapter by Amy Kind.

14. The line is from a letter Swift wrote to Alexander Pope. The line is widely quoted, as for instance in Henry Craik, *The Life of Jonathan Swift, Dean of St. Patrick's, Dublin*, vol. 2, p. 119. Swift was indeed a clergyman – and he got nicknamed 'the mad parson'.

15. The Hume quote is from his *Treatise of Human Nature*. For a fuller quotation of the passage, see section 4 of the chapter by Amy Kind. The Kant is from his *Critique of Pure Reason*, Bxvi (i.e. page xvi of the preface to the second edition of that book). Incidentally: one aim of Kant's shift of perspective was to invalidate the results that Hume had reached via *his* change of perspective! On Husserl, see section 4.a.i. of Joll, 'Contemporary Metaphilosophy'. As to pragmatism, William James said this: '"The true" is that which, "in almost any fashion", but "in the long run and on the whole", is *"expedient in the way of our thinking"*' (James, *Pragmatism*, p. 86). That statement is rather notorious, but that is partly because, too often, it is quoted without the caveats (namely the 'in *almost* any fashion' and 'in the long run and on the whole').

16. The 'imaginative solution' is to send the useless third of the population off into space on some pretence involving a giant space-goat,

or something, and with a false promise that the other two-thirds of the population – the third that does all the work and the third that runs things – will follow later. The Wonko material is from *Life*, esp. ch. 15. We note that it was finding instructions on a pack of toothpicks that finally convinced Wonko that the world at large was insane. But perhaps Nicholas Joll can top that. Recently he bought some bananas that came in a plastic packet bearing the instruction, 'Peel fruit from top.' Note also the following bit of philosophy of science* from Wonko. 'I'm not trying to prove anything, by the way. I'm a scientist and I know what constitutes proof. But the reason I call myself by my childhood name [presumably John Watson was called 'Wonko' as a child] is to remind myself that a scientist must also be absolutely like a child. If he sees a thing, he must say that he sees it, whether it was what he thought he was going to see or not. See first, think later, then test. But always see first. Otherwise you will only see what you were expecting. Most scientists forget that' (*So Long*, ch. 31, our addition).

17. Another thing Voltaire had against Leibniz was, perhaps, the rivalry between Leibniz and Newton as to who had discovered calculus. Voltaire greatly admired Newton.

18. We apologise if this sounds as if copied off the back of a packet of breakfast cereal. Leibniz was of course a far more accomplished member 'of the Amalgamated Union of Philosophers, Sages, Luminaries and Other Thinking Persons' than this summary suggests. On the problem of evil, see further section 2.3 of Michèle Friend's chapter. There is more on Leibniz in the chapters by Michèle Friend and Andrew Aberdein.

19. The following extracts (*Candide*, pp. 100–6) give an impression of the poem's tone.

> Oh wretched man, earth-fated to be cursed;
> Abyss of plagues, and miseries the worst!
> Horrors on horrors, griefs on griefs must show,
> That man's the victim of unceasing woe,
> And lamentations which inspire my strain,
> Prove that philosophy is false and vain.
> Approach in crowds, and meditate awhile
> Yon shattered walls, and view each ruined pile [. .]

There follow some lines about the earthquake itself – and then this:

> Leibniz can't tell me from what secret cause
> In a world governed by the wisest laws,
> Lasting disorders, woes that never end

With our vain pleasures real sufferings blend;
Why ill the virtuous with the vicious shares?

20. 'Philosophical tale' (French: *conte philosophique*) is a term often applied to some of Voltaire's output.

21. All these quotations are from *Candide*, ch. 1. We've slightly altered the translation of the passage we inset. The quotation in the next paragraph is from *Candide*'s fourth chapter.

22. 'Bit upset': *Hitchhiker's*, ch. 5. 'Commissioned, paid for, and run by mice': *Hitchhiker's*, ch. 24. 'Blown up' etc.: *Life*, ch. 22. On Arthur's coming to doubt most things he had thought true, compare Mrs E. Kapelsen in *So Long*, ch. 26.

23. It might be worth expanding a little upon some of these points. So: when Candide tells Martin 'yet there is some good in the world', Martin replies, 'Maybe so, but it has escaped my knowledge' (*Candide*, ch. 20). Elsewhere – and echoing an aspect of the pessimistic philosophy of Schopenhauer – Martin declares: 'man was born to endure either the convulsions of anxiety or the lethargy of boredom' (*Candide*, ch. 30). Manichaeism (also spelt Manicheism, i.e. without the 'a') is the view that the cosmos is a battleground between a good deity and an evil one, and that the outcome is not predetermined. This view arose as a variation of Christianity in the third century after Christ but resembled the much older Zoroastrian religion. The mainstream Church branded Manichaeism a heresy – whereas Schopenhauer thought the idea fairly sensible. See his 'On the Sufferings of the World', in which he rates creation stories by blackness. The grimmer the story – the more it fits with what Schopenhauer takes to be the terrible state of things – the more he likes it. Still, *Candide*'s Martin has a rival for the title of 'most perfect instantiation of Schopenhauer's pessimism'. The rival is of course Marvin. Marvin claims to be 'fifty thousand times more intelligent' (*Hitchhiker's*, ch. 19) than human beings, and, famously, opines thus: 'Life, loathe it or ignore it, you can't like it' (*Hitchhiker's*, ch. 20). Compare Schopenhauer: 'knowledge is no way out of the vale of tears of life. The higher the manifestation of life, the heavier and more obvious is the suffering' (Störig, *Kleine Weltgeschichte der Philosophie*, p. 511; translation by Jutta Pistor). There's a bit more about Schopenhauer in chapter 3 above.

24. Doesn't everyone, or just about everyone, pursue happiness? Not according to Nietzsche. 'Man does *not* strive after happiness; only the Englishman does that' (*Twilight of the Idols*, 'Maxims and Arrows', section 12, p. 33).

25. See especially *Restaurant*, ch. 20 and the references given in note 30 below. The quest for the Ultimate Question seems to get bound up with the quest to find the Ruler of the Universe. On that latter quest,

see especially *Hitchhiker's*, chs 14–16 and 29, *Restaurant*, chs 3, 12, 27–29, and *Life*, Epilogue. Perhaps the idea is that the Ruler will know the purpose of the Universe, or will *give* it a purpose.

26. Still: in the final analysis, the idea of a cosmic lack of significance may not actually make sense. Timothy Chappell (in section 2 of his chapter in this book) gives us one reason for that doubt. He asserts: 'Quite simply, size is one thing, significance another.' *However*, often size *does* affect significance. Rickmansworth is a less significant town than London because, or because of things to do with, the relative sizes of those places. But there is a different reason for thinking that the idea of a lack of cosmic significance does not make sense. It's this. Perhaps, from the point of view of the Universe, nothing either has *or lacks* significance. If so, then from that perspective, human doings neither matter nor fail to matter. (One might say: from that *so-called* perspective. For another way to put the point is this: there *is* no point of view of the Universe, no view *sub specie aeternitatis*, as philosophers sometimes say.) That said, it is arguable that this result, whereby we are not even candidates for *failing* to matter, just makes things *worse*. It is a shame that this material, which relates to the cover of the book, has ended up in an endnote. But that's just the way the cookie crumbles.

27. Actually, it turns out that there's more of a reason than that. But the extra reason, which is given in the following passage, is itself somewhat perverse (*Restaurant*, ch. 4).

> Ten light years away, Gag Halfrunt jacked up his smile by several notches. As he watched the picture on his vision screen, relayed across the sub-ether from the bridge of the Vogon ship, he saw the final shreds of the Heart of Gold's force-shield ripped away, and the ship itself vanish in a puff of smoke.
>
> Good, he thought.
>
> The end of the last stray survivors of the demolition he had ordered on the planet Earth, he thought.
>
> The final end of this dangerous (to the psychiatric profession) and subversive (also to the psychiatric profession) experiment to find the Question to the Ultimate Question of Life, the Universe, and Everything, he thought.
>
> There would be some celebration with his fellows tonight, and in the morning they would meet again their unhappy, bewildered and highly profitable patients, secure in the knowledge that the Meaning of Life would not now be, once and for all, well and truly sorted out, he thought.

For further satire of psychiatrists, see *The Long Dark Tea-Time of the Soul*, ch. 11.

28. Compare Roberts, '42', p. 49. On our Golgafrincham ancestry being the explanation of our stupidities, compare Jones's Foreword to *Restaurant* and Rosen, 'The Holy Trilogy', p. 74.

29. That said: were the Answer 'zero', 'one' or 'infinity' (Roberts, '42', pp. 55–6), or perhaps 'two', then it *could* be interpreted as speaking to the 'purpose' and/or 'how to live' questions. For then the Answer might express, respectively, the Emptiness of Everything, or the Oneness of All Things (or fundamental interconnectedness of all things, as in *Dirk Gently's Holistic Detective Agency*), or the Unlimitedness of Things, or the Duality of all Things – although each of these notions (especially perhaps the one about unlimitedness) would call for more explanation. But it seems to us that those numbers would not, here, be operating really as mere numbers. Still, infinity is a funny kind of number anyway (as too, perhaps, is zero). On infinity, see Andrew Aberdeen's chapter. Our source for molybdenum being the 42nd most common element in the universe is Gill, *42*, p. 166.

30. The 'good and happy place' formulation owes to the near identical prefaces to *Hitchhiker's Guide* and *So Long*. That construal of the Question is proposed – proposed explicitly *as* an interpretation of the Question – in a conversation between Arthur and Ford (*Restaurant*, ch. 26). But they reject the construal on the ground that it doesn't fit the answer – or 'Answer' – '42'. On the idea that the Answer makes sense of everything, see *So Long*, ch. 20. There's also the story (in the same chapter) about the animals and the raft – which, frankly, foxes us. (Actually, Nick Joll wrote that last bit. But Alex Pawlak concurs; he says that the story 'otters' him.)

31. In fact, there's one more pie (another one!) we haven't mentioned. It consists in this: one of the various accounts of how Adams came to pick 42 as the Ultimate Answer is *itself* deliberately absurd. To wit: he chose 42 because it was the funniest of the two-digit numbers. This wonderful joke is compatible with another explanation that Adams gave of why he picked 42, namely, that 42 is an entirely unremarkable number. On such matters, see Gill, *42*, pp. 316–21, and Simpson, *Hitchhiker*, pp. 12–13.

32. For more on the idea of complexity-from-simplicity, though, see section 3 of this book's Introduction.

33. Nicholas Joll would like to thank James Robson and Naoko Yamagata and the other classicists whom those two members of the Open University's Department of Classical Studies enlisted upon this book's behalf. Alexander Pawlak's acknowledgements run as follows. Hoopy thanks to Jutta Pistor, Carrie Mowatt and Viola Küstner for reading

drafts and for providing valuable comments and corrections; thanks also to Christine Mayer for the *Star Trek* quote. A galactic 'thank you' to my co-writer Nicholas for his patience and helpfulness and for giving me the chance to be part of this wholly remarkable book. His froody contribution turned my bric-a-brac into consistent text. I am sure that the great publishing houses of Ursa Minor would be proud of an editor of his capabilities.

Glossary

One of the major selling points of that wholly remarkable travel book, *The Hitchhiker's Guide to the Galaxy* [. .] is its compendious and occasionally accurate glossary.

(*The Restaurant at the End of the Universe*, chapter 19)

Our job, as we see it, is to get these words down from the heights of academe and into the mouths of babes and sucklings and so on, where they can start earning their keep in everyday conversation (well, OK, maybe not quite *everyday* conversation) and make a more positive contribution to society.

(Adams and Lloyd, *The Meaning of Lif The Deeper Meaning of Liff*, Preface; somewhat altered)

The purpose of the alphabetically ordered glossary below is to explain pieces of philosophical jargon. The titles of the glossary entries are in small capitals, LIKE THIS. The same goes for cross-references within entries, i.e. references, within entries, to terms that have their own definitions *elsewhere* in the glossary. So: if, for instance, you come across 'ETHICS' – written like that, but without the quotation marks – *within* an entry, then that means that 'ethics' has its own entry in the glossary.

The glossary is a kind of philosophical Babel fish. But the vocabulary of this fish is limited. For the glossary features *only* those terms that the main text has stuck an asterisk next to. (The word 'philosophy' is an exception. It gets a glossary entry but it's not asterisked in the book.) However, this fish does go on a bit – in that the glossary's explanations err on the side of generosity. In order to avoid the cry of 'this is just far too much!' (*Hitchhiker's*, chapter 14), *the more difficult or less important stuff is safely partitioned off through the use of a special font*, namely, `this` `one`. So, the normal font means 'don't panic!', whereas `this` `font` means either 'panic!' or 'if you're not very interested, you might find this "quite sensationally dull"' (*Life, the Universe and Everything*, chapter 22). Finally: if you need a philosophical Babel fish with a wider vocabulary, then please see the section at the end of the glossary that is called 'Further resources (everything you never wanted to know about philosophy but may be forced to find out)'.

AESTHETICS, AESTHETIC. Something is aesthetic if it has to do with beauty or appearance or – and this is the most philosophical sense of the term – with the discipline called 'aesthetics'. Aesthetics is the philosophical investigation of art and of the beauty (and, indeed, the 'sublimity') of nature. Questions of aesthetics include: What is beauty? What makes something sublime? What is art? What makes, say, Lallafa's *Songs of the Long Land* better than, say, Vogon poetry? `The word 'aesthetics' derives from the ancient Greek word for perception or sensation (`*`aisthesis`*`).`

ANALYTIC. There are various definitions of 'analyticity' (or 'analytic truth'). Roughly, though, a statement is analytic if, and only if, it is true by definition. Examples of statements often thought to be analytic (there's disagreement about what is analytic and even about whether *anything* is analytic) are: 'A bachelor is an unmarried man'; 'Circles are round'; '2 + 2 = 4'; and (!) 'God exists'. One could almost include 'hitchhikers have no money' and 'Arthur has had an accident'. An 'analytic untruth', or something that is analytically false, would be something that is false by definition. A matter of particular dispute, and a central question of METAPHYSICS and EPISTEMOLOGY, is whether all A PRIORI knowledge (if indeed there is any such knowledge) is analytic (if indeed there is any such thing as analytic knowledge).

A POSTERIORI. EPISTEMOLOGICAL term that means known (or at least know*able*) through experience. Literally (from the Latin) 'from what comes after'. Contrast A PRIORI.

A PRIORI (sometimes written without the space as 'apriori'). EPISTEMOLOGICAL term that means known, or at least know*able*, without experience. The question of whether anything is known a priori, and, if so, what, has been debated since at least Plato. A very literal translation of the Latin 'a priori' is 'from the prior', i.e. from that which comes earlier.

BEG THE QUESTION. To beg the question is to assume the very thing one is claiming to *demonstrate* – and, thus, to argue in a circle. See further note 4 to chapter 7.

CONDITIONS, NECESSARY AND/OR SUFFICIENT. A necessary condition for something is a 'without which not'. For instance: you can't be a woman who is cleverer than Trillian if you are not a woman; being a woman is a necessary condition for being such a person. So is being cleverer than Trillian. But neither of these conditions, on its own, *suffices* for being a woman who is cleverer than Trillian. Rather, you need to satisfy *both* conditions; together, but only together, the conditions are *sufficient* for the thing in question (being a woman who is cleverer than Trillian). Some conditions, though, are sufficient on their own. For instance, having the chromosome combination called 'XX' is sufficient for being biologically a human female. All of this may sound dull and obvious. But many philosophers have been very keen on doing necessary-and-sufficient-condition analysis.

The idea was that thereby one achieves a nice scientific precision and can even get at the *essences* of things (or, at least, at the essences of the *concepts* of things). Wittgenstein poured cold water on this idea by maintaining that very few concepts actually have necessary and sufficient conditions. His famous example was the concept game. ('Try and find necessary and sufficient conditions for *that*!', he said. In effect.) Compare the line quoted from Nietzsche in chapter 9, note 2.

DETERMINISM. The view that every event is necessitated by prior events. Hence if determinism is true then the future is entirely determined (fixed) before it happens. Many but not all philosophers believe that determinism rules out FREE WILL.

EMPIRICAL, EMPIRICISM. Something is called 'empirical' if it is a matter of experience and, especially, of verifiable observation (i.e. observation that can be publicly and/or scientifically reproduced and checked). EMPIRICISM is the EPISTEMOLOGICAL view that all or at least most knowledge is empirical, i.e. A POSTERIORI.

ENLIGHTENMENT. 'The Enlightenment': cultural and intellectual movement associated historically especially with eighteenth-century Europe and characterised by opposition to authoritarianism and belief in reason as against dogma and superstition. 'Enlightenment' (without the 'the'): the state of apprehending the truth or the achieving of that state. Sometimes, especially when the word is written with a capital letter, and particularly in the context of Eastern religions, the reference is to a state of specifically spiritual or religious enlightenment or salvation.

EPISTEMIC, EPISTEMOLOGICAL, EPISTEMOLOGY. 'Epistemic' means to do with knowledge. Epistemology is the branch of philosophy that studies knowledge. So something is epistemological if, and only if, it has to do with *that* – with the philosophical study of knowledge. That said, sometimes 'epistemic' and 'epistemological' are used inter-changeably. Much epistemology tries to counter various forms of philosophical SCEPTICISM.

ETHICS/ETHIC. In one sense: MORAL PHILOSOPHY, i.e. roughly, the study of how one should live. In another sense: any *particular* account of how one should live, i.e. 'ethics' in the sense of *an* ethics/an ethic. In this second sense, 'ethics' is at least largely synonymous with MORALITY.

EUDAIMONIA (EUDAIMON, EUDAIMONES). *Eudaimonia* is an Ancient Greek word that is associated especially with Aristotle. Sometimes it is translated as 'happiness'. Alternative translations are 'living well' and – perhaps the best translation – 'flourishing'. So to possess *eudaimonia* (to be *'eudaimon'*) is to flourish (and *'eudaimones'* are those who flourish). See also THEORIA.

FORMAL LOGIC. See LOGIC.

FREE WILL. The view that the human will is, at least on occasion, free. Often (but, in fact, not always!), free will is thought to be incompatible with DETERMINISM.

INDUCTION. Induction is INFERENCE 'from a finite number of particular cases to a further case or to a general conclusion' (Mautner, *Dictionary of Philosophy*, p. 273). Example: it has rained on Rob McKenna every day of his life; hence it will rain on him tomorrow. Strictly speaking, inductive arguments are not the kind of arguments that can be VALID. Is that a failing? Perhaps VALIDITY, which pertains only to so-called deductive argument, is just *irrelevant* to inductive argument. Compare: it is no criticism of a painting that it can never be a good piece of music!

INFERENCE. To make an inference is to infer – derive – something from something else. See further LOGIC, PREMISE and VALID.

INVALID. See **VALID.**

IPSO FACTO. This Latin phrase, which is not confined to philosophy, means 'by that very fact'.

LIBERTARIAN, LIBERTARIANISM. In POLITICAL PHILOSPHY, a libertarian is one who believes that the power of the state should be minimal in order to maximise individual freedom. In METAPHYSICS, a libertarian is someone who holds that DETERMINISM is false and that FREE WILL exists.

LOGIC. Roughly, the study of reasoning or inference. Less roughly, logic is normally construed as a NORMATIVE study of reasoning, i.e. as a study of *correct* reasoning rather than the psychological study of how people *actually* reason (even if logic books normally include a list of reasoning errors). Logic gets counted as part of PHILOSOPHY, even though other disciplines including, especially, mathematics claim it as well. 'Formal logic' often involves the use of symbols and may be defined as the study of VALID argument forms. Sometimes philosophical problems raised by logic are, themselves, counted as part of logic.

LOGICAL POSSIBILITY. Something is logically possible just in case the laws of LOGIC allow it. An example of something that is *not* logically possible, is (according to most philosophers, anyway!) that something both have and lack some single specified property, e.g. be both 20 years old and not 20 years old. In a looser sense, which might better deserve the name 'conceptual impossibility', something is logically (or conceptually) impossible when it is impossible given certain basic (but not logical) principles of facts. An example of something that is impossible in that sense is for a human being to have no age at all. Logic alone doesn't rule that out. Nonetheless, there is an important sense in which it does not *just happen to be the case* that it is impossible.

METAPHYSICS. Something like: the study of ultimate reality. Explaining or defending or bettering that definition is hard. One problem is showing how *physics* leaves any work for metaphysics. The Introduction (section 2) contains a definition of metaphysics that might begin to indicate that (contrary to SCIENTISM) there *is* some work for metaphysics to do. Anyhow, philosophers ancient and modern engage with topics that they file under the heading of 'metaphysics' – and those topics are, at least partly, not addressed by science. Those topics include: the difference between appearance and reality; PERSONAL IDENTITY; POSSIBLE WORLDS; 'meta-ethical' questions (see MORAL PHILOSOPHY); the relation between mind and matter; MODALITY; FREE WILL and DETERMINISM; the nature of space and time (some clear overlap with science there!) and the nature of such things as causation, numbers and identity. The origin of the *word* 'metaphysics' is thought to be as follows. In the first century BCE, a librarian placed some of Aristotle's texts after Aristotle's works on physics. Those texts that were placed after the stuff on physics became known as the 'metaphysics', 'after' being one meaning of the Greek word *meta*. Aristotle's *Metaphysics* (as it became known) treats what he called 'first philosophy'. Aristotle construed first philosophy as the study of (i) the most general features of beings, (ii) how it is that beings have those features, and – because of (ii) – (iii) God.

MODALITY, MODAL. Something is called 'modal' when it concerns either actuality or possibility (or impossibility) or necessity. But just *what is it* for something to be actual or possible or necessary? The study of modality, which is conducted by METAPHYSICS and LOGIC, aims to answer that question. See also POSSIBLE WORLD(S).

MORALITY. Often used as a synonym for ETHICS. When so used, the study of morality is the study of ethics, i.e. of how one should live (and *an* ethic/ethic is, for its part, *a* morality or some single account of morality). However, various philosophers have distinguished morality from ethics in various ways. One view is that morality is *a part of* ethics. The thinking here is something like this. Morality very much stresses 'permissibility' and 'impermissibility', i.e. what one may and may not do, along with obligation, i.e. what one *must* do. But there are ethical questions – questions about how best to live – that seem to take in *much more* than those things. A related idea is that morality is *one type* of ethic, in that morality involves an especially strong notion of obligation, whereby obligations are commands that trump all other considerations. See further the entry EUDAIMONIA – and note that morality in this 'overriding obligation' sense may be a Judaeo-Christian invention.

MORAL PHILOSOPHY. Branch of philosophy that studies how one should live, together with various questions of a more METAPHYSICAL (or 'meta-ethical') type such as: is there such a thing as moral truth? And, if there is, is it somehow relative to individuals or to groups? Often, moral philosophy is called ETHICS. Nonetheless, there may be some difference between ethics and MORALITY.

NON SEQUITUR. Latin for 'it does not follow'. A non sequitur is an INFERENCE that is INVALID. Tends to be used of inferences that *obviously* do not follow – as in, say, 'My dog is called Charlie; hence it will rain tomorrow.'

NORMATIVE, NORMATIVITY. Something is normative if it has to do with a norm or standard. Thus (as various versions of the *Oxford English Dictionary* indicate) 'prescriptive' is a near synonym for 'normative'. Normativity comes in various varieties. For instance, *logical* normativity is a matter of what LOGIC obliges one to do (or to think). By contrast, *ethical* normativity is a matter of the requirements of ETHICS. However, philosophers use the word 'normative' in what might be called a 'live' sense. On that usage, the *mere description* or neutral investigation of some norm(s) is not a normative investigation, whereas the assessment of a norm's *adequacy* is indeed a normative business. 'What are Ford's ethics?' does not count as a normative question in this live sense, but 'How adequate are Ford's ethics?' does.

NUMERICALLY IDENTICAL. Two things are numerically identical if and only if they are in fact one and the same thing. Contrast the 'qualitative identity' that consists in two things sharing properties and even perhaps (for whether this is possible without numerical identity is a question of METAPHYSICS) sharing *all* the same qualities.

PARADOX. The word 'paradox' derives from a Greek term meaning 'contrary to opinion'. Accordingly, sometimes *any statement that contradicts received opinion* is taken to be a paradox (to be a paradoxical statement or to yield a paradoxical statement) – at least if that statement seems to be true. Thus, if one comes to think that eternal life would be meaningless, then one has a paradox, because according to received opinion eternal life is desirable (and thus presumably not meaningless). (Compare chapter 4, section 2.) Still: a paradox of this type could be dissolved – rendered unparadoxical – simply by the discovery that one or the other view (the received opinion or the opinion that challenges it) is false. A more problematic form of paradox arises when one is faced with two contradictory ideas (two ideas that contradict one another) that resist that treatment; that is, each of them very much seems to be true. Sometimes a paradox of that type is called an 'antinomy'. A striking form of antimony occurs in the so-called 'liar paradox', in which one has an antimony *within a single statement*. The liar paradox (in one form, anyway) runs thus: 'This sentence is false.' If that statement is *true*, then seemingly it – that very same statement! – is false; and if the statement is *false*, then that would seem to make the statement . . true! So it seems that, whichever way you take the statement (the statement, 'This sentence is false'), it is both true and false. *Hitchhiker's* contains something that at least approximates a version of the liar paradox. It's this: 'a solitary old man who claimed repeatedly that nothing was true, though he was later discovered to be lying' (*Hitchhiker's Guide*, chapter 21). See also chapter 15 of *Restaurant* on the paradoxes of time travel – or rather for the claim that the main problem in that area is simply grammar!

PERMISSIBILITY (in the sense of morally permissible). See MORALITY.

PERSONAL IDENTITY. Personal identity is the relation that holds between two people when those people are NUMERICALLY IDENTICAL, i.e. one and the same person. That may sound a strange thing to say. But consider: what does such identity consist in? Under what conditions does it obtain – or fail to obtain? If my body/brain were to wake up with your memories, and you died at that same moment, would I be you? And what if you didn't die? Would we both be you? 'Diachronic' personal identity (mentioned in chapter 4) is personal identity *over time*. Am I the same person that I was 20 years ago? (Or better, because strictly that formulation BEGS THE QUESTION: am I identical to the person of 20 years ago whom I am apt to *say* that I was?)

PHILOSOPHY. Word deriving from an Ancient Greek word the literal meaning of which is 'love of wisdom'. For something approaching a definition of philosophy, see the Introduction, section 2. Branches of philosophy include AESTHETICS, EPISTEMOLOGY, ETHICS, LOGIC, METAPHYSICS and POLITICAL PHILOSOPHY.

PHILOSOPHY, MORAL. See MORAL PHILOSOPHY.

POLITICAL PHILOSOPHY. Branch of philosophy that considers the nature of political legitimacy, the nature of political power, the best form of government, and the like. If there is any difference between political philosophy and so-called 'political theory', it might be that the former tends to be quite NORMATIVE whereas the latter tends to be (more) descriptive.

POSSIBLE, LOGICALLY. See LOGICAL POSSIBILITY.

POSSIBLE WORLD(S). In the words of philosopher David Lewis, possible worlds are 'ways things could have been' (see chapter 8, section 5). See also MODALITY.

PREMISE (alternative spelling 'premiss', plural 'premises'/'premisses'). A premise is something that an argument asserts to be true and in that way presupposes. The following argument illustrates:

(1) Rob McKenna is a Rain God.

(Premise)

(2) Wherever a Rain God goes, it rains.

(Premise)

Hence

(3) Wherever Rob McKenna goes, it rains.

(Conclusion, reached by an INFERENCE, and in fact a VALID one, from the two premises)

SCEPTICISM (American spelling: skepticism). In the ordinary sense: an attitude of doubt. In the *philosophical* sense: a *wide* and/or *deep* doubt – about some or all of that which people claim to know. Hence scepticism is an EPISTEMOLOGICAL term (even though one can be sceptical about, say, *moral* knowledge). In modern philosophy, scepticism is often closely associated with EMPIRICISM. One form of scepticism in ancient philosophy was Pyrrhonian scepticism, named after Pyrrho of Elis (thought to have lived sometime around 360–272 BCE). 'The Pyrrhonist achieves peace of mind by finding that the arguments for and against an opinion balance evenly' (Mautner, *Dictionary of Philosophy*, p. 461).

Scientism. The view that science can solve many or all philosophical problems. 'Scientism' is often derogatory, i.e. a label used to *disparage* the view at issue. See the Introduction, section 3.

Sound. Soundness is a kind of 'validity+'. For an argument is sound only if (1) it is VALID *and* (2) all of its PREMISES are true. Consider the following argument: all vegetables are very clear that they do not want to be eaten; all carrots are vegetables; hence all carrots are very clear that they do not want to be eaten. This argument is valid, but it is unsound. It is unsound because, at least outside the *Hitchhiker* universe (*Restaurant*, chapter 17), the first premise is false.

Syllogism. Very roughly: an argument. Less roughly: any argument with two PREMISES. The specific nature of those premises determines the *type* of syllogism at issue. Types of syllogism include disjunctive, hypothetical and categorical syllogisms. Categorical syllogisms are the most familiar of these forms. A categorical syllogism is a syllogism wherein the two premises, and the conclusion, are 'categorical propositions'. Categorical propositions assert or deny that some or all of the members of one category belong to another. Here is a famous categorical syllogism. (1) All men are mortal. (2) Socrates is a man. Hence (3) Socrates is mortal.

Theism, theist. Theism: belief that there is a God (or more than one God). Theist: someone who holds that view. (An *atheist* is someone who believes that there is no God.)

Theodicy. Any attempt to square the existence of God – specifically, an all-good, all-knowing and all-powerful God – with the existence of evil. On a broader usage, any attempt to demonstrate God's justice. The term was invented by Leibniz by conjoining the Greek terms for God (*theos*) and justice (*dike*).

THEORIA. Ancient Greek term meaning contemplation or the contemplative life. Aristotle can seem to have held that the contemplative life is the best life (the life that is most *EUDAIMON*; 'can seem' because Aristotle is difficult to interpret on this point).

TROPES. In the usual sense of word, a trope is any rhetorical or literary device. But in METAPHYSICS, a trope is a *property* (or aspect) of something, but where that aspect/property is understood in a certain way. Some philosophers take properties to be UNIVERSALS. On that view, if a leaf is green it is because the universal *greenness* inheres in that leaf - and the very same universal is present in every other green thing. But 'trope theorists' reject multi-located universals in favour of *particularised properties*. They view each occurrence of green as a distinct entity in its own right. The general property *green* consists of all those particular instances of green which exactly resemble one another.

UNIVERSAL(S). In METAPHYSIC(S): a non-particular thing to which a concept at least seems to refer. For instance, redness (as distinct from all particular red things), circularity (as distinct from all particular circles or circular things), justice (as distinct from all particular just things or particular just states of affairs) and even, say, treeness (as distinct from all particular trees). The nature and even the existence of universals have been debated for a very long time. In LOGIC (or so-called philosophy of language), 'universal' is a word that denotes . . a certain type of word, namely, a word (such as the word 'red' or the word 'circle') that *refers to a universal* in the *metaphysical sense* (or that at least seems so to do; the logician can class certain words as universals without taking a stand on the metaphysical dispute about whether there really are any things that are universals). See also (if you are brave) TROPES.

UNSOUND. See SOUND.

VALID. In a broad or everyday sense: correct or well founded. In a moral or legal sense (as in 'valid consent'): having moral or legal force. In the strict sense used in LOGIC, only inferences and arguments can be valid (or 'invalid', i.e. not valid). An INFERENCE is valid only if it conforms to the laws of LOGIC. Valid *arguments* are arguments where the truth of the premises is a guarantee of the truth of the conclusion. That is: a valid argument is one in which the argument's underlying logical form just can't be filled out in such a way that the premises are true and the conclusion false (and arguments which aspire to having that form are called 'deductive arguments'). Take the following argument as an example. 'Jeltz is a Vogon; all Vogons are green; therefore, Jeltz is green.' No matter what we replace the non-logical words 'Jeltz', 'Vogon' (/'Vogons') and 'green' with, we cannot simultaneously make the premises true and the conclusion false. Whatever we feed into the logical form 'J is V; all V are G; therefore J is G', we can't get the result that the premises are true while the conclusion is false. Note that this does *not* mean that the conclusion of a valid argument must be true. Rather it means this: the conclusion of a valid argument must be true *if all its premises are true*. So an argument can be valid even if it has a false conclusion. What matters is that the conclusion *would* be true were the premises true. See also SOUND.

Further resources (everything you never wanted to know about philosophy but may be forced to find out)

Mautner, *Dictionary of Philosophy*

This slim-ish Penguin book is a useful resource for philosophical terminology.

The Oxford Companion to Philosophy, edited by Ted Honderich

Bigger and in that way better than the Mautner; less of a dictionary and more of an encylopedia.

Internet Encyclopedia of Philosophy (http://www.iep.utm.edu/)

This really is an encylopedia. That said: it is not, yet, fully comprehensive in its coverage.

Stanford Encyclopedia of Philosophy (http://plato.stanford. edu/; UK mirror at http://www.seop.leeds.ac.uk/)

A wide range of articles, written by leading philosophers. A warning, though: it does rather drop one in at the deep end! (Still, if *philosophy* can't have a deep end, what can?)

Whyte, *Bad Thoughts. A Guide to Clear Thinking*

Accessible, fairly cheap, generally marvellous and doesn't require a fleet of trucks to carry around. The American version has the wonderful title *Crimes against Logic: Exposing the Bogus Arguments of Politicians, Priests, Journalists, and Other Serial Offenders.* Let 'em have it!

Warburton, *Thinking from A to Z*

Slim, helpful, fairly accessible. Recommended reading for Open University philosophy students.

Morwood, *A Dictionary of Latin Words and Phrases*

This book is neither specifically about philosophical terms nor comprehensive. But it can be useful for, *inter alia,* decoding academic writing that uses phrases like *'inter alia'* (which – to give the game away – means 'among other things').

Peters, *Greek Philosophical Terms*

Good at what it does.

Further details of all these works can be found in the Bibliography that follows.[†]

[†]Well, except in the cases of the *Internet Encylopedia of Philosophy* and the *Stanford Encyclopedia of Philosophy*. Those two encylopedias, which exist only online, do not get entries to themselves in the bibliography (though they are mentioned in those bibliographical entries that detail *particular articles* from them).

Bibliography – of Adams, Philosophy and Everything

Well, not quite everything, obviously. But a lot. To be more specific: this bibliography contains every work mentioned anywhere in this book (with a few exceptions, including the Bible and a few poems; and the bibliography contains no works that are *not* mentioned in the book). Dates in square brackets are dates of first publication (which are given when it was thought helpful to do so).

Works by or about Douglas Adams are in bold. Also, and by the happy circumstance that 'Adams' begins with the letter 'A', works by Adams appear at the start of the bibliography. For a fuller list of works by Adams or to which he contributed, see pp. 293–300 of Alexander Pawlak's book *Die Wissenschaft bei Douglas Adams*. (That book is available only in German – bad news if you don't read German and you lack a Babel fish. But some use can be made of Alex's fine bibliography even without knowledge of German. The book's title translates as 'Science in Douglas Adams'.)

For *guidance on philosophical reading*, see the 'For deeper thought' sections at end of each of the chapters above and also the 'Further resources' part of the Glossary (p. 282).

Adams, Douglas, *Dirk Gently's Holistic Detective Agency* (London: Pan Macmillan, 1988 [1987]).

Adams, Douglas, 'Douglas Adams' Last Interview', May 2001. Directed and edited by Barton Bishoff. Interviewer Scott McGrew. Available at http://www.bartonbishoff.com/video_past_business_douglasadams.html and on YouTube (http://www.youtube.com/watch?v=6RNnXYwqIwA). Pages retrieved 09/09/2011. The interview first appeared on the *Tech Now!* programme on KNTV (an affiliate of the US television channel NBC).

Adams, Douglas, *Life, the Universe and Everything* (London: Pan Macmillan, (2001 [1982]).

Adams, Douglas, *Mostly Harmless* (London: Pan Macmillan, 2001 [1992]).

Adams, Douglas, 'Parrots, the Universe and Everything', talk given at the University of California, Santa Barbara, 2001. Video available at http://www.youtube.com/watch?v=_ZG8HBuDjgc. Video also available, with a transcript, at http://navarroj.com/parrots/. Pages retrieved 09/09/2011.

Adams, Douglas, Preface to Mike Russell (ed.), *Digging Holes in Popular Culture: Archaeology and Science Fiction* (Oxford: Oxbow Books, 2002).

Adams, Douglas, 'Re: Get a Professorship Now, and Beat the Rush', post on douglasadams.com forum; wwwe.douglasadams.com/cgi-bin/mboard/info/dnathread.cgi?425,1. The post is dated 20 March 1999. Web page retrieved 09/09/2011.

Adams, Douglas, *So Long, and Thanks for All the Fish* (London: Pan Macmillan, 2001 [1984]).

Adams, Douglas, *The Hitchhiker's Guide to the Galaxy* (London: Pan Macmillan, 2001 [1979]).

Adams, Douglas, *The Hitch-Hiker's Guide to the Galaxy: the Original Radio Scripts* (London: Pan, 1985).

Adams, Douglas, *The Long Dark Tea-Time of the Soul* (London: Pan Macmillan, 1989 [1988]).

Adams, Douglas, *The Restaurant at the End of the Universe* (London: Pan Macmillan, 2001 [1980]).

Adams, Douglas, *The Salmon of Doubt: Hitchhiking the Galaxy One Last Time* (London: Pan Macmillan, 2002). This posthumously published book includes a 'Prologue' by Nicholas Wroe, an 'Editor's Note' by Peter Guzzardi, an 'Introduction' by Stephen Fry, a quasi-draft of an unfinished Dirk Gently novel (assembled from bits and bobs), and, among other things, Adams's speech 'Is There an Artificial God?, which was given to the conference 'Digital Biota 2' at Cambridge (1998) and which has a transcript available here: http://www.biota.org/people/douglasadams. The only thing *Salmon* doesn't contain, just about, is a proper table of contents.

Adams, Douglas and Fincham, Peter (eds), *The Utterly Utterly Merry Comic Relief Christmas Book* (London: Fontana Press, 1986).

Adams, Douglas et al. (Richard Dawkins, Daniel Dennett, Jared Diamond and Steven Pinker), 'Evolutionary Perspectives': discussion, at the conference *Der Digitale Planet* (Munich, 1998). Recording available on YouTube: http://www.youtube.com/watch?v=diua4tWaW4Y. Web page retrieved 09/09/2011.

Adams, Douglas and Lloyd, John, *The Meaning of Liff* (London: Pan, 1983).

Adams, Douglas and Lloyd, John, *The Deeper Meaning of Liff* (London: Pan, 1990). This is an expanded edition of *The Meaning of Liff*.

Adams, Douglas and Carwardine, Mark, *Last Chance to See* (London: Pan Macmillan, new edn, 1991 [1990]).

Adams, Douglas, with Shircore, Ian, 'The First and Last Tapes', transcript of an interview of Adams by Ian Shircore, in *Darker Matter: Online Science Fiction Magazine*, Issue 1: March 2007, http://www.darkermatter.com/issue1/douglas_adams.php. Web page retrieved 09/09/2011.

Adams, Douglas with Shirley, John, 'A Talk with Douglas Adams' in Glenn Yeffeth (ed.), *The Anthology at the End of the Universe: Leading Science Fiction Authors on Douglas Adams' Hitchhiker's* Guide to the Galaxy (Dallas: BenBella, 2005), pp. 169–78.

Adorno, Theodor T., 'Free Time', in his *Critical Models: Interventions and Catchwords* (New York: Columbia University Press, 1998; first presented, as a radio lecture, in 1969). Translated by Henry W. Pickford.

Adorno, Theodor W., *Minima Moralia. Reflections from Damaged Life* (London: Verso, 1979 [1951]).

Annas, Julia, *Plato: a Very Short Introduction* (Oxford: University Press, 2003).

Asimov, Isaac, *Foundation* (London: Panther, 1960 [1951]).

Ayer, A. J., *Language, Truth and Logic* (London: Penguin, new edn, 2001 [1936]). There's a cheaper edition too – by Dover Publications.

Ayer, A. J., 'The Claims of Philosophy', *Polemic* 7: 18–33, 1947. Reprinted in Klemke and Cahn (eds), *The Meaning of Life*, pp. 199–202.

Barker, Martin and Petley, Julian (eds), *Ill Effects. The Media/Violence Debate* (London and New York: Routledge, 2nd edn, 2011).

Baron-Cohen, Simon, *Mindblindness* (Harvard: MIT Press, 1995).

Bayne, Tim and Nagasawa, Yujin, 'Grounds of Worship', *Religious Studies* 42: 299–313, 2006.

BBC, 'German Cannibal Tells of Fantasy', http://news.bbc.co.uk/1/hi/3286721.stm, 2003. Web page retrieved 09/09/2011.

BBC (Audiobooks), *The Hitchhiker's Guide to the Galaxy: the Complete Radio Series* [first series first broadcast 1978; second series first broadcast 1980], 2005. Compact discs.

Bett, Richard, 'Pyrrho', *The Stanford Encyclopedia of Philosophy* (Winter 2010 edn), Edward N. Zalta (ed.); URL = <http://plato.stanford.edu/archives/win2010/entries/pyrrho/>.

Bok, Sissela, *Mayhem: Violence as Public Entertainment* (Reading, Mass.: Perseus, 1998).

Borgmann, Albert, *Technology and the Character of Everyday Life: a Philosophical Inquiry* (Chicago and London: University of Chicago Press, 1984).

Bostrom, Nick, 'Are You Living in a Computer Simulation?', *Philosophical Quarterly* 53(211): 243–55, 2003.

Burley, Mikel, 'Immortality and Meaning: Reflections on the Makropulos Debate', *Philosophy* 84: 529–47, 2009.

Byrne, Mike, 'Beware of the Leopard' in Yeffeth (ed.), *The Anthology at the End of the Universe*, pp. 2–10.

Calude, Cristian, S., *Information and Randomness: an Algorithmic Perspective* (Berlin: Springer, 1994).

Camus, Albert, 'The Myth of Sisyphus' [1942], in Justin O'Brien (trans.), *The Myth of Sisyphus and Other Essays* (New York: Vintage Books, 1991), pp. 1–138. Excerpt reprinted in Klemke and Cahn (eds), *The Meaning of Life*, pp. 72–81.

Cathcart, Tom and Klein, Daniel, *Plato and a Platypus Walk into a Bar: Understanding Philosophy through Jokes* (New York: Abrams Image, 2007).

Chalmers, David, 'The Matrix as Metaphysics', in Grau (ed.), *Philosophers Explore the Matrix*.

Channel 4, *Break the Science Barrier*, 1996. Television documentary presented by Richard Dawkins and featuring Douglas Adams. Available in two parts on YouTube (http://www.youtube.com/watch?v=1KR8SigWQuY). Available to buy at http://store.richarddawkins.net/products/break-the-science-barrier.

Chappell, Timothy, 'Infinity Goes up on Trial: Must Immortality Be Meaningless?', *European Journal of Philosophy* 17(1): 30–44, 2007.

Chappell, Timothy, 'On the Very Idea of Criteria for Personhood', *Southern Journal of Philosophy* 49: 1–27, 2010.

Christian, Brian, *The Most Human Human: What Talking with Computers Teaches Us about What It Means to Be Alive* (New York: Knopf, 2011).

Cialdini, Robert B., *Influence: the Psychology of Persuasion* (New York: HarperCollins, rev. edn, 2007).

Conee, Earl and Sider, Theodore, *Riddles of Existence: a Guided Tour of Metaphysics* (Oxford and New York: Oxford University Press, 2007).

Connery, Brian and Combe, Kirk (eds), *Theorizing Satire: Essays in Literary Criticism* (Basingstoke and New York: Palgrave Macmillan, 1996).

Copeland, B. J. (ed.), *The Essential Turing* (Oxford: Oxford University Press, 2004).

Craig, William Lane, 'The Absurdity of Life without God', in William Lane Craig, *Reasonable Faith: Christian Truth and Apologetics* (Wheaton, Ill.: Good News Publishers/Crossways Books, 1994), pp. 57–75.

Craik, Henry, *The Life of Jonathan Swift, Dean of St. Patrick's, Dublin*, vol. 2 (London and New York: Macmillan, 1894).

Crawford, Matthew, *The Case for Working with Your Hands: or Why Office Work is Bad for Us and Fixing Things Feels Good* (London: Penguin, 2009).

Dainton, Barry, 'On Singularities and Simulations', *Journal of Consciousness Studies*, forthcoming.

Damasio, Antonio, *Descartes' Error: Emotion, Reason and the Human Brain* (London: Picador Books, 1994).

Damasio, Antonio, *The Feeling of What Happens: Body, Emotion and the Making of Consciousness* (London: Vintage Press, 1999).

Dawkins, Richard, *The Selfish Gene* (Oxford and New York: Oxford University Press, 1989, new edn [1976]).

Day, Vox, 'The Subversive Dismal Scientist: Douglas Adams and the Rule of Unreason', in Yeffeth (ed.), *The Anthology at the End of the Universe*, pp. 117–23. 'Vox Day' is a pseudonym of Theodore Beale.

DeGrazia, David, *Animal Ethics: a Very Short Introduction* (Oxford: Oxford University Press, 2002).

Dellamonica, A. M., 'Digital Watches May Be a Pretty Neat Idea, But Peanuts and Beer Are what Get You through the Apocalypse' in Yeffeth (ed.), *The Anthology at the End of the Universe*, pp. 133–43.

Dennett, Daniel, *Brainchildren* (London: Penguin, 1998).

Dennett, Daniel, *Brainstorms* (London: Penguin, 1997).

Dennett, Daniel, *Darwin's Dangerous Idea: Evolution and the Meanings of Life* (London: Penguin, 1995).

Descartes, René, *Descartes: Philosophical Writings*, vol. 1 (Cambridge: Cambridge University Press, 1985). Translated by J. Cottingham, R. Stoothoff and D. Murdoch.

Descartes, René, *Descartes: Selected Philosophical Writings* (Cambridge: Cambridge University Press, 1988). Edited and translated by J. Cottingham, R. Stoothoff and D. Murdoch.

Descartes, René, *Discourse on the Method*, in Descartes, *Descartes: Selected Philosophical Writings*, pp. 20–56. Translated by R. Stoothoff.

Descartes, René, *Meditations on First Philosophy*, in Descartes, *Descartes: Selected Philosophical Writings*, pp. 72–122. Translated by J. Cottingham.

Descartes, René, 'The Passions of the Soul', in Descartes, *Descartes: Philosophical Writings*, vol. 1, pp. 328–404. Translated by R. Stoothoff. An abridged version of this text is collected in Descartes, *Descartes: Selected Philosophical Writings*.

Deutsch, David, *The Fabric of Reality: the Science of Parallel Universes – and its Implications* (London: Allen Lane., 1997).

Di Muzio, Gianluca, 'The Immorality of Horror Films', *International Journal of Applied Philosophy* 22(1): 149–57, 2006.

Doctorow, Cory, 'Wikipedia: a Genuine H2G2 – minus the Editors', in Yeffeth (ed.), *The Anthology at the End of the Universe*, pp. 26–34.

Edmonds, David and Eidinow, John, *Wittgenstein's Poker: the Story of a Ten-Minute Argument between Two Great Philosophers* (New York: HarperCollins, 2001).

Epicurus, 'Letter to Menoeceus', in Joel Feinberg and Russ Shafer-Landau (eds), *Reason and Responsibility: Readings in Some Basic Problems of Philosophy* (Belmont, Calif.: Wadsworth, 14th edn, 2011).

Feenberg, Andrew, *Questioning Technology* (London and New York: Routledge, 1999).

Feinberg, Joel, 'Absurd Self-Fulfillment' [1980], in Joel Feinberg, *Freedom and Fulfillment* (Princeton: Princeton University Press, 1992), pp. 297–330. Reprinted in Klemke and Cahn (eds), *The Meaning of Life*, pp. 153–83.

Frayn, Michael, *Constructions: Making Sense of Things* (London: Faber and Faber, 2009 [1974]).

Fredkin, Edward, 'Digital Mechanics: an Informational Process Based on Reversible Universal Cellular Automata' in Howard Gutowitz (ed.), *Cellular Automata: Theory and Experiment* (Cambridge, Mass.: MIT Press, 1991).

Gaiman, Neil, *Don't Panic: Douglas Adams and the* Hitchhiker's Guide to the Galaxy (London: Titan Books, 2nd rev. edn, 1993 [1988]). Additional material by David K. Dickson.

Galilei, Galileo, *Dialogues Concerning Two New Sciences* (New York: Dover, 1954 [1638]). Translated by H. Crew and A. de Salvio.

Gill, Peter, *42. Douglas Adams' Amazingly Accurate Answer to Life, the Universe and Everything* (London: Beautiful Books, 2011).

Gleik, James, *The Information: a History, a Theory, a Flood* (New York: Pantheon Books, 2011).

Graham, Gordon, *Philosophy of the Arts: an Introduction to Aesthetics* (London and New York: Routledge, 3rd edn, 2005).

Grau, Christopher (ed.), *Philosophers Explore the Matrix* (Oxford: Oxford University Press, 2005).

Gutting, Gary, 'Voltaire', in *A Companion to Early Modern Philosophy* (Oxford: Blackwell, 2002).

'H2G2' http://h2g2.com/.

H2G2, entry on 'The Hitchhiker's Guide to the Galaxy', http://h2g2.com/dna/h2g2/A5815. Page retrieve 28/04/2012.

Haddon, Mark, *The Curious Incident of the Dog in the Night-Time* (London: Vintage Books, 2004).

Häkkänen, Kalle, 'Physics and Metaphysics in the Hitchhiker Series (1979–1992) by Douglas Adams', Pro Gradu thesis, University of Jyväskylä, Finland, 2006. (The author has made this thesis available on the web at https://jyx.jyu.fi/dspace/bitstream/handle/123456789/7291/urn_nbn_fi_jyu-2006314.pdf?sequence=1.)

Hanley, Richard, *Is Data Human? The Metaphysics of Star Trek* (London: Boxtree, 1998). First published simply as *The Metaphysics of Star Trek* (New York: Basic Books, 1997).

Hanlon, Michael, *The Science of* The Hitchhiker's Guide to the Galaxy (Basingstoke and New York: Palgrave Macmillan, 2005).

Hayes, Brian, 'Computational Creationism', *American Scientist* 87(5): 392, 1999.

Heath, Thomas L., *The Thirteen Books of Euclid's Elements* (New York: Barnes & Noble, 2006 [1908]).

Heidegger, Martin, *Being and Time* (Oxford: Blackwell Publishers, 1962 [1927]). Translated by John Macquarrie and Edward Robinson.

Heidegger, Martin, *The Fundamental Concepts of Metaphysics: World, Finitude, Solitude* (Bloomington and Indianapolis: Indiana University Press, 1995 [From lectures of 1929–30]). Translated by William McNeill and Nicholas Walker.

Hills, Alison, *Do Animals Have Rights?* (Cambridge: Icon Books, 2005).

Hobbes, Thomas, *Leviathan* (London and Melbourne: Dent, 1973).

Hodgart, Matthew, *Satire* (London: World University Library, 1969). Reissued with an introduction by Brian Connery as *Satire: Origins and Principles* (New Brunswick, USA: Transaction Publishers, 2009).

Honderich, Ted (ed.), *The Oxford Companion to Philosophy* (Oxford and New York: Oxford University Press, 2nd expanded edn, 2005).

Hornby, Nick, *Nick Hornby: the Omnibus – Fever Pitch; High Fidelity; About a Boy* (London: Orion, 2000).

Hourihan, Margery, *Deconstructing the Hero: Literary Theory and Children's Literature* (Abingdon and New York: Routledge, 1997). (Indignant child: 'Leave my hero alone!')

Hume, David, *An Enquiry Concerning Human Understanding* [1748] in Hume, *An Enquiry Concerning Human Understanding and Concerning the Principles of Morals*, ed. P. H. Nidditch (Oxford: Oxford University Press, 1975).

Hume, David, *A Treatise of Human Nature*, ed. P. H. Nidditch (Oxford and New York: Oxford University Press, 1978 [1739/1740]).

Hurley, Susan, 'Imitation, Media Violence, and Freedom of Speech', *Philosophical Studies* 117: 165–218, 2004.

Huxley, Aldous, *Brave New World*. Various editions. First published 1932.

Huxley, Aldous, *Brave New World Revisited*. Various editions. First published 1958.

James, William, *Pragmatism: a New Name for Some Old Ways of Thinking* (New York: Dover Publications, 1995).

Joll, Nicholas, 'Contemporary Metaphilosophy', *The Internet Encyclopedia of Philosophy*, ISSN 2161-0002, http://www.iep.utm.edu/con-meta. Web page retrieved 09/09/2011.

Jones, Terry, Foreword to *The Restaurant at the End of the Universe* (London: Pan, 2009), '30th anniversary edition', pp. vii–ix.

Juvenal, *Satires*. Various editions.

Kant, Immanuel, *Immanuel Kant's Critique of Pure Reason* (London: Palgrave Macmillan, 2007 [first German edition published 1781]). Translated by Norman Kemp Smith.

Katz, Jerrold J., *Cogitations: a Study of the* Cogito *in Relation to the Philosophy of Logic and Language and a Study of them in Relation to the* Cogito (New York: Oxford University Press, 1988).

Kelly, Kevin, 'God is the Machine', *Wired* magazine issue 10 (12), December 2002.

Kierkegaard, Søren, *Fear and Trembling* (London: Penguin, 2005 [1843]). Translated by Alastair Hannay.

Kirk, Robert, *Zombies and Consciousness* (Oxford: Oxford University Press, 2007).

Klemke, E.D. and Steven M. Cahn (eds), *The Meaning of Life: a Reader* (Oxford: Oxford University Press, 3rd edn, 2007).

Kreider, S. Evan, 'The Virtue of Horror Films: a Response to Di Muzio', *International Journal of Applied Philosophy* 20(2): 277–94, 2008.

Kristol, Irving, 'Pornography, Obscenity, and the Case for Censorship', *The New York Times Magazine*, 28 March 1971. Reprinted in Burton F. Porter, *The Voice of Reason. Fundamentals of Critical Thinking* (Oxford: Oxford University Press, 2010), pp. 274–80 of the 'international edition' of the book.

Kropf, Carl R., 'Douglas Adams's "Hitchhiker" Novels as Mock Science Fiction', *Science Fiction Studies* 44 (Volume 15, Part 1): 61–70, March 1988.

Kurzweil, Raymond, *The Singularity Is Near: When Humans Transcend Biology* (New York: Viking, 2005).

Lakatos, Imre, *Proofs and Refutations: the Logic of Mathematical Discovery*, ed. J. Worrall and E. Zahar (Cambridge: Cambridge University Press, 1976).

Larkin, Philip and Thwaite, Anthony, *Further Requirements: Interviews, Broadcasts, Statements and Book Reviews, 1952–85* (Ann Arbor, Mich.: University of Michigan Press, 2004).

Leahy, Michael, *Against Liberation: Putting Animals in Perspective* (London: Routledge, 1994).

Leavitt, David, *The Man Who Knew Too Much: Alan Turing and the Invention of the Computer* (New York: W. W. Norton, 2006). There are other editions by Atlas and Phoenix.

Leibniz, Gottfried Wilhelm, *Theodicy – Essays on the Goodness of God, the Freedom of Man and the Origin of Evil* [1710]. Various editions.

Lem, Stanislaw, *Microworlds: Writings on Science Fiction and Fantasy*, ed. Franz Rottensteiner (San Diego: Harcourt, 1984).

Lewis, David, *Counterfactuals* (Oxford: Oxford University Press, 1973).

Lloyd, Seth, *Programming the Universe* (New York: Knopf, 2006).

Locke, John, *Two Treatises of Government*. Various editions.

Lukes, Steven, *The Curious Enlightenment of Professor Caritat: a Comedy of Ideas* (London and New York: Verso, 1995).

Lukes, Steven, *Power: a Radical View* (Basingstoke and New York: Palgrave Macmillan, 2nd edn, 2005).

Mackie, J. L., *Ethics: Inventing Right and Wrong* (London: Penguin, 1990 [1977]).

Mackie, J. L., *The Miracle of Theism: Arguments for and against the Existence of God* (Oxford, Clarendon Press, 1983).

Malcolm, Norman, *Ludwig Wittgenstein: a Memoir* (Oxford University Press, London, 1958).

Manson, Neil and O'Neill, Onora, *Rethinking Informed Consent in Bioethics* (Cambridge: Cambridge University Press, 2007).

Maor, Eli, *To Infinity and Beyond: a Cultural History of the Infinite* (Princeton, USA: Princeton University Press, 1991).

Marx, Karl, 'The German Ideology' in David McLellan (ed.), *Karl Marx: Selected Writings* (Oxford University Press, 2nd edn, 2000), pp. 175–208.

Mautner, Thomas, *The Penguin Dictionary of Philosophy* (London: Penguin, 1997).

Metz, Thaddeus, 'Could God's Purpose Be the Source of Life's Meaning?' *Religious Studies* 36: 293–313, 2000.

Metz, Thaddeus, 'The Immortality Requirement for Life's Meaning', *Ratio* 16: 161–77, 2003.

Mill, John Stuart, *On Liberty* [1859]. Various editions.

Miller, Richard, 'Beneficence, Duty and Distance', *Philosophy & Public Affairs* 32, 357–83, 2004.

Minsky, Marvin, 'Jokes and their Relation to the Cognitive Unconscious', in R. Groner, M. Groner and W.F. Bischof (eds), *Methods of Heuristics* (Hillsdale, USA: Lawrence Erlbaum Associates, 1983).

Moore, Adrian, 'Williams, Nietzsche, and the Meaninglessness of Immortality', *Mind* 115: 311–30, 2006.

Moore, Andrew and Scott, Michael (eds), *Realism and Religion: Philosophical and Theological Perspectives* (Aldershot, UK and Burlington, USA: Ashgate, 2007).

Morwood, James, *A Dictionary of Latin Words and Phrases* (Oxford and New York: Oxford University Press, 1998).

Murdoch, Iris, *Metaphysics as a Guide to Morals* (London: Penguin, new edn, 1993 [1992]).

Murray, John P., 'Media Violence: the Effects Are Both Real and Strong', *American Behavioral Scientist* 51 (8): 2008.

Nagel, Thomas, 'Death', *Noûs* 4: 73–80, 1970. Reprinted in Nagel's *Mortal Questions* (Cambridge: Cambridge University Press, 1979), pp. 1–10.

Nagel, Thomas, *Mortal Questions* (Cambridge: Cambridge University Press, 1979).

Nagel, Thomas, 'The Absurd', *Journal of Philosophy* 68: 716–27, 1971. Reprinted in Klemke and Cahn (eds), *The Meaning of Life*, pp. 143–52 and in Nagel's *Mortal Questions* (Cambridge: Cambridge University Press, 1979), pp. 11–23.

Nagel, Thomas, *The View from Nowhere* (Oxford: Oxford University Press, 1986).

Nietzsche, Friedrich, *On the Genealogy of Morality* (Cambridge: Cambridge University Press, 1994 [1887]).

Nietzsche, Friedrich, *Twilight of the Idols* [1889]/*The Anti-Christ* [1895] (London, Penguin: 1968).

Nozick, Robert, *Anarchy, State, and Utopia* (Malden, USA and Oxford, UK: Wiley Blackwell, new edn, 2004 [1974]).

Nozick, Robert, 'Philosophy and the Meaning of Life', in his *Philosophical Explanations* (Cambridge, USA: Harvard University Press, 1981), pp. 571–650. Excerpt reprinted in Klemke and Cahn (eds), *The Meaning of Life*, pp. 143–52.

O'Neill, Onora, 'Between Consenting Adults', *Philosophy & Public Affairs* 14: 252–77, 1985.

Parfit, Derek, *Reasons and Persons* (Oxford: Oxford University Press, 2nd edn, 1987).

Paulos, John Allen, *I Think, Therefore I Laugh: the Flip Side of Philosophy* (London: Penguin, 2001).

Pavić, Milorad, *Dictionary of the Khazars: a Lexicon Novel in 100,000 Words* (New York: Knopf, 1984). Translated by Christina Pribicevic-Zoric.

Pawlak, Alexander, *Die Wissenschaft bei Douglas Adams* (Weinheim: Wiley, 2010).

Peters, F. E., *Greek Philosophical Terms: a Historical Lexicon* (New York: New York University Press, 1967).

Pettit, Philip, 'Consequentialism' in Peter Singer (ed.), *A Companion to Ethics* (Oxford: Blackwell, 1993), pp. 230–40.

Philips, D. Z. and Tessin, Timothy (eds), *Religion without Transcendence?* (Basingstoke: Macmillan, 1997).

Plato, 'Apology' in Plato, *Five Dialogues*. Available in other collections/editions.

Plato, *Five Dialogues: Euthyphro, Apology, Crito, Meno, Phaedo* (Hackett: Indianapolis, rev. edn, 2002). Translated by G. M. A. Grube.

Plato, 'Phaedo' in Plato, *Five Dialogues*. Available in other collections/editions.

Postman, Neil, *Amusing Ourselves to Death. Public Discourse in the Age of Show Business* (London: Heinemann, 1986).

Poundstone, William, *The Recursive Universe: Cosmic Complexity and the Limits of Scientific Knowledge* (New York: Morrow, 1985).

Quintero, Ruben (ed.), *A Companion to Satire Ancient and Modern* (Malden, Oxford and Carlton: Routledge, 2007).

Rachels, James, with Rachels, Stuart, *The Elements of Moral Philosophy* (New York: McGraw-Hill, 6th edn, 2009).

Rae, Alastair, *Quantum Physics: Illusion or Reality?* (Cambridge: Cambridge University Press, 1994).

Read, Stephen, *Thinking about Logic: an Introduction to the Philosophy of Logic* (Oxford and New York: Oxford University Press, 1995).

Real, Hermann J. and Vienken, Heinz J., *Jonathan Swift, Gulliver's Travels*, p. 88. (This is a book *about* Swift's book – not a version *of* that book.)

Ripstein, Arthur, 'Beyond the Harm Principle', *Philosophy & Public Affairs* 34: 215–45, 2006.

Roberts, Adam, '42', in Yeffeth (ed.), *The Anthology at the End of the Universe*, pp. 48–64.

Rosen, Selina, 'The Holy Trilogy' in Yeffeth (ed.), *The Anthology at the End of the Universe*, pp. 73–81.

Rousseau, Jean-Jacques, *Discourse on Inequality* (Oxford: World's Classics, 1994 [1755]). Translated by Franklin Philip.

Rowlands, Mark, *Animals Like Us* (London: Verso, 2002).

Rowling, J. K., *Harry Potter and the Philosopher's Stone* (London: Bloomsbury Publishing, 1997).

Rucker, Rudy, *Infinity and the Mind: the Science and Philosophy of the Infinite* (Princeton: Princeton University Press, new edn, 2004).

Ryle, Gilbert, *The Concept of Mind* (London: Penguin, 2000 [1949]).

Saramago, José, *The Gospel According to Jesus Christ*. Translated by Giovanni Pontiero (New York, Harcourt Brace Company, 1994).

Savage, Joanne and Yancey, Christina, 'The Effects of Media Violence Exposure on Criminal Aggression: a Meta-Analysis', *Criminal Justice and Behavior* 35: 772–91, 2008.

Scharrer, Erica, 'Media Exposure and Sensitivity to Violence in News Reports: Evidence of Desensitization?', *Journalism & Mass Communication Quarterly* 85(2): 291–310, 2008.

Schopenhauer, Arthur, 'On the Sufferings of the World' [1851], in Klemke and Cahn (eds), *The Meaning of Life*, pp. 45–54. (This is not quite the same text as the one called 'On The Suffering of the World' (*sic*) in Schopenhauer's *Essays and Aphorisms*.)

Schopenhauer, Arthur, 'On the Vanity of Existence' [1851], in his *Essays and Aphorisms* (London: Penguin, 1970). Translated by R. J. Hollindale.

Scruton, Roger, *Animal Rights and Wrongs*. Various editions.

Sellars, Wilfred, *Science, Perception and Reality* (London and New York: Routledge & Kegan Paul: Humanities Press, 1963).

Shirley, John, 'Douglas Adams and the Wisdom of Madness' in Yeffeth (ed.), *The Anthology at the End of the Universe*, pp. 157–68.

Shusterman, Richard, 'Entertainment: a Question for Aesthetics', *British Journal of Aesthetics* 43(3): 289–307, 2003.

Simmons, A. John, *Moral Principles and Political Obligation* (Princeton: Princeton University Press, 1981).

Simpson, David, 'Francis Bacon', *The Internet Encyclopedia of Philosophy*, ISSN 2161-0002, http://www.iep.utm.edu/bacon/. Web page retrieved 20/09/2011.

Simpson, M. J., *Hitchhiker. A Biography of Douglas Adams* (London: Coronet Books, 2003). Revised and updated edition. Foreword by John Lloyd.

Singer, Peter, *Animal Liberation* (London: Thorsons, 2nd edn, 1991 [1975]). The first edition bore the subtitle *A New Ethics for our Treatment of Animals*.

Singer, Peter, 'Famine, Affluence and Morality', *Philosophy & Public Affairs* 1: 229–43, 1972. Reprinted in many places including Hugh LaFollette (ed.), *Ethics in Practice* (Oxford: Blackwell, 3rd edn, 2007).

Singer, Peter, *How Are We to Live? Ethics in an Age of Self-Interest* (Amherst, USA: Prometheus Books, 1995).

Singer, Peter and Mason, Jim, *Eating: What We Eat and Why it Matters* (London: Arrow, 2006). First published as *The Way We Eat: Why Our Food Choices Matter* by Rochdale Inc. in the United States in 2006.

Sokol, Daniel, 'The Harms of Violent Imagery', *Think* Spring 2006: 66–67, 2006.

Sorell, Tom, *Descartes: a Very Short Introduction* (Oxford: Oxford University Press, 2000). Previously published, in 1987 and 1996, in slightly different formats by the same press.

Staude-Müller, Frithjof, Bliesener, Thomas and Luthman, Stefanie, 'Hostile and Hardened? An Experimental Study on (De-)Sensitization to Violence and Suffering through Playing Video Games', *Swiss Journal of Psychology* 67(1): 41–50, 2008.

Störig, Hans Joachim, *Kleine Weltgeschichte der Philosophie* (Frankfurt am Main: Fischer, 1990).

Stroud, Barry, *Hume* (London: Routledge, 1977).

Swift, Jonathan, *Gulliver's Travels* (London: Penguin, rev. edn, 2003 [1726; original full title *Gulliver's Travels into Several Remote Nations of the World. In Four Parts. By Lemuel Gulliver*]). Other editions are available.

Thomson, Judith Jarvis, 'A Defence of Abortion', *Philosophy & Public Affairs* 1: 47–66, 1971. Reprinted in numerous collections.

Tolstoy, Leo, *My Confession* [1905], excerpt reprinted in Klemke and Cahn (eds), *The Meaning of Life*, pp. 7–16.

Tomassi, Paul, *Logic* (New York: Routledge, 1996).

Tooley, Michael, 'Abortion and Infanticide', *Philosophy & Public Affairs* 2: 37–65, 1972.

Turing, Alan, 'Computing Machinery and Intelligence', in Copeland (ed.), *The Essential Turing*, pp. 441–64. Originally published in *Mind* 59: 433–60, 1950.

Voltaire, *Candide, Or Optimism* (London: Penguin, 2005 [1759]). Translated and edited by Theo Cuffe, with an introduction by Michael Wood. This edition includes Voltaire's *Poem on the Lisbon Disaster*.

Wallace, David Foster, *Everything and More: a Compact History of* ∞ (New York: W. W. Norton, 2003).

Warburton, Nigel, *Thinking from A–Z* (Abingdon, UK and New York: Routledge, 3rd edn, 2007).

Watson, George, 'The Cosmic Comic: Douglas Adams (1952–2001)', *Michigan Quarterly Review* 43 (1): 112–16, 2004.

Webb, Nick, *Wish You Were Here: the Official Biography of Douglas Adams* (London: Headline, 2003). Note: this informative and interesting book is often somewhat unreliable in the few things that it says about philosophy.

Webb, Nick, 'Exclusive Interview with Nick Webb'; transcript of an interview about Douglas Adams with 'the Douglas Adams Continuum';

http://www.douglasadams.se/exclusive/nick.html. No date. Web page retrieved 08/09/ 2011.

Welsh, Irvine, *The Acid House* (London: Vintage, 2009).

Weinberg, Steven, 'Is the Universe a Computer?', *New York Review of Books* 24 October, 2002.

Westphal, Jonathan and Cherry, Christopher, 'Is Life Absurd?', *Philosophy* 65: 199–203, 1990. Reprinted in Westphal and Levenson (eds), *Life and Death*, pp. 98–103.

Westphal, Jonathan and Levenson, Carl (eds), *Life and Death* (Indianapolis: Hackett, 1993).

Wheeler, John A., 'Information, Physics, Quantum: the Search for Links' in Wojciech H. Zurek (ed.), *Complexity, Entropy and the Physics of Information* (Reading, USA: Addison-Wesley, 1990), pp. 3–29.

Whyte, Jamie, *Bad Thoughts. A Guide to Clear Thinking* (London: Corvo, 2003)/*Crimes against Logic: Exposing the Bogus Arguments of Politicians, Priests, Journalists, and Other Serial Offenders* (New York: McGraw-Hill, 2004).

Williams, Bernard, *Descartes: the Project of Pure Enquiry* (Abingdon, Oxon, and New York: Routledge, rev. edn, 2005 [1978]).

Williams, Bernard, 'The Makropoulos Case: Reflections on the Tedium of Immortality', in Bernard Williams, *Problems of the Self* (Cambridge: Cambridge University Press, 1973), pp. 82–100. Reprinted in *The Metaphysics of Death*, ed. John Martin Fischer (Stanford, USA: Stanford University Press, 1993), pp. 73–92.

Williams, Bernard, *Philosophy as a Humanistic Discipline* (Cambridge: Cambridge University Press, 2006).

Wisdom, John, 'The Meanings of the Questions of Life' [1965] in Klemke and Cahn (eds), *The Meaning of Life*, pp. 220–3.

Wittgenstein, Ludwig, *Philosophical Investigations* (Oxford: Basil Blackwell, 1967 [1953]). Translated G. E. M. Anscombe.

Wittgenstein, Ludwig, *Tractatus Logico-Philosophicus* (London: Routledge and Kegan Paul, 1922). Translated by C. K. Ogden.

Wolfram, Stephen, *A New Kind of Science* (Champaign, USA: Wolfram Media Inc., 2002).

Woolf, Virginia, *Orlando: a Biography* (various editions).

Wright, Robert, *Three Scientists and their Gods: Looking for Meaning in an Age of Information* (New York: Times Books, 1988).

Yeffeth, Glenn (ed.), *The Anthology at the End of the Universe: Leading Science Fiction Authors on Douglas Adams'* Hitchhiker's Guide to the Galaxy (Dallas: BenBella, 2005).

Zimmerman, Michael E. et al (eds), *Environmental Philosophy: From Animal Rights to Radical Ecology* (Upper Saddle River: Prentice Hall, 2nd edn, 1988).

Zuse, Konrad, *Calculating Space* (Cambridge, USA: MIT Technical Translation, 1970).

Indexes

There are (don't panic!) four indexes:

(1) **an index of works by Douglas Adams** (or at least partly by him, and taking 'works' broadly; for details of the works, see the Bibliography);

(2) **an index of characters, things and places in** *Hitchhiker's*;

(3) **an index of (non-fictional!) philosophers, sages, luminaries and other thinking persons** (i.e. people – so long as they're either thinkers or famous);

(4) **a general index** (everything else, which turns out mostly to be topics).

In those indexes, unadorned numbers refer to pages, and 'n.' refers to endnotes. 'Passim' means 'throughout'. Page numbers in *italics* refer to pages in the Glossary.

1   Index of works by Douglas Adams

2   Index of characters, things and places in *Hitchhiker's*

3 Index of (non-fictional!) philosophers, sages, luminaries and other thinking persons

4 General index